2017 SQA Specimen and Past Papers with Answers

National 5
HISTORY

2016 & 2017 Exams
and 2017 Specimen Question Paper

HODDER GIBSON
AN HACHETTE UK COMPANY

This book contains the official SQA 2016 and 2017 Exams, and the 2017 Specimen Question Paper for National 5 History, with associated SQA-approved answers modified from the official marking instructions that accompany the paper.

In addition the book contains study skills advice. This has been specially commissioned by Hodder Gibson, and has been written by experienced senior teachers and examiners in line with the new National 5 syllabus and assessment outlines. This is not SQA material but has been devised to provide further guidance for National 5 examinations.

Hodder Gibson is grateful to the copyright holders, as credited on the final page of the Answer section, for permission to use their material. Every effort has been made to trace the copyright holders and to obtain their permission for the use of copyright material. Hodder Gibson will be happy to receive information allowing us to rectify any error or omission in future editions.

Hachette UK's policy is to use papers that are natural, renewable and recyclable products and made from wood grown in sustainable forests. The logging and manufacturing processes are expected to conform to the environmental regulations of the country of origin.

Orders: please contact Bookpoint Ltd, 130 Park Drive, Milton Park, Abingdon, Oxon OX14 4SE. Telephone: (44) 01235 827720. Fax: (44) 01235 400454. Lines are open 9.00–5.00, Monday to Saturday, with a 24-hour message answering service. Visit our website at www.hoddereducation.co.uk. Hodder Gibson can be contacted direct on: Tel: 0141 333 4650; Fax: 0141 404 8188; email: hoddergibson@hodder.co.uk

This collection first published in 2017 by
Hodder Gibson, an imprint of Hodder Education,
An Hachette UK Company
211 St Vincent Street
Glasgow G2 5QY

Typeset by Aptara, Inc.

Printed in the UK

A catalogue record for this title is available from the British Library

ISBN: 978-1-5104-2193-6

2 1

2018 2017

Introduction

National 5 History

This book of SQA past papers contains the question papers used in the 2016 and 2017 exams (with answers at the back of the book). The National 5 History exam is being extended by 20 marks for 2018 onwards, following the removal of unit assessments from the course. A new specimen question paper, which reflects the requirements of the revised exam, is also included. The specimen question paper reflects the content and duration of the exam in 2018.

All of the question papers included in the book (2016, 2017 and the new specimen question paper) provide excellent representative exam practice for the final exams. Using the 2016 and 2017 past papers as part of your revision will help you to develop the vital skills and techniques needed for the exam, and will help you to identify any knowledge gaps you may have.

It is always a very good idea to refer to SQA's website for the most up-to-date course specification documents. These are available for each subject at www.sqa.org.uk/nqsubjects

The course requirements

The Assignment – how to be successful

The Assignment is an essay written under exam conditions and then sent to the SQA to be marked.

The Assignment counts for 20 marks out of a total of 100 so doing well in it can provide you with a very useful launch pad for future success.

How long does my essay have to be?

There are NO word limits in the Assignment – it is whatever you can write in one hour!

What should I write about?

First, it makes sense to choose a question from the topics you have been learning about. It is also sensible to choose a question from a past exam paper.

Second, your essay title should be based on a question that allows you to use your evidence to answer the question. You must avoid titles that are just statements such as "The Slave Trade" or "Appeasement". They do not allow you to use information to provide an overall answer to your title question.

Finally, try NOT to make up questions that are too complicated or that ask two questions within the same title.

What is the Resource Sheet?

Your Resource Sheet provides a framework and notes for your essay.

It shows the marker

- that you have researched, selected and organised your information
- that you have thought about your work and reached a decision about the question in your title
- which sources you have used and demonstrates how you have used them.

Your Resource Sheet MUST be sent to the SQA with your finished essay.

Your Resource Sheet should NOT be just a collection of facts, figures and quotes. It should outline the main parts of your essay and remind you what to write. Remember that this has a limit of 200 words.

The Exam Paper

The question paper is made up of three **sections**:

Section 1 – Historical Study: Scottish
Section 2 – Historical Study: British
Section 3 – Historical Study: European and World.

In each **section** you will select **one** part to answer questions on:

Section 1: Historical Study: Scottish

Part 1: The Wars of Independence, 1286–1328
Part 2: Mary Queen of Scots and the Scottish Reformation, 1542–1587
Part 3: The Treaty of Union, 1689–1715
Part 4: Migration and Empire, 1830–1939
Part 5: The Era of the Great War, 1900–1928

Section 2: Historical Study: British

Part 1: The Creation of the Medieval Kingdoms, 1066–1406
Part 2: War of the Three Kingdoms, 1603–1651
Part 3: The Atlantic Slave Trade, 1770–1807
Part 4: Changing Britain, 1760–1914
Part 5: The Making of Modern Britain, 1880–1951

Section 3: Historical Study: European and World

Answering the Exam Questions

The first rule is simple and is the most important thing that will get you marks:

Answer the question that you are asked, NOT what you would like it to ask.

The Exam paper has six types of questions.

TYPE 1 – the **"Describe"** question, worth **4 marks**.

In this type of question you must describe what happened by using five or six pieces of your own knowledge, known as **recall**. There is no source to help you with information so your answer will be based on your own recall.

TYPE 2 – the **"Explain"** question, worth **6 marks**.

To be successful with this type of question you must give five or six reasons why something happened. Once again, there is no source to help you. Use recall that is correct and accurate.

(**Note:** question types 3, 4 and 5 are very similar in nature, but remember to pay close attention to the wording of the question – and make sure you answer it!)

TYPE 3A – the **"To what extent…"** question, worth **9 marks**.

To be successful with this type of question you must write a balanced answer. That means you must decide how important a particular factor was in explaining why something happened. Include at least five pieces of relevant information and give a short conclusion which sums up your answer to the question, including a reason to support your conclusion.

TYPE 3B – the **"how successful"** question, worth **9 marks**.

To be successful with this type of question you must write a balanced answer. That means you must decide how successful a particular factor was in explaining why something happened. Include at least five pieces of relevant information and give a short conclusion which sums up your answer to the question, including a reason to support your conclusion.

TYPE 3C – the **"how important"** question, worth **9 marks**.

To be successful with this type of question you must write a balanced answer. That means you must decide how important a particular factor was in explaining why something happened. Include at least five pieces of relevant information and give a short conclusion which sums up your answer to the question, including a reason to support your conclusion.

TYPE 4 – the **"Evaluate the usefulness…"** question, worth **5 marks**. This question will ask "Evaluate the usefulness of a source as evidence of …."

Evaluate means **to judge** how good a source is as evidence for finding out about something. The short answer is that it will always be partly useful but it will never be entirely useful in giving all the information you need.

In this type of question it is never enough just to **describe** what is in a source. It might be helpful to base your answer around the following guide questions.

WHO produced the source? Why is the AUTHORSHIP of the source relevant and therefore useful in assessing the value of a source?

WHEN was the source produced and how might that help in the evaluation of the source?

WHAT'S NOT THERE? What important information is missing from the source that makes you think the source was not as useful as it could be?

TYPE 5 – the **"Compare"** question, worth **4 marks.**

You will always get one question that asks you to compare two sources in your exam. To be successful with this type of question you must make clear connections between sources but do not just describe the two sources.

These questions are easy to spot because they are the only ones that will refer to TWO sources. For this type of question you must say whether you think the sources agree or not and then support your decision by making two comparisons using evidence from the sources.

TYPE 6 – the **"How fully..."** question, worth **6 marks**.

To be successful with this type of question you must select information from the source which is relevant to the question – usually there will be three points of information in the source for you to use. Use recall that is accurate and relevant to make your answer more balanced. You will never get a source that gives the full story so it is up to you to say that the source PARTLY explains or describes something but there is more information needed to give the full story. That's where you show off your recalled extra knowledge.

Good luck!

Remember that the rewards for passing National 5 History are well worth it! Your pass will help you get the future you want for yourself. In the exam, be confident in your own ability. If you're not sure how to answer a question, trust your instincts and just give it a go anyway. Keep calm and don't panic! GOOD LUCK!

Study Skills – what you need to know to pass exams!

Pause for thought

Many students might skip quickly through a page like this. After all, we all know how to revise. Do you really though?

Think about this:

"IF YOU ALWAYS DO WHAT YOU ALWAYS DO, YOU WILL ALWAYS GET WHAT YOU HAVE ALWAYS GOT."

Do you like the grades you get? Do you want to do better? If you get full marks in your assessment, then that's great! Change nothing! This section is just to help you get that little bit better than you already are.

There are two main parts to the advice on offer here. The first part highlights fairly obvious things but which are also very important. The second part makes suggestions about revision that you might not have thought about but which WILL help you.

Part 1

DOH! It's so obvious but …

Start revising in good time

Don't leave it until the last minute – this will make you panic.

Make a revision timetable that sets out work time AND play time.

Sleep and eat!

Obvious really, and very helpful. Avoid arguments or stressful things too – even games that wind you up. You need to be fit, awake and focused!

Know your place!

Make sure you know exactly **WHEN and WHERE** your exams are.

Know your enemy!

Make sure you know what to expect in the exam.

How is the paper structured?

How much time is there for each question?

What types of question are involved?

Which topics seem to come up time and time again?

Which topics are your strongest and which are your weakest?

Are all topics compulsory or are there choices?

Learn by DOING!

There is no substitute for past papers and practice papers – they are simply essential! Tackling this collection of papers and answers is exactly the right thing to be doing as your exams approach.

Part 2

People learn in different ways. Some like low light, some bright. Some like early morning, some like evening / night. Some prefer warm, some prefer cold. But everyone uses their BRAIN and the brain works when it is active. Passive learning – sitting gazing at notes – is the most INEFFICIENT way to learn anything. Below you will find tips and ideas for making your revision more effective and maybe even more enjoyable. What follows gets your brain active, and active learning works!

Activity 1 – Stop and review

Step 1

When you have done no more than 5 minutes of revision reading STOP!

Step 2

Write a heading in your own words which sums up the topic you have been revising.

Step 3

Write a summary of what you have revised in no more than two sentences. Don't fool yourself by saying, "I know it, but I cannot put it into words". That just means you don't know it well enough. If you cannot write your summary, revise that section again, knowing that you must write a summary at the end of it. Many of you will have notebooks full of blue/black ink writing. Many of the pages will not be especially attractive or memorable so try to liven them up a bit with colour as you are reviewing and rewriting. **This is a great memory aid, and memory is the most important thing.**

Activity 2 – Use technology!

Why should everything be written down? Have you thought about "mental" maps, diagrams, cartoons and colour to help you learn? And rather than write down notes, why not record your revision material?

What about having a text message revision session with friends? Keep in touch with them to find out how and what they are revising and share ideas and questions.

Why not make a video diary where you tell the camera what you are doing, what you think you have learned and what you still have to do? No one has to see or hear it, but the process of having to organise your thoughts in a formal way to explain something is a very important learning practice.

Be sure to make use of electronic files. You could begin to summarise your class notes. Your typing might be slow, but it will get faster and the typed notes will be easier to read than the scribbles in your class notes. Try to add different fonts and colours to make your work stand out. You can easily Google relevant pictures, cartoons and diagrams which you can copy and paste to make your work more attractive and **MEMORABLE**.

Activity 3 – This is it. Do this and you will know lots!

Step 1

In this task you must be very honest with yourself! Find the SQA syllabus for your subject (www.sqa.org.uk). Look at how it is broken down into main topics called MANDATORY knowledge. That means stuff you MUST know.

Step 2

BEFORE you do ANY revision on this topic, write a list of everything that you already know about the subject. It might be quite a long list but you only need to write it once. It shows you all the information that is already in your long-term memory so you know what parts you do not need to revise!

Step 3

Pick a chapter or section from your book or revision notes. Choose a fairly large section or a whole chapter to get the most out of this activity.

With a buddy, use Skype, Facetime, Twitter or any other communication you have, to play the game "If this is the answer, what is the question?". For example, if you are revising Geography and the answer you provide is "meander", your buddy would have to make up a question like "What is the word that describes a feature of a river where it flows slowly and bends often from side to side?".

Make up 10 "answers" based on the content of the chapter or section you are using. Give this to your buddy to solve while you solve theirs.

Step 4

Construct a wordsearch of at least 10 × 10 squares. You can make it as big as you like but keep it realistic. Work together with a group of friends. Many apps allow you to make wordsearch puzzles online. The words and phrases can go in any direction and phrases can be split. Your puzzle must only contain facts linked to the topic you are revising. Your task is to find 10 bits of information to hide in your puzzle, but you must not repeat information that you used in Step 3. DO NOT show where the words are. Fill up empty squares with random letters. Remember to keep a note of where your answers are hidden but do not show your friends. When you have a complete puzzle, exchange it with a friend to solve each other's puzzle.

Step 5

Now make up 10 questions (not "answers" this time) based on the same chapter used in the previous two tasks. Again, you must find NEW information that you have not yet used. Now it's getting hard to find that new information! Again, give your questions to a friend to answer.

Step 6

As you have been doing the puzzles, your brain has been actively searching for new information. Now write a NEW LIST that contains only the new information you have discovered when doing the puzzles. Your new list is the one to look at repeatedly for short bursts over the next few days. Try to remember more and more of it without looking at it. After a few days, you should be able to add words from your second list to your first list as you increase the information in your long-term memory.

FINALLY! Be inspired...

Make a list of different revision ideas and beside each one write **THINGS I HAVE** tried, **THINGS I WILL** try and **THINGS I MIGHT** try. Don't be scared of trying something new.

And remember – "FAIL TO PREPARE AND PREPARE TO FAIL!"

NATIONAL 5

2016

National Qualifications 2016

X737/75/11

History

FRIDAY, 20 MAY
1:00 PM – 2:45 PM

Total marks — 60

SECTION 1 — SCOTTISH CONTEXTS — 20 marks

Attempt ONE part.

SECTION 2 — BRITISH CONTEXTS — 20 marks

Attempt ONE part.

SECTION 3 — EUROPEAN AND WORLD CONTEXTS — 20 marks

Attempt ONE part.

Write your answers clearly in the answer booklet provided. In the answer booklet you must clearly identify the question number you are attempting.

Use **blue** or **black** ink.

Before leaving the examination room you must give your answer booklet to the Invigilator; if you do not, you may lose all the marks for this paper.

SECTION 1 — SCOTTISH CONTEXTS
PARTS

SECTION 2 — BRITISH CONTEXTS
PARTS

SECTION 3 — EUROPEAN AND WORLD CONTEXTS
PARTS

MARKS

SECTION 1 — SCOTTISH CONTEXTS — 20 marks

Part A — The Wars of Independence, 1286–1328

Answer the following questions using recalled knowledge and information from the sources where appropriate.

1. Explain the reasons why King John Balliol had problems ruling Scotland between 1292 and 1296.   6

Source A is an extract from a letter written by Wallace and Murray as Guardians of Scotland in 1297.

Source A

> From Andrew Murray and William Wallace, greetings to our beloved friends the mayors in Lubeck and in Hamburg. We ask that you announce to your merchants that they may safely trade their goods to all ports in the kingdom of Scotland, because the kingdom has been freed by war from the power of the English. In return, our merchants will bring their trade to you.

2. Evaluate the usefulness of **Source A** as evidence of Wallace's leadership.   6

    (You may want to comment on what type of source it is, who wrote it, when they wrote it, why they wrote it, what they say and what has been missed out.)

3. To what extent had Bruce dealt successfully with opposition by 1314?   8

    (You must use recalled knowledge to present a **balanced assessment** of the influence of different factors and come to a **reasoned conclusion**.)

[Now go to SECTION 2 starting on *Page eight*]

MARKS

SECTION 1 — SCOTTISH CONTEXTS — 20 marks

Part B — Mary Queen of Scots and the Scottish Reformation, 1542–1587

Answer the following questions using recalled knowledge and information from the sources where appropriate.

4. Explain the reasons why Protestantism grew in Scotland up to 1560.

   6

5. To what extent did Mary's marriage to Darnley play a part in her downfall in 1567?

   8

   (You must use recalled knowledge to present a **balanced assessment** of the influence of different factors and come to a **reasoned conclusion.**)

Source A is from a letter written in 1586 by Mary Queen of Scots to Anthony Babington.

Source A

> When everything is prepared and the forces are ready both in this country and abroad, then you must set the six gentlemen to work. Give orders that when the act is done, they get me away from here. At the same time get all your forces into battle order to protect me while we wait for help from abroad. May God grant success to our plans.

6. Evaluate the usefulness of **Source A** as evidence of why Mary Queen of Scots was executed in 1587.

   6

   (You may want to comment on what type of source it is, who wrote it, when they wrote it, why they wrote it, what they say and what has been missed out.)

[Now go to SECTION 2 starting on *Page eight*]

MARKS

SECTION 1 — SCOTTISH CONTEXTS — 20 marks

Part C — The Treaty of Union, 1689–1715

Answer the following questions using recalled knowledge and information from the sources where appropriate.

7. To what extent was anger over the Darien Scheme the most important reason in explaining worsening relations between Scotland and England by 1707?   8

   (You must use recalled knowledge to present a **balanced assessment** of the influence of different factors and come to a **reasoned conclusion**.)

Source A is from a petition by Stirling Town Council against the Union presented on 18 November 1706.

Source A

> We want a lasting friendship with England. But we judge that this Union will bring a high burden of taxation upon this land. Scotland would be under the rules of the English in the Parliament of Britain. The English may discourage our trade, if they think it will be in competition with their own. The Union will ruin our industry, our religion, laws and liberties.

8. Evaluate the usefulness of **Source A** as evidence of the arguments used by Scots against the Union.   6

   (You may want to comment on what type of source it is, who wrote it, when they wrote it, why they wrote it, what they say and what has been missed out.)

9. Explain the reasons why the Scots Parliament passed the Treaty of Union.   6

[Now go to SECTION 2 starting on *Page eight*]

MARKS

SECTION 1 — SCOTTISH CONTEXTS — 20 marks

Part D — Migration and Empire, 1830–1939

Answer the following questions using recalled knowledge and information from the sources where appropriate.

10. To what extent were the Clearances the most important factor for people leaving the Highlands?

    (You must use recalled knowledge to present a **balanced assessment** of the influence of different factors and come to a **reasoned conclusion**.)

8

11. Explain the reasons why so many immigrants came to Scotland after 1830.

6

Source A is from a song written by a Scottish emigrant to Canada in the 1920s.

Source A

> The winter night is long for me.
> I see only bleak empty prairie,
> There's no sound of waves breaking on the shore.
> In the evening darkness
> My spirit sinks with homesickness
> Thinking how far away
> Is everything I want to be visiting -
> The happy wee *ceilidh** house
> With the peat fire on the floor
> Where cheerful folk gathered for a gossip.
> But there's no *ceilidh** on the prairie.
> It seems like forever since I left Lewis.
>
> **ceilidh* = a friendly gathering, like a party

12. Evaluate the usefulness of **Source A** as evidence of how well Scots settled in their new countries.

6

    (You may want to comment on what type of source it is, who wrote it, when they wrote it, why they wrote it, what they say and what has been missed out.)

[Now go to SECTION 2 starting on *Page eight*]

MARKS

SECTION 1 — SCOTTISH CONTEXTS — 20 marks

Part E — The Era of the Great War, 1900–1928

Answer the following questions using recalled knowledge and information from the sources where appropriate.

13. Explain the reasons why so many Scots volunteered to fight in the Great War.   6

14. To what extent did food shortages have the biggest impact on Scottish civilians during the Great War?   8

     (You must use recalled knowledge to present a **balanced assessment** of the influence of different factors and come to a **reasoned conclusion**.)

Source A is from "*Scotland and the Impact of the Great War 1914–1928*" a book written by the historian John Kerr in 2010.

Source A

> The 1918 Representation of the People Act gave some women over 30 the vote in national elections. They had to be either householders or the wives of householders, occupiers of property with an annual rent of £5 or graduates of British universities. The electorate increased to about 21 million, of which 8·4 million were women. By the end of the 1920s women over 21 were also given the vote.

15. Evaluate the usefulness of **Source A** as evidence of the extension of the right to vote by 1918.   6

     (You may want to comment on what type of source it is, who wrote it, when they wrote it, why they wrote it, what they say and what has been missed out.)

[Now go to SECTION 2 starting on *Page eight*]

MARKS

SECTION 2 — BRITISH CONTEXTS — 20 marks

Part A — The Creation of the Medieval Kingdoms, 1066–1406

Answer the following questions using recalled knowledge and information from the sources where appropriate.

16. Explain the reasons why William, Duke of Normandy, claimed he had a right to the English throne.

5

Sources A and **B** are about how William I dealt with rebellion.

Source A

> When William's army reached York it brutally crushed the rebellion. Every home and farmland was burnt and all livestock destroyed. So many people were massacred that their bodies filled the streets. William made no attempt to control his anger and punished everyone whether they were innocent or guilty. Within weeks the whole of Yorkshire had become a wasteland. The few who had survived now faced starvation.

Source B

> William marched north with an army of experienced soldiers. Hundreds of people were slaughtered when William's men went from village to village to end the uprising. Crops were set on fire, herds of animals were slaughtered and supplies of food ruined. Whole families died of hunger as a result of William's harsh actions. The north never rebelled again and William was able to spend his time dealing with problems elsewhere in his kingdom.

17. Compare the views of **Sources A** and **B** about how William I dealt with rebellion. (Compare the sources overall and/or in detail.)

4

18. Describe the actions taken by Henry II to increase his power when he became king in 1154.

5

Source C explains why the Church was important in medieval times.

Source C

> Harvest failure and disease meant life was often short and brutal for medieval people. The Church offered support and comfort during difficult times and encouraged people not to give up. Every Sunday, priests preached about the afterlife and taught people how to be good Christians. Priests also heard confessions and issued penance for those who wanted their sins forgiven. In this way the Church was able to control the way people behaved in society allowing most communities to live in peace.

19. How fully does **Source C** explain why the Church was important in medieval times? (Use the source and recall to reach a judgement.)   6

[Now go to SECTION 3 starting on *Page eighteen*]

MARKS

SECTION 2 — BRITISH CONTEXTS — 20 marks

Part B — War of the Three Kingdoms, 1603–1651

Answer the following questions using recalled knowledge and information from the sources where appropriate.

Sources A and **B** are about the reign of King Charles I.

Source A

> The reign of Charles I began with an unpopular friendship with the Duke of Buckingham. He used his influence with the King to control the nobility. Buckingham was assassinated in 1628. There was ongoing tension with Parliament over money, made worse by the costs of war abroad. Religious tensions led to further resentment of Charles I as he preferred Anglican forms of worship which made Puritans suspicious.

Source B

> Charles I was a very religious man who enjoyed Anglican church services full of ritual, and this led to clashes with Puritans who preferred plain and simple services. Charles also angered many by having favourites at court, particularly the Duke of Buckingham. In 1628 Buckingham was assassinated. Charles' constant arguments with Parliament led him to rule without Parliament for eleven years. Charles also angered many with the methods he used to raise money.

20. Compare the views of **Sources A** and **B** about the reign of King Charles I. (Compare the sources overall and/or in detail.) **4**

21. Explain the reasons why there was opposition to the methods used by Charles I to raise money. **5**

22. Describe the reaction in Scotland to the introduction of the New Prayer Book in 1637. **5**

MARKS

Source C is about the Battle of Edgehill in 1642.

Source C

> The King ordered his army to occupy the high ridge on Edgehill, hoping that the Parliamentarian army would be forced to attack uphill. Instead the Parliamentarian army was arranged on flat ground 2 miles away, waiting for the King to make the first move. The Parliamentary army was commanded by the Earl of Essex who had gained experience of commanding an army during the First Bishops' War. Essex's decision to wait forced the King to take action. The King moved his army down off the ridge and attacked.

23. How fully does **Source C** describe the events of the Battle of Edgehill in 1642? (Use the source and recall to reach a judgement.)

6

[Now go to SECTION 3 starting on *Page eighteen*]

MARKS

SECTION 2 — BRITISH CONTEXTS — 20 marks

Part C — The Atlantic Slave Trade, 1770—1807

Answer the following questions using recalled knowledge and information from the sources where appropriate.

Source A is about conditions on board ships during the Middle Passage.

Source A

> Slave ships left from British ports on the triangular trade. When the ships arrived in Africa, captains exchanged guns or alcohol for slaves. Slaves were often tightly packed below deck for the journey across the Atlantic Ocean. This was known as the middle passage. Conditions below deck were horrendous and slaves were denied basic sanitation. Disease was common and many died from conditions such as dysentery. Slaves were given enough food to sustain them during the voyage. However, the food was unfamiliar and many slaves simply refused to eat.

24. How fully does **Source A** describe the conditions on board ships during the Middle Passage? (Use the source and recall to reach a judgement.)   6

25. Explain the reasons why the slave trade was important to British cities.   5

MARKS

Sources **B** and **C** are about resistance on the plantations.

Source B

> Slaves hated the way they were treated. They were not paid for their work and saw no reason for working hard. They sabotaged their owners by working slowly and inefficiently. They broke tools and let animals loose. They were harshly punished for such behaviour. As well as whipping, some slaves had their ears, noses and limbs cut off. Many slaves attempted to run away. In mountainous islands like Jamaica, runaways fled to the mountains.

Source C

> The West Indian plantations relied on slaves to do the work. Although the slaves outnumbered the Whites they still felt isolated and powerless. However, they resisted their situation in many ways. The mildest forms of resistance were doing a job slowly or badly. Other slaves ran away when they saw a chance. The punishments for slaves who resisted were very harsh. Plantation records show that punishments such as hanging, mutilation or lashing were common.

26. Compare the views of **Sources B** and **C** about resistance on the plantations. (Compare the sources overall and/or in detail.)   4

27. Describe the methods used by abolitionists to try and end the slave trade.   5

[Now go to SECTION 3 starting on *Page eighteen*]

MARKS

SECTION 2 — BRITISH CONTEXTS — 20 marks

Part D — Changing Britain, 1760–1914

Answer the following questions using recalled knowledge and information from the sources where appropriate.

Sources **A** and **B** are about the Peterloo massacre in 1819.

Source A

> In 1819 a meeting was due to be addressed by Henry Hunt in Manchester. People had gathered from all over Lancashire in St Peter's Fields. The magistrates wrongly believed that people had been marching and drilling like soldiers in preparation. They ordered the army to charge the crowd. In the stampede that followed, 11 people were killed and hundreds injured. The press nicknamed the tragedy "Peterloo" in mocking memory of the Battle of Waterloo.

Source B

> I saw a large crowd that had gathered from miles around and was moving towards St Peter's Fields. I laughed at the fears of the magistrates as the so-called "marching" protest was actually a procession of men with their wives, sisters and children. After that there was just noise and confusion and I could see that many people had been hurt. I will always be haunted by the sight of those trampled bodies.

28. Compare the views of **Sources A** and **B** about the events of the Peterloo massacre in 1819. (Compare the sources overall and/or in detail.)   4

29. Explain the reasons why working in mills was harmful to the health of textile workers.   5

MARKS

Source C describes the benefits that railways brought to Britain.

Source C

> Railways changed the lives of nearly everyone in Britain. As early as 1852, all the present-day main lines had been laid. Even the most remote country areas were brought into contact with towns and cities. Industries benefited greatly from being able to transport their raw materials and goods quickly and cheaply. Farmers were able to sell their fresh produce over greater distances. Faster travel meant that people could live further from their jobs, so towns spread as suburbs were built.

30. How fully does **Source C** explain the benefits brought to Britain by railways? (Use the source and recall to reach a judgement.)   6

31. Describe the changes made to voting and representation by 1867.   5

[Now go to SECTION 3 starting on *Page eighteen*]

MARKS

SECTION 2 — BRITISH CONTEXTS — 20 marks

Part E — The Making of Modern Britain, 1880—1951

Answer the following questions using recalled knowledge and information from the sources where appropriate.

32. Describe the problems facing the poor by the early 1900s.   5

Source A is about changing attitudes to poverty.

Source A

> In 1900 the Labour Party was formed. This new party campaigned for reforms to tackle poverty. Other parties were afraid that they might lose votes to Labour if they did not show that they wanted to help the poor. Most working class men now had the vote, so it was possible that they could vote for Labour. Trade unions put pressure on the Liberals and Conservatives to do more to help the poor. Society was beginning to accept that some people became poor through no fault of their own.

33. How fully does **Source A** explain the reasons for changing attitudes to poverty by the 1900s? (Use the source and recall to reach a judgement.)   6

34. Explain the reasons why the reforms of the Liberal government of 1906—1914 did not fully meet the needs of the British people.   5

MARKS

Sources **B** and **C** are about the success of the reforms of the Labour Government of 1945–1951.

Source B

> There is some disagreement amongst historians about how successful the Labour reforms actually were. However, their record of success is difficult to argue with. The National Health Service was the greatest achievement of the Labour welfare state, giving free medical and dental treatment to all. Considerable progress was made in tackling the housing shortage. Between 1948 and 1951, around 200,000 homes were built per year.

Source C

> Labour came to power in 1945. Their reputation of being the creator of the modern welfare state is not entirely deserved. Labour's record on house building was poor when compared to previous governments. Labour claimed the credit for maintaining low levels of unemployment, but this was mainly due to booming private industry and exports. By 1951, charges had to be introduced for some dental treatment, spectacles and prescriptions, meaning the NHS was not entirely free.

35. Compare the views of **Sources B** and **C** about the success of the reforms of the Labour Government of 1945–1951. (Compare the sources overall and/or in detail.)   4

[Now go to SECTION 3 starting on *Page eighteen*]

MARKS

SECTION 3 — EUROPEAN AND WORLD CONTEXTS — 20 marks

Part A — The Cross and the Crescent: the Crusades, 1071–1192

Answer the following questions using recalled knowledge and information from the sources where appropriate.

36. Describe the role of a knight in medieval times.   **5**

37. Explain the reasons why the People's Crusade failed.   **5**

Source A describes Muslim disunity.

Source A

> After capturing Antioch, the Crusader army had an easy march south. Local Muslim communities did not attack the Crusaders and some even gave them money to keep the peace. Unwilling to end their bitter rivalries, the Muslim leaders refused to join together and thought only of their own land. By the time the Crusaders reached Jerusalem, the Seljuk Turks had been defeated by an Egyptian force and had lost the city. The Egyptians asked for help but no Muslim armies came to their aid.

38. How fully does **Source A** describe Muslim disunity during the First Crusade? (Use the source and recall to reach a judgement.)   **5**

Source B is from a chronicle written by a Crusader in 1187.

Source B

> Desperate to help the Christians in Tiberias, King Guy gathered a large Crusader army and left for the city. Whilst on their way, the Crusaders were constantly attacked by Saladin's men. Exhausted by their journey, King Guy made a terrible mistake and made camp near Hattin. Without water and supplies the Crusaders could neither carry on nor turn back. Saladin's army surrounded the Crusaders' camp and slaughtered nearly all those inside.

39. Evaluate the usefulness of **Source B** as evidence of the Battle of Hattin.   **5**

    (You may want to comment on what type of source it is, who wrote it, when they wrote it, why they wrote it, what they say and what has been missed out.)

MARKS

SECTION 3 — EUROPEAN AND WORLD CONTEXTS — 20 marks

Part B — "Tea and Freedom": the American Revolution, 1774–1783

Answer the following questions using recalled knowledge and information from the sources where appropriate.

40. Explain the reasons why the colonists had become unhappy with British rule by the 1770s.   5

41. Describe the events at Bunker Hill in 1775.   5

Source A is about the events in Lexington and Concord in 1775.

Source A

> By early 1775 many in the colonies had started to prepare for war. Spies had informed the British commander in Boston about a store of gunpowder and weapons that the colonists had been collecting at Concord. British soldiers were dispatched to seize the supplies. When the British arrived at Lexington they were confronted by a group of minutemen. These were colonists who had been training and preparing for war. Shots were fired and several colonists were killed. The British then marched on to Concord where they destroyed any remaining supplies.

42. How fully does **Source A** describe the events at Lexington and Concord in 1775? (Use the source and recall to reach a judgement.)   5

Source B is from a diary written by an American army officer in December 1777.

Source B

> The army now continues to grow sickly from the exhaustion they have suffered in this campaign. We are sick — discontented — and out of humour. Poor food — cold weather — nasty clothes — nasty cooking — the Devil's in it! I can't endure it! Why are we sent here to starve and freeze? Despite all of this, the men still show a spirit not to be expected from such young troops.

43. Evaluate the usefulness of **Source B** as evidence of the condition of the American army during the winter of 1777.   5

    (You may want to comment on what type of source it is, who wrote it, when they wrote it, why they wrote it, what they say and what has been missed out.)

MARKS

SECTION 3 — EUROPEAN AND WORLD CONTEXTS — 20 marks

Part C — USA, 1850–1880

Answer the following questions using recalled knowledge and information from the sources where appropriate.

44. Describe the problems faced by the different groups who travelled west after 1850.   **5**

45. Explain the reasons why the Southern States seceded from the Union in 1861.   **5**

Source A is from a letter written by George Fitzhugh, a Southern lawyer, in 1857.

Source A

> The slaves of the South are the happiest and are, in many ways, the most free people in the world. The children, the aged and the sick do not work at all. They have all the comforts and necessaries of life provided for them such as food and housing. The slave women do little hard work. On average the slave men and boys do not work more than nine hours a day in good weather.

46. Evaluate the usefulness of **Source A** as evidence of slave life on plantations before 1861.   **5**

(You may want to comment on what type of source it is, who wrote it, when they wrote it, why they wrote it, what they say and what has been missed out.)

Source B is part of a speech made by Frederick Douglass, a former slave, in 1880.

Source B

> Slaves were made free in 1865. At first there were great hopes for change. But today, in most of the Southern States, the Fourteenth and Fifteenth Amendments to the Constitution are almost totally ignored. The right of citizenship granted in the Fourteenth Amendment is practically a mockery. The right to vote, provided for in the Fifteenth Amendment, is under attack. The old ruling class is victorious today and the newly freed slaves are little better off than they were before the rebellion of the Southern States against the Union.

47. How fully does **Source B** describe the impact of Reconstruction in the South after 1865? (Use the source and recall to reach a judgement.)   **5**

MARKS

SECTION 3 — EUROPEAN AND WORLD CONTEXTS — 20 marks

Part D — Hitler and Nazi Germany, 1919—1939

Answer the following questions using recalled knowledge and information from the sources where appropriate.

48. Explain the reasons why the German people were opposed to the Treaty of Versailles.

5

49. Describe the treatment of the Jews in Nazi Germany.

5

Source A is from the diary of Ernst Thalmann, a Communist leader writing about his arrest in 1933 by the Gestapo.

Source A

> Every cruel method of blackmail was used against me to obtain details about my comrades. But the approach proved unsuccessful. I was then assaulted and in the process had four teeth knocked out. They tried hypnosis which was also ineffective. Finally, a Gestapo officer with a whip in his hand beat me with measured strokes. Driven wild with pain, I screamed at the top of my voice.

50. Evaluate the usefulness of **Source A** as evidence of the use of intimidation by the Nazis.

(You may want to comment on what type of source it is, who wrote it, when they wrote it, why they wrote it, what they say and what has been missed out.)

5

Source B is about the activities of the Hitler Youth.

Source B

> Boys learned military skills such as practising with weapons. To toughen them up, they were taken on cross country hikes and runs. One member of the Hitler Youth remembered that anyone who got a stitch while running was punished and humiliated as a weakling. Boys were also tested on their knowledge of Nazism and those who passed the test were given a dagger marked "Blood and Honour". Most members of the Hitler Youth joined because they thought it was fun and exciting. However they did not all enjoy the endless marching.

51. How fully does **Source B** describe the activities of the Hitler Youth? (Use the source and recall to reach a judgement.)

5

MARKS

SECTION 3 — EUROPEAN AND WORLD CONTEXTS — 20 marks

Part E — Red Flag: Lenin and the Russian Revolution, 1894—1921

Answer the following questions using recalled knowledge and information from the sources where appropriate.

Source A is about the conditions for workers and peasants in Russia before 1905.

Source A

> Tsar Nicholas II, I do not wish to die without having told you and the people of Russia what I think of your activities up to the present. Police brutality is steadily growing. The prisons are filled to overflowing with hundreds of thousands of common criminals. Many workers are now imprisoned along with political prisoners. The treatment of millions of peasants, on whom the power of Russia depends, leads to them becoming poorer every year. Famine is now normal throughout the country.

52. How fully does **Source A** describe the conditions of workers and peasants in Russia before 1905? (Use the source and recall to reach a judgement.)   5

53. Describe the reforms which were introduced in Russia after the 1905 Revolution.   5

54. Explain the reasons why the Bolsheviks were able to seize power in Petrograd in October 1917.   5

Source B is from the diary of Leon Trotsky written in 1921.

Source B

> We formed an army out of peasants, workers and refugees escaping from the Whites. We believed that this flabby, panicky mob could be changed into a useful force. What was needed were good commanders and a few experienced fighters. The mob would fight as long as they had boots for the barefooted, a bathhouse, food, underwear, tobacco and a dozen or so Communists ready to make any sacrifice to inspire them.

55. Evaluate the usefulness of **Source B** as evidence of the reasons for the Bolshevik victory in the Civil War.   5

    (You may want to comment on what type of source it is, who wrote it, when they wrote it, why they wrote it, what they say and what has been missed out.)

MARKS

SECTION 3 — EUROPEAN AND WORLD CONTEXTS — 20 marks

Part F — Mussolini and Fascist Italy, 1919–1939

Answer the following questions using recalled knowledge and information from the sources where appropriate.

56. Explain the reasons why Mussolini was able to secure power in Italy by 1925.   5

57. Describe the policies introduced by Mussolini to try to control the lives of young Italians.   5

Source A is about the cult of "Il Duce".

Source A

> When the Fascists came to power in 1922, a leadership cult was established in Italy. The media played a very important role, making Mussolini the centre of every story. The cult built popular support for him and secured continuing support for his dictatorship. Benito Mussolini was shown as a man chosen by destiny to save Italy and its people from Communism and Socialism. He was the new Caesar — a man of genius, a man of action.

58. How fully does **Source A** describe the cult of "Il Duce". (Use the source and recall to reach a judgement.)   5

Source B is part of a speech made by Mussolini in 1922.

Source B

> There is much for us to do in this country. Perfect unity in Italy cannot be spoken of until Fiume and Dalmatia and other territories have come back to us, fulfilling the proud dream which we carry in our hearts. Violence may have to be used. Violence is sometimes necessary. Italy, in order to become a Mediterranean power, must have control over the Adriatic Sea.

59. Evaluate the usefulness of **Source B** as evidence of Mussolini's foreign policy.   5

(You may want to comment on what type of source it is, who wrote it, when they wrote it, why they wrote it, what they say and what has been missed out.)

MARKS

SECTION 3 — EUROPEAN AND WORLD CONTEXTS — 20 marks

Part G — Free at Last? Civil Rights in the USA, 1918—1968

Answer the following questions using recalled knowledge and information from the sources where appropriate.

60. Describe the ways that the Jim Crow laws segregated black and white Americans.   5

61. Explain the reasons why many Americans were against immigration by the 1920s.   5

Source A is about the actions of the Ku Klux Klan.

Source A

> The original Ku Klux Klan was a white supremacist organisation founded in 1866. Wearing white robes and pointed hats, the Klan of the 1920s looked similar to the original. During elections, the Klan would wait outside the voting place to beat up blacks if they came near. Women considered immoral were also targeted by the Klan. A divorced woman in Texas was tarred and feathered for remarrying. A massive march in Washington DC in 1925 was a demonstration of the Klan's power.

62. How fully does **Source A** describe the actions of the Ku Klux Klan in the 1920s? (Use the source and recall to reach a judgement.)   5

Source B is from a newspaper interview with a black American taxi driver from New York in 1961.

Source B

> I like Malcolm the best. I can believe in a leader who comes from the street, Malcolm is one of us. Malcolm isn't afraid to stand up to the FBI and the cops. Those black Muslims make more sense than the NAACP and all of the rest of them put together, you don't see Malcolm tip-toeing around the whites like he's scared of them.

63. Evaluate the usefulness of **Source B** as evidence of the reasons why Malcolm X was popular amongst many black Americans.   5

(You may want to comment on what type of source it is, who wrote it, when they wrote it, why they wrote it, what they say and what has been missed out.)

MARKS

SECTION 3 — EUROPEAN AND WORLD CONTEXTS — 20 marks

Part H—Appeasement and the Road to War, 1918–1939

Answer the following questions using recalled knowledge and information from the sources where appropriate.

64. Describe the ways in which Hitler rearmed Germany between 1933 and 1935.   5

Source A is from an article by the historian Professor Neil Gregor in *"20th Century History Review"*, published in 2008.

Source A

> The Anschluss had a number of significant consequences and was notable for several reasons. Most obviously, it marked the beginning of Germany's territorial expansion, starting a chain of events which continued with the occupation of the Sudetenland. The lack of meaningful opposition from Britain and France underlined again for Hitler that he could do as he pleased. The persecution of Jews by the Nazis was greatly intensified following the Anschluss, especially in Austria.

65. Evaluate the usefulness of **Source A** as evidence of the consequences of the Anschluss.   5

    (You may want to comment on what type of source it is, who wrote it, when they wrote it, why they wrote it, what they say and what has been missed out.)

Source B is about the British policy of appeasement in the 1930s.

Source B

> Appeasement was a policy which involved making concessions to Hitler. The main reason for such a stance was a belief that given the harsh treatment of Germany at Versailles, Hitler's demands were not unreasonable. The policy was motivated by several other factors. The British public were still haunted by memories of World War One and unwilling to back military action. Chiefs of the armed forces advised that the British military was unprepared for war. The Treasury meanwhile warned against the financial consequences of war.

66. How fully does **Source B** explain the reasons why Britain followed a policy of appeasement? (Use the source and recall to reach a judgement.)   5

67. Explain the reasons why Hitler declared war on Poland in 1939.   5

MARKS

SECTION 3 — EUROPEAN AND WORLD CONTEXTS — 20 marks

Part I — World War II, 1939—1945

Answer the following questions using recalled knowledge and information from the sources where appropriate.

68. Explain the reasons why Hitler launched an attack on Russia in June 1941.   **5**

69. Describe the attack on Pearl Harbour by Japanese forces in December 1941.   **5**

Source A is about the preparation for the Normandy Landings of June 1944.

Source A

> Operation Overlord was a complex operation. It involved the land, sea and air forces of the USA, Britain and Canada. Preparations began in 1943 under the overall command of General Eisenhower of the United States. Normandy was chosen as the site for the landings because of its open beaches that were not as well defended as those at Calais. Normandy was also chosen because it had a fairly large port, Cherbourg. It was also opposite the main ports of southern England. The intended date for the invasion was May 1944.

70. How fully does **Source A** describe the preparations for the Normandy Landings of June 1944? (Use the source and recall to reach a judgement.)   **5**

Source B is from a leaflet dropped by the US Government over Japan on 16 August 1945.

Source B

> TO THE JAPANESE PEOPLE: We are in possession of the most destructive explosive devised by man. We have just begun to use this weapon against your country. If you still have any doubts, ask what happened to Hiroshima when just one atomic bomb fell on that city. You should take steps now to surrender. Otherwise we shall use this bomb again to promptly and forcefully end the war. EVACUATE YOUR CITIES.

71. Evaluate the usefulness of **Source B** as evidence of the use of atomic bombs against Japan in 1945.   **5**

(You may want to comment on what type of source it is, who wrote it, when they wrote it, why they wrote it, what they say and what has been missed out.)

MARKS

SECTION 3 — EUROPEAN AND WORLD CONTEXTS — 20 marks

Part J — The Cold War, 1945—1989

Answer the following questions using recalled knowledge and information from the sources where appropriate.

Source A is from a leaflet published by the East German Government in 1962.

Source A

> We could no longer stand by and see so many of our doctors, engineers and skilled workers persuaded by corrupt methods to work in West Germany or West Berlin. These dirty tricks cost East Germany annual losses amounting to 3·5 thousand million marks. But we prevented something much more important with the Wall — West Berlin could have become the starting point for military conflict.

72. Evaluate the usefulness of **Source A** as evidence of why the Berlin Wall was built.   5

    (You may want to comment on what type of source it is, who wrote it, when they wrote it, why they wrote it, what they say and what has been missed out.)

Source B is about the Cuban missile crisis.

Source B

> During the Cuban missile crisis it was said that the world held its breath. There was a crisis in Cuba because by the early 1960s the USA and the Soviet Union were bitter rivals. Many in the United States believed that the Soviet actions in Cuba provided proof of a determination to spread Communism all around the world. Cuba was very close to the American mainland and this explains why Americans were so concerned by events there. Both sides were afraid to back down in case they lost face.

73. How fully does **Source B** explain the reasons for the Cuban missile crisis? (Use the source and recall to reach a judgement.)   5

74. Describe the differing American views on the Vietnam War.   5

75. Explain the reasons why the USA and the Soviet Union followed a policy of détente after 1968.   5

[END OF QUESTION PAPER]

[BLANK PAGE]

DO NOT WRITE ON THIS PAGE

NATIONAL 5

2017

National Qualifications 2017

X737/75/11

History

TUESDAY, 9 MAY
1:00 PM — 2:45 PM

Total marks — 60

SECTION 1 — SCOTTISH CONTEXTS — 20 marks

Attempt ONE part.

SECTION 2 — BRITISH CONTEXTS — 20 marks

Attempt ONE part.

SECTION 3 — EUROPEAN AND WORLD CONTEXTS — 20 marks

Attempt ONE part.

Write your answers clearly in the answer booklet provided. In the answer booklet you must clearly identify the question number you are attempting.

Use **blue** or **black** ink.

Before leaving the examination room you must give your answer booklet to the Invigilator; if you do not, you may lose all the marks for this paper.

MARKS

SECTION 1 — SCOTTISH CONTEXTS — 20 marks

Part A — The Wars of Independence, 1286–1328

Answer the following **four** questions using recalled knowledge and information from the sources where appropriate.

1. Explain the reasons why many Scots were unhappy to accept the Maid of Norway as their queen.   **5**

Source A is from a textbook written by a modern historian in 2009.

Source A

> After the Scots asked for his help, King Edward I called for a parliament to be held in May 1291 to settle the future of the Scottish crown. The location he chose was Norham Castle on the English side of the River Tweed. He said that the proceedings would not start until the Guardians and the claimants to the throne had acknowledged his position as overlord of Scotland. The Scots were stunned.

2. Evaluate the usefulness of **Source A** as evidence of problems the Scots faced when judging the Great Cause.   **5**

    (You may want to comment on what type of source it is, who wrote it, when they wrote it, why they wrote it, what they say and what has been missed out.)

3. Describe the actions Edward I took to assert his authority over Scotland in 1296.   **5**

Source B is about what happened to William Wallace after the Battle of Falkirk.

Source B

> For many years, little was known about Wallace's activities between his defeat at Falkirk and his death. He certainly left Scotland. Historians found a "safe conduct" which was given to Wallace in 1300 by the King of France. Wallace travelled to France as part of his campaign to free John Balliol. Wallace apparently planned to visit the Pope to get him on Balliol's side. His campaign failed however and Wallace was back in Scotland well before 1305 where he continued to fight against Edward's rule.

4. How fully does **Source B** describe what happened to William Wallace after the Battle of Falkirk? (Use the source and recall to reach a judgement.)   **5**

[Now go to SECTION 2 starting on *Page eight*]

MARKS

SECTION 1 — SCOTTISH CONTEXTS — 20 marks

Part B — Mary Queen of Scots, and the Scottish Reformation, 1542–1587

Answer the following **four** questions using recalled knowledge and information from the sources where appropriate.

5. Explain the reasons why Mary, Queen of Scots left Scotland for France in 1548.   5

6. Describe the events that led to Scotland becoming a Protestant country in 1560.   5

Source A is from a textbook written by a modern historian in 2013.

Source A

> On the night Darnley was killed, everyone in the palace was woken by a deafening noise that shook the entire area. Mary asked what cannon were firing as she thought they were under attack. But no one knew what was happening. All over town, people hurried outside to discover what dreadful disaster had occurred. Those who lived in Kirk o' Field stared in disbelief at the house where Darnley was staying, which was now rubble.

7. Evaluate the usefulness of **Source A** as evidence of the death of Darnley in 1567.   5

   (You may want to comment on what type of source it is, who wrote it, when they wrote it, why they wrote it, what they say and what has been missed out.)

Source B describes the events relating to the abdication of Mary, Queen of Scots in 1567.

Source B

> Many of the Scottish nobles were outraged that Mary had married the Earl of Bothwell. Some of the Protestant nobles decided to rebel against Mary and Bothwell, including her half-brother the Earl of Moray. The Protestant nobles raised an army and so did Mary and her new husband. The two armies met at Carberry on 15th June 1566. The nobles said they would withdraw if Mary gave up Bothwell but she refused. Bothwell escaped to Denmark and Mary surrendered to the Scottish nobles.

8. How fully does **Source B** describe the events relating to the abdication of Mary, Queen of Scots? (Use the source and recall to reach a judgement.)   5

[Now go to SECTION 2 starting on *Page eight*]

MARKS

SECTION 1 — SCOTTISH CONTEXTS — 20 marks

Part C — The Treaty of Union, 1689–1715

Answer the following **four** questions using recalled knowledge and information from the sources where appropriate.

Source **A** describes the causes of tension between Scotland and England up to 1707.

Source A

> Relations between Scotland and England were very poor in these years. In England there was a lot of resentment at the level of support for the Jacobites in Scotland. The Scots were angry at not being consulted by the English over the Act of Settlement of 1701. As the smaller partner in the union of crowns the Scots felt their interests were ignored. The Scots were also annoyed that they had not been consulted over entry into the war of Spanish Succession.

9. How fully does **Source A** describe the causes of tension between Scotland and England up to 1707? (Use the source and recall to reach a judgement.)   5

10. Describe the arguments used by the opponents of Union in Scotland.   5

11. Explain the reasons why many Scots were in favour of Union with England.   5

Source **B** is from a textbook written by a modern historian in 1996.

Source B

> Many Kirk ministers were very concerned about the possibility of union. But when Parliament passed an Act for the Security of the Kirk many of them changed their tune. The Equivalent was the biggest incentive for many as it led to the sum of over three hundred thousand pounds sterling to be sent in cash to Scotland. English guarantees over the independence of the Scots legal system also soothed most fears within the Scottish legal profession.

12. Evaluate the usefulness of **Source B** as evidence of the reasons why the Scots Parliament passed the Treaty of Union.   5

    (You may want to comment on what type of source it is, who wrote it, when they wrote it, why they wrote it, what they say and what has been missed out.)

[Now go to SECTION 2 starting on *Page eight*]

MARKS

SECTION 1 — SCOTTISH CONTEXTS — 20 marks

Part D — Migration and Empire, 1830–1939

Answer the following **four** questions using recalled knowledge and information from the sources where appropriate.

13. Describe the impact the Empire had on Scotland between 1830 and 1939.   5

Source A describes the importance of the Catholic Church to Irish immigrants in Scotland.

Source A

> Seventy five percent of Irish immigrants to Scotland were Catholic and by 1902 there were 234 priests ministering to the Irish community in Glasgow. The church enabled them to keep their religious identity in Scotland through worshipping in their traditional way. It was the centre of social life for many Irish immigrants, offering a friendly environment where people could meet and be made welcome. The church also established youth groups. The church also attempted to tackle some of the issues Scottish society faced, such as the problem of poverty.

14. How fully does **Source A** describe the importance of the Catholic Church to Irish immigrants in Scotland? (Use the source and recall to reach a judgement.)   5

Source B is from a textbook written by a modern historian in 2007.

Source B

> Jewish immigrants usually lacked the experience needed to work in heavy industry but instead they supplied goods and services. The Census of 1891 showed that in the Gorbals in Glasgow, where most of the working class Jews lived, 195 Jews worked in the clothing industry. Another 116 made a living selling door to door or running small shops. Many had practised these occupations in their native country so they brought these skills with them.

15. Evaluate the usefulness of **Source B** as evidence of the work done by immigrants in Scotland.   5

(You may want to comment on what type of source it is, who wrote it, when they wrote it, why they wrote it, what they say and what has been missed out.)

16. Explain the reasons why many Scots were attracted to start new lives overseas.   5

[Now go to SECTION 2 starting on *Page eight*]

MARKS

SECTION 1 — SCOTTISH CONTEXTS — 20 marks

Part E — The Era of the Great War, 1900–1928

Answer the following **four** questions using recalled knowledge and information from the sources where appropriate.

17. Describe the conditions Scottish soldiers faced in the trenches.   5

18. Explain the reasons why rationing was introduced during the Great War.   5

Source A describes the changing role of women during the Great War.

Source A

> The Great War was a crucial time for women. This is because it gave women an opportunity to prove themselves in a male-dominated society, doing more than cleaning the house and looking after children. With so many men going to war, there was a large gap in employment and women responded by replacing men in the workplace. The Women's Royal Air Force was created, where women worked on planes as mechanics. Some of the less well known roles of women in the war included selling war bonds.

19. How fully does **Source A** describe the changing role of women during the Great War? (Use the source and recall to reach a judgement.)   5

Source B is from a textbook written by a modern historian in 1989.

Source B

> The Great War had a considerable impact on Scotland's fishing industry. By 1919 the hundreds of fishing boats that had been working for the Royal Navy were free again to go fishing. It meant there were far more boats chasing the same amount of fish, and many boats could not make enough money to stay in business. On top of that it was far more difficult to sell fish. Before the war most of the herring that were caught were sold to Germany and Russia.

20. Evaluate the usefulness of **Source B** as evidence of the effects of the Great War on Scotland's industries.   5

   (You may want to comment on what type of source it is, who wrote it, when they wrote it, why they wrote it, what they say and what has been missed out.)

[Now go to SECTION 2 starting on *Page eight*]

MARKS

SECTION 2 — BRITISH CONTEXTS — 20 marks

Part A — The Creation of the Medieval Kingdoms, 1066–1406

Answer the following **three** questions using recalled knowledge and information from the sources where appropriate.

21. Explain the reasons why David I was influenced by the Normans during his reign.   6

22. To what extent were illegal castles Henry II's greatest problem when he became king in 1154?   8

    (You must use recalled knowledge to present a **balanced assessment** of the influence of different factors and come to a **reasoned conclusion**.)

Source A is from a chronicle, written by a monk in 1381.

Source A

> King Richard II was eager to end the revolt and so agreed to meet the peasants. Whilst at the meeting, a fight broke out and the peasants' leader, Wat Tyler was killed. The peasants immediately took up their weapons to fight but the king rode toward them and persuaded them to put their weapons away. The king promised the peasants that they would be treated fairly and so they agreed to go home.

23. Evaluate the usefulness of **Source A** as evidence of the reasons for the failure of the Peasants' Revolt.   6

    (You may want to comment on what type of source it is, who wrote it, when they wrote it, why they wrote it, what they say and what has been missed out.)

[Now go to SECTION 3 starting on *Page fourteen*]

MARKS

SECTION 2 — BRITISH CONTEXTS — 20 marks

Part B — War of the Three Kingdoms, 1603–1651

Answer the following **three** questions using recalled knowledge and information from the sources where appropriate.

Source A is from the Protestation of 1621, a statement from the House of Commons of England.

Source A

> After many years of growing discontent we the members assemble in Parliament to make our protest formally. The privileges of Parliament are our ancient birth right. Matters concerning the king, state, defence, the church and the making of laws are for debating in Parliament only. And that, if any of its members are questioned for anything said or done in Parliament, the same is to be applied to the king.

24. Evaluate the usefulness of **Source A** as evidence of the arguments between Parliament and King James VI and I.

    (You may want to comment on what type of source it is, who wrote it, when they wrote it, why they wrote it, what they say and what has been missed out.)

    6

25. Explain the reasons why Charles I was unpopular in Scotland.

    6

26. To what extent were financial disputes between Charles I and Parliament the main reason for the outbreak of the Civil War?

    8

    (You must use recalled knowledge to present a **balanced assessment** of the influence of different factors and come to a **reasoned conclusion**.)

[Now go to SECTION 3 starting on *Page fourteen*]

MARKS

SECTION 2 — BRITISH CONTEXTS — 20 marks

Part C — The Atlantic Slave Trade, 1770—1807

Answer the following **three** questions using recalled knowledge and information from the sources where appropriate.

27. To what extent was increased employment the main benefit the slave trade brought to Britain?

    (You must use recalled knowledge to present a **balanced assessment** of the influence of different factors and come to a **reasoned conclusion**.)

    8

28. Explain the reasons why the slave trade had a negative impact on the Caribbean islands.

    6

Source A is from an Abolitionist speech made by William Wilberforce to the House of Commons on the 12th May 1789.

Source A

> Let anyone imagine to himself 600 of these unfortunates chained two and two. The right ankle of one is connected with the left ankle of another by a small iron fetter. The slaves are so miserable at leaving their country, that they set sail at night, unaware of their departure. For exercise, these miserable people, loaded down by chains and suffering from disease, are forced to dance by the terror of the whip.

29. Evaluate the usefulness of **Source A** as evidence used by the abolitionists to argue against the slave trade.

    6

    (You may want to comment on what type of source it is, who wrote it, when they wrote it, why they wrote it, what they say and what has been missed out.)

[Now go to SECTION 3 starting on *Page fourteen*]

MARKS

SECTION 2 — BRITISH CONTEXTS — 20 marks

Part D — Changing Britain, 1760–1914

Answer the following **three** questions using recalled knowledge and information from the sources where appropriate.

30. To what extent was a lack of clean water the main reason for poor health in towns during the nineteenth century?

    (You must use recalled knowledge to present a **balanced assessment** of the influence of different factors and come to a **reasoned conclusion**.)

8

Source A is an extract from the Factory Act passed by the government in 1833.

Source A

> • No children under the age of 9 are permitted to work in textile mills
> • Children aged 9–13 must not work more than 8 hours each day
> • Children aged 14–18 must not work more than 12 hours each day
> • Children under 18 must not work at night
> • Government factory inspectors will be given the power to demand entry to textile mills and enforce these rules

31. Evaluate the usefulness of **Source A** as evidence of the ways working conditions in factories were improved by 1900.

    (You may want to comment on what type of source it is, who wrote it, when they wrote it, why they wrote it, what they say and what has been missed out.)

6

32. Explain the reasons why the Chartists failed to achieve their aims.

6

[Now go to SECTION 3 starting on *Page fourteen*]

MARKS

SECTION 2 — BRITISH CONTEXTS — 20 marks

Part E — The Making of Modern Britain, 1880–1951

Answer the following **three** questions using recalled knowledge and information from the sources where appropriate.

33. To what extent were the reports of Booth and Rowntree the main reason for changing attitudes to poverty around 1900?

    (You must use recalled knowledge to present a **balanced assessment** of the influence of different factors and come to a **reasoned conclusion**.)

    8

34. Explain the reasons why the Liberal Reforms of 1906–1914 improved the lives of some British people.

    6

Source A is a government advertisement published in May 1948.

Source A

> ### YOUR NEW
> ### NATIONAL HEALTH SERVICE
>
> On 5th July the new National Health Service starts for the benefit of the public all over Britain.
>
> Anyone can use it — men, women and children. There are no age limits. You can use any part of it, or all of it, as you wish. Your right to use the National Health Service does not depend upon any weekly payments.
>
> Choose your doctor now.

35. Evaluate the usefulness of **Source A** as evidence of the introduction of the National Health Service in 1948.

    (You may want to comment on what type of source it is, who wrote it, when they wrote it, why they wrote it, what they say and what has been missed out.)

    6

[Now go to SECTION 3 starting on *Page fourteen*]

[BLANK PAGE]

DO NOT WRITE ON THIS PAGE

MARKS

SECTION 3 — EUROPEAN AND WORLD CONTEXTS — 20 marks

Part A — The Cross and the Crescent: the Crusades, 1071–1192

Answer the following **four** questions using recalled knowledge and information from the sources where appropriate.

Sources **A** and **B** are about Pope Urban II's speech in 1095.

Source A

> In 1095, Pope Urban II held a meeting in France. At the meeting, the Pope said that Jerusalem must be recaptured and protection given to Christian churches and shrines there. The Pope warned that every Christian in the west must fight or the Muslims could advance into Europe. He appealed to the knights to stop their violent behaviour towards each other and use their military skills against God's enemy in the east.

Source B

> Pope Urban II's speech at Clermont shocked all those who heard it. The Pope said a Christian army must be called to stop the Muslims before they captured every city they attacked. Pope Urban told the knights of Europe to stop fighting amongst each other and unite against the infidel. The Pope said Jerusalem was the most important city in the world and that it must be taken back from the Muslims.

36. Compare the views of **Sources A** and **B** about Pope Urban II's call for the First Crusade in 1095. (Compare the sources overall and/or in detail.)   **4**

MARKS

Source C explains why Jerusalem was difficult to capture in 1099.

Source C

> The Crusaders' joy at reaching Jerusalem did not last long. The Muslims were well prepared for an attack and had strengthened the wall around the city. As well as this, the Muslims had collected the harvest early and had enough food to last for several months. The Crusaders attacked Jerusalem but the Muslims fought back and forced them to retreat. The Crusaders did not have scaling ladders or siege machines and so could not launch another attack until supplies arrived from Europe.

37. How fully does **Source C** explain the reasons why Jerusalem was difficult to capture in 1099? (Use the source and recall to reach a judgement.)   6

38. Explain the reasons why the Crusaders had problems after the First Crusade.   5

39. Describe the Battle of Arsuf in 1191.   5

MARKS

SECTION 3 — EUROPEAN AND WORLD CONTEXTS — 20 marks

Part B — "Tea and Freedom": the American Revolution, 1774–83

Answer the following **four** questions using recalled knowledge and information from the sources where appropriate.

40. Explain the reasons why some British people sympathised with America during the American Revolution.

5

Sources A and **B** are about the Continental Army.

Source A

> The Continental Army was led by George Washington, who was an experienced soldier. The troops themselves were usually inexperienced in battle and for many it was their first time fighting. Many soldiers left to return home, leaving the army without enough men. The Continental Army always lacked sufficient cavalry and artillery. Washington was always short of money to buy much needed supplies or to pay his soldiers.

Source B

> The army needed troops even more than fortifications, and Washington appealed to Congress to provide them. Many of the soldiers needed practice with their weapons, so early in July he ordered that each man was to fire two rounds — hardly extensive training but all that supplies permitted. The Continental Army was always short of ammunition. Gunpowder was always in short supply but houses were stripped of lead for bullets.

41. Compare the views of **Sources A** and **B** about the capabilities of the Continental Army. (Compare the sources overall and/or in detail.)

4

42. Describe the events of the British defeat at Saratoga.

5

MARKS

Source C is about help given to the colonists after the British defeat at Saratoga.

Source C

> After the British defeat at Saratoga, many in Europe were keen to take advantage of British weakness. France, in particular, wanted revenge for the loss of her colonies. In order to help the colonists France offered financial support. France also gave military assistance in the form of soldiers and gunpowder to put more pressure on Britain. Spain saw an opportunity to try to retake Gibraltar to distract Britain. Finally, France and Spain joined forces and threatened to invade Britain in 1779.

43. How fully does **Source C** explain the reasons why help was given to the colonists in their war against Britain? (Use the source and recall to reach a judgement.)

6

MARKS

SECTION 3 — EUROPEAN AND WORLD CONTEXTS — 20 marks

Part C — USA, 1850–1880

Answer the following **four** questions using recalled knowledge and information from the sources where appropriate.

Sources **A** and **B** are about the treatment of slaves on Southern Plantations.

Source A

> The cotton planter gave me meat and bread with the other slaves, which was not half enough for me to live upon. He flogged me nearly every day. He set me to work without any shirt in the cotton field, in a very hot sun. When a slave runs away, the master always adopts a more strict system of flogging. When I was caught, I got a severe flogging of one hundred lashes each time.

Source B

> The usual method of punishing slaves was using a system of floggings, beatings and in some severe cases, hanging. As well as the beatings, slaves were given the absolute minimum amount of food to survive. Some slaves were punished by being tied to trees on the plantation, often in the burning heat of the sun. However, some slaves were treated better on plantations by their masters.

44. Compare the views of **Sources A** and **B** about the treatment of slaves on Southern Plantations. (Compare the sources overall and/or in detail.)   **4**

MARKS

Source C is about the reasons for Southern secession in 1861.

Source C

> Why did the Confederate states secede? Some writers argued they seceded to escape the high taxes that they thought would come with a Republican election victory. The main reason for secession was that the Southerners had come to feel themselves a separate community. They had come more and more to dislike and despise, to hate and fear, their northern neighbours. There was also a feeling in the South that there would be more advantages to secession than staying in the union.

45. How fully does **Source C** explain the reasons for Southern secession in 1861? (Use the source and recall to reach a judgement.)   6

46. Describe the activities of the Freedmen's Bureau.   5

47. Explain the reasons why there was conflict between white settlers and Native Americans.   5

MARKS

SECTION 3 — EUROPEAN AND WORLD CONTEXTS — 20 marks

Part D — Hitler and Nazi Germany, 1919–1939

Answer the following **four** questions using recalled knowledge and information from the sources where appropriate.

48. Describe the appeal of Adolf Hitler to many Germans between 1929 and 1933.   5

Sources A and **B** are about the Night of the Long Knives in 1934.

Source A

> On the night of 29–30 June, units of the SS arrested the leaders of the SA as well as political opponents. The arrests carried on for two more nights. In total 77 men were executed on charges of treason. Röhm was shot and others were beaten to death. The SA was placed under the command of the army. Hitler received an oath of allegiance from all those who served in the army.

Source B

> Members of the SS stormed a hotel where the SA had gathered, pulled Röhm and his henchmen from their beds and had them arrested. Some were promptly executed. Röhm was taken to a Munich prison, along with other SA leaders, and there awaited his fate. He was given a chance to shoot himself, but did not take it. An SS officer entered his cell and shot Röhm at point blank range.

49. Compare the views of **Sources A** and **B** about the events of the Night of the Long Knives. (Compare the sources overall and/or in detail.)   4

50. Explain the reasons why there was a lack of effective opposition in Nazi Germany between 1933 and 1939.   5

MARKS

Source C is about Nazi education policies.

Source C

> Education played a very important part in Nazi Germany. Schools tried to develop a loyal following for Hitler. Geography taught pupils about the land that Germany lost in 1919 to make them understand the need for more living space. The science curriculum was changed so shooting had to be studied as well as bridge building and the impact of poisonous gasses. Girls had a different curriculum as they studied domestic science and racial studies. Both of these were to prepare a young girl to be the perfect wife and mother.

51. How fully does **Source C** explain Nazi education policies? (Use the source and recall to reach a judgement.)

6

MARKS

SECTION 3 — EUROPEAN AND WORLD CONTEXTS — 20 marks

Part E — Red Flag: Lenin and the Russian Revolution, 1894–1921

Answer the following **four** questions using recalled knowledge and information from the sources where appropriate.

52. Describe the events of Bloody Sunday in January 1905.   5

Source A is about Stolypin's reforms.

Source A

> Stolypin's government did gradually bring about a number of economic and social reforms in Russia. He ordered the Zemstvos to carry out a huge expansion of health services to the provinces. In 1912 a system of health insurance was set up for workers. Compulsory universal education within ten years became a declared aim. By 1914 the government had established 50,000 additional primary schools, administered and funded by the Zemstvos. There was also an expansion of secondary and higher educational institutions.

53. How fully does **Source A** explain the impact of Stolypin's reforms? (Use the source and recall to reach a judgement.)   6

54. Explain the reasons why Tsar Nicholas II abdicated in March 1917.   5

Sources **B** and **C** are about the Russian Civil War.

Source B

> The territory held by the Bolsheviks was a great advantage to them — their control of central areas meant shorter lines of supply and communication. However the White forces stretched right out along the edges of Russia — in Siberia, the western borderlands and along the Volga in the South. The Bolsheviks were better prepared to mobilise their troops and acquire resources. In contrast the Whites were disorganised in battle. Eventually the Bolsheviks were victorious.

Source C

> During the Civil War, Russian people suffered greatly, families were torn apart and there were huge numbers of casualties. The Bolsheviks won the Civil War largely because they were well prepared and disciplined. In comparison the Whites were disorganised, lacking in the ability to properly mobilise and lead their troops. The Bolsheviks held better territory and had access to railways for their communication and supply lines.

55. Compare the views of **Sources B** and **C** about the reasons why the Bolsheviks won the Civil War. (Compare the sources overall and/or in detail.)   **4**

MARKS

SECTION 3 — EUROPEAN AND WORLD CONTEXTS — 20 marks

Part F — Mussolini and Fascist Italy, 1919–1939

Answer the following **four** questions using recalled knowledge and information from the sources where appropriate.

56. Describe Mussolini's economic policies up to 1939.

5

Sources A and **B** are about Fascist propaganda.

Source A

> Italian Fascists relied a great deal on propaganda to maintain support. Mussolini was portrayed as athletic, strong and courageous and most Italians believed this. The Fascist regime was very successful in controlling the output of radio and cinema. One admirer of him was the British Foreign Secretary, Austen Chamberlain, who was widely reported as saying that Mussolini was "a wonderful man working for the greatness of his country".

Source B

> Fascist propaganda made many claims about Mussolini. Few Italians believed the ridiculous claims that Mussolini was a brilliant athlete and musician. While the Fascist regime did its best to control the media, in reality Italians watched American films which certainly did not support Fascist ideas. Foreigners could see through the Fascist's crude propaganda attempts and in the European press Mussolini was often presented as a figure of fun.

57. Compare the views of **Sources A** and **B** on the effectiveness of Fascist propaganda. (Compare the sources overall and/or in detail.)

4

MARKS

Source C is from a history textbook.

Source C

> Benito Mussolini's Fascist regime came to power in Italy in 1922. He quickly set about removing democratic rights and freedoms. It took Mussolini some time to fully develop his foreign policy. His main aim was to make Italy respected as a world power. To achieve this he wanted to build up the Italian armed forces to make Italy feared. Mussolini was determined that one day Italy would be the dominant power in the Mediterranean. He was particularly keen to extend Italian influence in the countries of the Balkans.

58. How fully does **Source C** explain the aims of Fascist foreign policy up to 1939? (Use the source and recall to reach a judgement.)   6

59. Explain the reasons why opposition never posed a serious threat to the Fascist state.   5

MARKS

SECTION 3 — EUROPEAN AND WORLD CONTEXTS — 20 marks

Part G — Free at Last? Civil Rights in the USA, 1918–1968

Answer the following **four** questions using recalled knowledge and information from the sources where appropriate.

Sources A and **B** describe the activities of the Ku Klux Klan.

Source A

> Dressed in their white hoods the Klan were very frightening — they looked like ghosts! They sneaked around at night when us blacks were in our beds. My father told me that I should avoid them at all costs. He said the Klansmen tied up the blacks that they caught and beat them. They left their victims with their hands tied in the air and the blood streaming out of their wounds.

Source B

> The Klan came to my house about ten o'clock. I was in bed at that time fast asleep. I jumped up, stepped to the door and looked out. As far as I could see they were all disguised, with white sheets pulled over their heads. The Klansmen came in and when I spoke they grabbed me. They took me out into the yard and struck me three times over the head with a pistol.

60. Compare the views of **Sources A** and **B** about the activities of the Ku Klux Klan. (Compare the sources overall and/or in detail.) 4

MARKS

Source C is about the growth of the civil rights movement after 1945.

Source C

> Soldiers in World War II experienced life in a more equal society when abroad and were determined to fight against discrimination when they returned. In the years that followed the war the campaign to gain equality for black Americans grew. Black Americans were better educated than previous generations and therefore better equipped to challenge discrimination. The success of the Montgomery Bus Boycott encouraged others to become involved in the fight for civil rights. The leadership of civil rights campaigner Martin Luther King inspired others to join the civil rights campaign.

61. How fully does **Source C** explain the reasons why there was a growth in the civil rights movement after 1945? (Use the source and recall to reach a judgement.)   **6**

62. Describe the events at Central High School in Little Rock, Arkansas in 1957.   **5**

63. Explain the reasons why race riots broke out in the ghettos of Northern cities in the 1960s.   **5**

MARKS

SECTION 3 — EUROPEAN AND WORLD CONTEXTS — 20 marks

Part H — Appeasement and the Road to War, 1918–1939

Answer the following **four** questions using recalled knowledge and information from the sources where appropriate.

64. Explain the reasons why France and Britain did not take military action against German rearmament up to 1938.

    5

65. Describe the events leading to Germany's Anschluss with Austria in 1938.

    5

Source A is about Neville Chamberlain and the policy of appeasement.

Source A

> In March 1939, Chamberlain abandoned appeasement and promised to defend Poland if the Nazis invaded. The main reason was the invasion of Czechoslovakia which proved that Hitler was a liar and that he did not just want land where Germans lived. In addition, many were influenced by Churchill's speeches which meant appeasement was losing the support of the British people. Kristallnacht proved that the Nazi regime was evil and ought to be resisted. Rearmament had strengthened Britain's armed forces too and gave Chamberlain the confidence to tackle Nazi aggression.

66. How fully does **Source A** explain the reasons why Chamberlain abandoned the policy of Appeasement? (Use the source and recall to reach a judgement.)

    6

MARKS

Sources **B** and **C** are about the reasons why Stalin signed the Nazi-Soviet Non-Aggression Pact in 1939.

Source B

> The agreement shocked the world as each nation had been the sworn enemy of the other. By signing the pact the Soviet Union gained time to prepare its defences against a future German attack. Stalin also gained the opportunity to take back lands Russia lost in the aftermath of the First World War. The half-hearted attempt of the British to come to an agreement with the Soviet Union was another factor in Stalin's decision.

Source C

> The British were unenthusiastic about a possible Anglo-Soviet agreement, and this encouraged Stalin to sign the Nazi-Soviet Pact. The pact gave the Soviet Union time to prepare for eventual German invasion. The chance to extend Soviet control over lands from which Russia had been excluded since the end of the First World War was another factor. The Nazi-Soviet Pact was therefore a logical result of Stalin protecting his country's interests.

67. Compare the views of **Sources B** and **C** on the reasons why Stalin signed the Nazi-Soviet Non-Aggression Pact in 1939. (Compare the sources overall and/or in detail.)

4

MARKS

SECTION 3 — EUROPEAN AND WORLD CONTEXTS — 20 marks

Part I — World War II, 1939–1945

Answer the following **four** questions using recalled knowledge and information from the sources where appropriate.

Source A is about why Japan attacked Pearl Harbour in December 1941.

Source A

> In 1937 America restricted oil supplies to Japan. Faced with severe shortages of oil, Japan became increasingly angry with America. The Japanese were also determined to push American influence out of the Pacific and planned an attack. The attack was also intended to damage US military strength. A surprise attack took place on the US Pacific fleet at Pearl Harbour on 7 December 1941. Japan was confident of defeating the US because they had rehearsed the attack for a year until they achieved an 80% hit rate.

68. How fully does **Source A** explain why Japan attacked Pearl Harbour in December 1941? (Use the source and recall to reach a judgement.)   6

69. Describe the treatment of Jews and other minorities in Nazi occupied Europe.   5

MARKS

Sources **B** and **C** are about collaboration in Nazi occupied Europe.

Source B

> People collaborated with the Nazis in occupied Europe in many different ways. In many cases it was simply a way to survive such as doing the laundry of German soldiers to earn extra food for your family. Others were more actively involved by informing the Germans of "enemies" within the community. Then there were those who supported the Nazi regime such as the local civilians and police who were recruited into the SS death squads.

Source C

> Collaboration on a large scale occurred in Vichy France where the authorities supplied information to help the Nazis round up "undesirables". Other examples of collaboration involved civilians working for the Germans in order to earn extra money or gain extra food rations. The most infamous example of collaboration was at Babi Yar near Kiev. Over 33,000 Jews were slaughtered there in September 1941 by Nazi SS forces, assisted by the Ukrainian police.

70. Compare the views of **Sources B** and **C** about collaboration in Nazi occupied Europe. (Compare the sources overall and/or in detail.)   4

71. Explain the reasons why the Normandy landings were successful.   5

MARKS

SECTION 3 — EUROPEAN AND WORLD CONTEXTS — 20 marks

Part J — The Cold War, 1945–1989

Answer the following **four** questions using recalled knowledge and information from the sources where appropriate.

72. Describe the attitude of Hungarians to the Soviet Union by 1956.   5

73. Explain the reasons why the Berlin Wall was built.   5

Source A is about American opposition to the war in Vietnam.

Source A

> There were many in the United States who opposed joining the war in Vietnam from the beginning. They felt it was not America's job to fight a war thousands of miles from home. Many remembered the Second World War and did not want a repeat of the casualties suffered in this conflict. By 1967, as many as 160 American soldiers were being killed every week. Some Americans opposed the conflict as they felt its huge cost meant the government was unable to spend money on health and housing.

74. How fully does **Source A** explain why many Americans opposed the war in Vietnam? (Use the source and recall to reach a judgement.)   6

MARKS

Sources **B** and **C** are about the policy of Glasnost.

Source B

> At only 54 years of age, Mikhail Gorbachev, was a breath of fresh air for the Soviet Union. Gorbachev was most famous for his policies of Glasnost and Perestroika. His intention was to give a boost to the Soviet economy, which was performing badly. The aim of Glasnost was to allow open discussion of social and economic issues. Gorbachev hoped this would strengthen the Communist system.

Source C

> Mikhail Gorbachev, who was appointed in 1985, was the last General Secretary of the Soviet Union. Gorbachev was responsible for the policy of Glasnost. Gorbachev remained a committed Communist and hoped that Glasnost would increase support for the system. He wanted to find new solutions to problems by allowing people to express their views freely. Ultimately, the hope was that Glasnost could help strengthen the Soviet economy.

75. Compare the views of **Sources B** and **C** on the aims of the policy of Glasnost. (Compare the sources overall and/or in detail.)   4

[END OF QUESTION PAPER]

[BLANK PAGE]

DO NOT WRITE ON THIS PAGE

NATIONAL 5

2017 Specimen
Question Paper

National
Qualifications
SPECIMEN ONLY

S837/75/11

History

Date — Not applicable

Duration — 2 hours 20 minutes

Total marks — 80

SECTION 1 — SCOTTISH CONTEXTS — 25 marks

Attempt ONE part.

SECTION 2 — BRITISH CONTEXTS — 26 marks

Attempt ONE part.

SECTION 3 — EUROPEAN AND WORLD CONTEXTS — 29 marks

Attempt ONE part.

Write your answers clearly in the answer booklet provided. In the answer booklet you must clearly identify the question number you are attempting.

Use **blue** or **black** ink.

Before leaving the examination room you must give your answer booklet to the Invigilator; if you do not, you may lose all the marks for this paper.

[BLANK PAGE]

DO NOT WRITE ON THIS PAGE

MARKS

SECTION 1 — SCOTTISH CONTEXTS — 25 marks

Part A — The Wars of Independence, 1286–1328

Answer the following **five** questions using recalled knowledge and information from the sources where appropriate.

Source A is from a textbook written by a modern historian in 2011.

Source A

> John Balliol claimed the strongest right to be King of Scots. Balliol argued this because he was descended from the eldest daughter in the family of David, Earl of Huntingdon, brother of King William the Lion. According to Balliol it didn't matter that he was a generation younger than Bruce because the feudal law of primogeniture always supported the eldest line of a family. Robert Bruce claimed he should be the next King. Bruce argued the feudal law of primogeniture did not apply to kingdoms.

1. Evaluate the usefulness of **Source A** as evidence of the succession problem following the death of the Maid of Norway.   **5**

   (You may want to comment on what type of source it is, who wrote it, when they wrote it, why they wrote it, what they say and what has been missed out.)

2. Explain the reasons why John Balliol was a failure as King of Scots.   **6**

3. Describe the actions of William Wallace during the Wars of Independence.   **4**

Source B is about the Battle of Bannockburn.

Source B

> Bruce's careful preparations for battle were ruined when Edward II moved his army to attack from the east and not from the south. However, this gave the much larger English army no room to move because they were surrounded by marshes and streams. Bruce decided to take advantage of this mistake and to attack them. The English were so jammed together and so tangled up that their leaders struggled to organise any defence. They lost all confidence in Edward II for leading them into this trap.

4. How fully does **Source B** explain why the Scots won the Battle of Bannockburn? (Use the source and recall to reach a judgement.)   **6**

MARKS

Sources **C** and **D** are about support for Robert Bruce in 1320.

Source **C**

> In the Declaration of Arbroath, Scottish nobles explained to the Pope why all the Scots thought Robert Bruce was their rightful king. They argued Bruce had royal blood. His actions had won him the support of the Scottish people. In addition, they argued that they wanted him as king because, by saving Scotland from being taken over by England, he proved that he was worthy of being King of Scotland.

Source **D**

> Even while the Declaration of Arbroath was being written, some Scottish nobles were plotting against Robert Bruce. They felt he was a ruthless thug who had murdered his main rival in a church and so he was unworthy of being King of Scots. Other Scottish nobles claimed their blood ties meant they were more closely related to the Scottish royal family than Robert Bruce. These disagreements caused problems in Scotland.

5. Compare the views of **Sources C** and **D** about support for Robert Bruce in 1320. (Compare the sources overall and/or in detail.)   4

[Now go to SECTION 2 starting on *Page fourteen*]

MARKS

SECTION 1 — SCOTTISH CONTEXTS — 25 marks

Part B — Mary Queen of Scots, and the Scottish Reformation, 1542–1587

Answer the following **five** questions using recalled knowledge and information from the sources where appropriate.

6. Describe the events of the "Rough Wooing".   4

Source A is about why Protestantism spread in Scotland in the 1540s and 1550s.

Source A

> In Germany, the ideas of Martin Luther had started the Reformation movement. Some Scots began to criticise the teachings of the Catholic Church. During the Rough Wooing, English invaders had further encouraged this. This was done by the distribution of English translations of the Bible which helped the growth of Protestantism in Scotland. The Catholic Church continued to use the Latin Bible. Religious pamphlets, smuggled into Scotland from Europe, also spread Protestant ideas. The "Good and Godly Ballads" made these ideas popular, encouraging the spread of Protestantism in Scotland.

7. How fully does **Source A** explain why Protestantism spread in Scotland in the 1540s and 1550s? (Use the source and recall to reach a judgement.)   6

Sources B and C are about how well Mary, Queen of Scots ruled Scotland.

Source B

> Mary returned to Scotland as Queen in 1561. Mary was a Roman Catholic who believed that she should rule England instead of her Protestant cousin, Elizabeth. She neglected the government of Scotland. Mary was happy to leave the running of the country to a group of Protestant nobles. Despite the fact that Mary was a Catholic, she showed little interest in the issue of religion in Scotland.

MARKS

Source C

> To begin with Mary had been a successful ruler in Scotland. That was until she allowed her heart to rule her head by marrying her English born first cousin, Lord Darnley. She had defeated the Protestant nobles who challenged her authority and had established a successful government under her half-brother Moray. Mary was a very devout Catholic, but she decided that she would tolerate Scotland's new Protestant church.

8. Compare the views of **Sources B** and **C** about how well Mary, Queen of Scots ruled Scotland. (Compare the sources overall and/or in detail.)   4

Source D is from a textbook written by a modern historian in 2007.

Source D

> Some Scots simply did not want to be ruled by a woman, as they believed that only men should be in positions of power. John Knox wrote a book against women in power. Others were suspicious of Mary's religion, as she was a Catholic, and so they also opposed her. At that time in Europe, rulers had the power to decide their country's religion. Eventually, Mary's half-brother, the Earl of Moray, forced her into giving up her power in favour of her infant son.

9. Evaluate the usefulness of **Source D** as evidence of why Mary, Queen of Scots, lost power over Scotland in 1567.   5

   (You may want to comment on what type of source it is, who wrote it, when they wrote it, why they wrote it, what they say and what has been missed out.)

10. Explain the reasons why Mary Queen of Scots was executed in 1587.   6

[Now go to SECTION 2 starting on *Page fourteen*]

MARKS

SECTION 1 — SCOTTISH CONTEXTS — 25 marks

Part C — The Treaty of Union, 1689–1715

Answer the following **five** questions using recalled knowledge and information from the sources where appropriate.

11. Explain the reasons why relations between Scotland and England got worse between 1689 and 1707.

6

Sources **A** and **B** are about Scottish attitudes to a possible Union of the Parliaments.

Source A

> The issue of a Union of Parliaments between Scotland and England stirred up heated debate. Supporters of the Union saw it as a way of settling the Protestant Succession and closing the door to the Jacobite claimant to the throne. They weren't worried about wanting a closer relationship with England. A Union would end the danger of future wars between Scotland and England. Other Scots saw the economic benefits of gaining access to England's colonies.

Source B

> Many Scots disliked the idea of entering a Union with "the Auld Enemy". This resulted from centuries of bad feeling between the two countries. They feared that Scotland's economy would be ruined by cheap goods flooding up from England. The Jacobites encouraged opposition to the Union in the hope of restoring their king to his throne. They organised petitions against the Union and burned copies of the Treaty to stir up opposition to the Union.

12. Compare the views of **Sources A** and **B** about Scottish attitudes to a possible Union of the Parliaments. (Compare the sources overall and/or in detail.)

4

13. Describe the unrest in Edinburgh and other parts of Scotland to the proposed Treaty of Union.

4

MARKS

Source C is about why the opponents of the Treaty of Union were unable to stop it being passed.

Source C

> At first, there was widespread public opposition in Scotland to the Union. Opposition to it in Parliament was led by the Duke of Hamilton who could have become king if Scotland and England separated. Hamilton however was indecisive and unreliable. One night, without any warning, he suddenly changed sides. There was widespread belief that, like many, Hamilton had been bribed to support the Union. Hamilton's activities kept the opponents of the Union disorganised. Opponents of the Union were unable to overcome the ruthless methods used by supporters of the Union.

14. How fully does **Source C** explain why opponents of the Treaty of Union were unable to stop it being passed? (Use the source and recall to reach a judgement.)   6

Source D is from a textbook written by a modern historian in 1994.

Source D

> For most people in Scotland after the Union, life in most matters was unchanged. Some however were soon disappointed. The Church of Scotland was outraged when patronage was reintroduced into the church and Episcopalians were to be tolerated. Within a few years other significant changes were made. Many Scots thought these changes also broke the terms of the Treaty of Union. They were unhappy with the introduction of the Malt Tax as this could have had serious consequences.

15. Evaluate the usefulness of **Source D** as evidence of reasons for Scottish disappointment with the Union.   5

(You may want to comment on what type of source it is, who wrote it, when they wrote it, why they wrote it, what they say and what has been missed out.)

[Now go to SECTION 2 starting on *Page fourteen*]

MARKS

SECTION 1 — SCOTTISH CONTEXTS — 25 marks

Part D — Migration and Empire, 1830–1939

Answer the following **five** questions using recalled knowledge and information from the sources where appropriate.

Source A is about why many Irish people moved to Scotland.

Source A

> Among those who moved to Scotland, the largest group of immigrants came from Ireland. The Irish potato famine of the mid-1840s led to a sharp increase in numbers moving to Scotland. Others left for Scotland as some landlords evicted those who could not pay their rent. Transport costs were cheap making it easy to travel to Scotland. The Irish were attracted to the west of Scotland as wages were higher than those in Ireland. However, by the end of the 19th century, it wasn't just Irish who were attracted to Scotland.

16. How fully does **Source A** explain why many Irish people moved to Scotland between 1830 and 1939? (Use the source and recall to reach a judgement.)   **6**

17. Describe how Scotland benefited from the Empire between 1830 and 1939.   **4**

Sources B and **C** are about Scottish attitudes to Irish immigration.

Source B

> By the mid-nineteenth century many Irish immigrants had settled in the Glasgow area. Newspapers were eager to describe the violent activities of groups of Irish men. They were also blamed for being dirty and responsible for spreading disease. Some Irish men and women came to Scotland and worked for part of the year and then returned home. Other Irish however were accused of being too lazy to work and for relying on charity.

MARKS

Source C

> In the nineteenth century many Irish came to Scotland to escape poverty back home. When they first came over they were, in general, very clean. The Irish in Paisley are almost all poor and I can only remember one Irish shopkeeper. But when more labourers are needed, the Irish are always ready to work hard for their pay. Although they live in the worst housing, the Irish are of good character and behave very well.

18. Compare the views of **Sources B** and **C** about Scottish attitudes to Irish immigration. (Compare the sources overall and/or in detail.)   4

Source D is from a textbook written by a modern historian in 1992.

Source D

> Scots were typical of emigrants throughout history in that they moved abroad for economic reasons. Many Scots had farms which they could sell to raise funds for emigration. Countries such as Canada were keen to attract Scots. Once settled, many emigrants were happy to help pay for relatives to come and join them. The journey became much easier and cheaper with the development of faster and more efficient steam ships. Only about a quarter of Scots returned home; most made a better living abroad.

19. Evaluate the usefulness of **Source D** as evidence of why many Scots were able to emigrate between 1830 and 1939.   5

    (You may want to comment on what type of source it is, who wrote it, when they wrote it, why they wrote it, what they say and what has been missed out.)

20. Explain the reasons why so many Scots were successful in the countries to which they emigrated.   6

[Now go to SECTION 2 starting on *Page fourteen*]

MARKS

SECTION 1 — SCOTTISH CONTEXTS — 25 marks

Part E — The Era of the Great War, 1900–1928

Answer the following **five** questions using recalled knowledge and information from the sources where appropriate.

21.   Describe the use of new technology on the Western Front during the First World War.   **4**

Source A is from a textbook written by a modern historian in 1984.

Source A

> In August 1914, Parliament passed the Defence of the Realm Act. This allowed the Government to introduce whatever restrictions were necessary to protect the country during wartime. British Summer Time was introduced to give more daylight working hours. Pub opening hours were limited to prevent drunkenness. People who believed, in 1914, that life in Britain would not be affected much, were quickly proved wrong. High casualties on the Western Front led to conscription, forcing unmarried men between 18 and 41 to join the armed forces.

22.   Evaluate the usefulness of **Source A** as evidence of Government control of everyday life in Britain during the war.   **5**

    (You may want to comment on what type of source it is, who wrote it, when they wrote it, why they wrote it, what they say and what has been missed out.)

Sources B and **C** are about the impact of the First World War on employment opportunities for women.

Source B

> Women wanted to be involved in the First World War from the start. From the outbreak of war there was a steady increase in the female workforce as men enlisted. Glasgow was the first city in Britain to employ women tram drivers. The vital role they played in the war helped change many people's attitude to women. When the war ended, many women voluntarily gave up their jobs to men returning from the fighting.

MARKS

Source C

> For women in particular, the First World War brought about many changes. At the beginning of the war, thousands of women were unemployed. Despite women's contribution to the war effort, it didn't change deep-seated beliefs many people had about the role of women. At the end of the war many newspapers became critical of women workers. Many women wanted to keep their jobs but when the fighting ended, large numbers of women were sacked.

23. Compare the views of **Sources B** and **C** about the impact of the First World War on employment opportunities for women. (Compare the sources overall and/or in detail.)

    4

Source D is about the decline of Scottish industries in the 1920s.

Source D

> Before the First World War, the Scottish economy was very dependent on the traditional industries. When the war ended, there was a sharp drop in demand for Clyde-built warships. This decline in shipbuilding in the 1920s had a damaging effect on the iron and steel industries. Many of the companies had depended on shipbuilding for their orders. Despite increased competition from abroad, Scotland's manufacturers failed to invest in new technology. Not surprisingly, overseas markets lost during the war often preferred to stay with their new suppliers.

24. How fully does **Source D** explain the reasons for the decline of Scottish industries in the 1920s? (Use the source and recall to reach a judgement.)

    6

25. Explain the reasons why women gained the vote in 1918.

    6

[Now go to SECTION 2 starting on *Page fourteen*]

MARK

SECTION 2 — BRITISH CONTEXTS — 26 marks

Part A — The Creation of the Medieval Kingdoms, 1066–1406

Answer the following **four** questions using recalled knowledge and information from the sources where appropriate.

Source A is from a chronicle written by William's priest in 1077.

Source A

> William went to various parts of his new kingdom. Wherever he went, the people surrendered to him. The remaining English Earls were confirmed in their lands and titles. There was limited resistance from the native population. To overcome this, his loyal Norman lords undertook a programme of castle building to maintain their hold on the kingdom. He gave rich fiefs to the men he had brought over from France but no Frenchman was given anything that had been unjustly taken from an Englishman.

26. Evaluate the usefulness of **Source A** as evidence of William's attempts to control England after 1066.

    (You may want to comment on what type of source it is, who wrote it, when they wrote it, why they wrote it, what they say and what has been missed out.)

    5

27. To what extent was the corruption in the legal system the most important problem facing Henry II?

    (Use recalled knowledge to introduce, then present a **balanced assessment** of the influence of different factors and come to a **reasoned conclusion.**)

    9

28. Explain the reasons why the Church was important in the Middle Ages.

    6

MARKS

Source B describes the effects of the Black Death on England.

Source B

> One in three of the population of England died. If the same proportion of people killed by the Black Death in England were affected today, then about 17 million people would die. Lords, who relied on their peasants to farm their land, became desperate to retain them. This meant Lords were forced to pay more to keep each peasant on their land. The labour shortage meant they were in greater demand, so some peasants left their own Lord's land in search of higher pay elsewhere.

29. How fully does **Source B** describe the effects of the Black Death on England? (Use the source and recall to reach a judgement.)

6

[Now go to SECTION 3 starting on *Page twenty-four*]

MARK$

SECTION 2 — BRITISH CONTEXTS — 26 marks

Part B — War of the Three Kingdoms, 1603–1651

Answer the following **four** questions using recalled knowledge and information from the sources where appropriate.

30. To what extent were financial grievances the main cause of dispute between King James I and Parliament?

    (Use recalled knowledge to introduce, then present a **balanced assessment** of the influence of different factors and come to a **reasoned conclusion**.)

    9

31. Explain the reasons why Charles I became unpopular in Scotland between 1629 and 1640.

    6

Source A is from a letter written by Sir John Eliot, a Member of Parliament, in the 1630s.

Source A

> It was an ill omen that Charles' first Parliament met against the background of a terrible outbreak of plague in London. Members of Parliament complained that the terms of Charles' marriage contract included unacceptable concessions to English Catholics. In addition we were suspicious of Charles' foreign policy which meant Parliament was reluctant to grant him funds. The king tried his best to manipulate Parliament. This didn't stop me launching a fierce criticism of Charles' favourite, Buckingham's mismanagement of the Cadiz expedition.

32. Evaluate the usefulness of **Source A** as evidence of growing opposition in England to the reign of King Charles I.

    5

    (You may want to comment on what type of source it is, who wrote it, when they wrote it, why they wrote it, what they say and what has been missed out.)

MARKS

Source B describes events between 1640 and 1642 that led to the outbreak of civil war.

Source B

> Charles called Parliament in April 1640. He then dismissed it because MPs refused to give him what he wanted. In November 1640 Charles was forced to recall Parliament. He still didn't get the money he wanted. Charles faced growing criticism in Parliament from Pym and other Puritan MPs regarding his religious policies. In May 1641 Parliament accused the King's chief Minister, Strafford, of treason and executed him. Many MPs were unhappy with the way Pym twisted the laws to get Strafford executed, which led to further disputes in Parliament.

33. How fully does **Source B** describe the events between 1640 and 1642 that led to the outbreak of the civil war? (Use the source and recall to reach a judgement.)   6

[Now go to SECTION 3 starting on *Page twenty-four*]

MARK

SECTION 2 — BRITISH CONTEXTS — 26 marks

Part C — The Atlantic Slave Trade, 1770–1807

Answer the following **four** questions using recalled knowledge and information from the sources where appropriate.

Source A is from a diary written by a slave ship's doctor in 1788.

Source A

> Some wet and windy weather had caused the port holes to be shut. This led to diarrhoea and fevers among the slaves. I often went down below deck among them. After some time the apartments became so extremely hot, as to be only bearable for a very short time. The floor of the place where the slaves lay was covered in blood and diarrhoea which had come from them because of their sickness. It looked like a slaughter house.

34. Evaluate the usefulness of **Source A** as evidence of the conditions faced by slaves during the Middle Passage.

    (You may want to comment on what type of source it is, who wrote it, when they wrote it, why they wrote it, what they say and what has been missed out.)

5

Source B is about the impact the slave trade had on the Caribbean islands.

Source B

> The slave trade had a long lasting effect on the islands of the Caribbean. The slaves outnumbered the white population about 20 to 1 which created a fear of rebellion among the white population. This fear of a slave uprising led to the introduction of a legal system which supported slavery. Slave laws were introduced which allowed slave owners to brutally punish or even execute slaves. Slaves were vital to work on the plantations. The concentration on sugar production did lasting damage to the Jamaican economy.

35. How fully does **Source B** describe the impact the slave trade had on the Caribbean islands? (Use the source and recall to reach a judgement.)   6

36. Explain the reasons why resistance was difficult for slaves on the plantations.   6

37. To what extent was Olaudah Equiano the main reason for the success of the abolitionist campaign?   9

    (Use recalled knowledge to introduce, then present a **balanced assessment** of the influence of different factors and come to a **reasoned conclusion**.)

[Now go to SECTION 3 starting on *Page twenty-four*]

MARKS

SECTION 2 — BRITISH CONTEXTS — 26 marks

Part D — Changing Britain, 1760–1914

Answer the following **four** questions using recalled knowledge and information from the sources where appropriate.

38. To what extent were medical advances the main reason for improved health by 1900?

    (Use recalled knowledge to introduce, then present a **balanced assessment** of the influence of different factors and come to a **reasoned conclusion**.)

    9

Source A describes the impact of factories upon the working conditions of textile workers.

Source A

> People used to working in their own homes found working in a factory very different. The powered machines went on hour after hour and many workers struggled to keep up with them. Owners had very strict rules and workers had to do what they were told to do. There was, however, no shortage of workers wanting employment in factories. Wages were usually better than farm work, but only when the factory was working. If business became slow then workers were laid off, with no income at all.

39. How fully does **Source A** describe the impact of factories upon the working conditions of textile workers? (Use the source and recall to reach a judgement.)

    6

MARKS

Source B is from the diary of a Scottish railway engineer written in the 1840s.

Source B

> We had to build the line to Perth over Lord Seafield's land. Lady Seafield very decidedly told us that she hated railways. "Cheap travel", she said, "brought together such an objectionable variety of people." Lord Seafield said the railway would frighten away the grouse from his moors. "Besides", he went on, "what would become of the men who have for many years been employed to float timber down the River Spey to the sea. Would a railway replace them?"

40. Evaluate the usefulness of **Source B** as evidence of different attitudes to the building of railways in 19th century Scotland.

    (You may want to comment on what type of source it is, who wrote it, when they wrote it, why they wrote it, what they say and what has been missed out.)

    5

41. Explain the reasons why more people gained the vote by 1867.

    6

[Now go to SECTION 3 starting on *Page twenty-four*]

SECTION 2 — BRITISH CONTEXTS — 26 marks

Part E — The Making of Modern Britain, 1880–1951

Answer the following **four** questions using recalled knowledge and information from the sources where appropriate.

Source A is from a report written by a social investigator about conditions in London in 1892.

Source A

> The building was spread over two floors. The two room apartment on the ground floor is occupied by Fletcher, a pedlar, his wife and six of his children. Eight feet square—that is about the average of many of these rooms. On the first floor are the Lawson and Bewley families. In most of the apartments the walls and ceilings are black with filth. In these buildings it is a common occurrence to find sewage running down the walls.

42. Evaluate the usefulness of **Source A** as evidence of poverty in Britain in the 1890s. 5

   (You may want to comment on what type of source it is, who wrote it, when they wrote it, why they wrote it, what they say and what has been missed out.)

MARKS

Source B is about the limitations of the Liberal welfare reforms of 1906—1914.

Source B

> The Liberal reforms were just a beginning. They were a long way short of solving all the problems. Medical care was only provided for the worker, it did not cover his wife or children. Other benefits were only to last for a short period of time. The amounts paid as benefits were not enough to live on. Old Age Pensions were paid for the first time in 1909. However as the pension only applied to people over 70, many elderly still received no help.

43. How fully does **Source B** describe the limitations of the Liberal welfare reforms of 1906—1914? (Use the source and recall to reach a judgement.) **6**

44. Explain the reasons why the Labour Government introduced the Welfare State in 1948. **6**

45. To what extent was the NHS the most beneficial social reform introduced by the Labour Government after 1948? **9**

    (Use recalled knowledge to introduce, then present a **balanced assessment** of the influence of different factors and come to a **reasoned conclusion**.)

[Now go to SECTION 3 starting on *Page twenty-four*]

MARKS

SECTION 3 — EUROPEAN AND WORLD CONTEXTS — 29 marks

Part A — The Cross and the Crescent: the Crusades, 1071–1192

Answer the following **five** questions using recalled knowledge and information from the sources where appropriate.

Source A is about the importance of castles in the twelfth century.

Source A

> During Henry II's reign, castles were built of stone and with extra walls and towers. These castles became a key symbol of power. They were also the administrative centres of each town. The numerous rooms inside a castle meant that it was an ideal base for the local garrison carrying out guard duty. During the civil war many castles had been built illegally. There was no doubt however that they were useful during times of attack when food, drink and other supplies could be stored there.

46. How fully does **Source A** describe the importance of castles in the twelfth century? (Use the source and recall to reach a judgement.)

6

MARKS

Sources **B** and **C** describe what happened to Jewish communities during the First Crusade.

Source B

> After a few weeks of travelling, Peter the Hermit and his followers came upon a Jewish community. Many Crusaders were poor and hungry so they began stealing food and possessions from the Jews. As the Crusaders thought the Jews were the enemy of Christ, most believed they could treat them as they wished. Some forced the Jews to change religion and become Christian. Others, against the orders of Peter the Hermit, slaughtered the Jews.

Source C

> A rumour spread among the Crusaders that whoever killed a Jew would have all their sins forgiven. Immediately, Peter the Hermit's army began attacking and killing Jewish men, women and children. Although some Jews tried to fight back they had few weapons and were easily defeated. In the riot that followed, Jewish houses were robbed and valuables stolen. Those Jews who survived the massacre were forced to give up their faith and become Christians.

47. Compare the views of **Sources B** and **C** about what happened to Jews during the First Crusade. (Compare the sources overall and/or in detail.)   4

48. To what extent were Muslim divisions the main reason for the success of the First Crusade?   9

    (Use recalled knowledge to introduce, then present a **balanced assessment** of the influence of different factors and come to a **reasoned conclusion**.)

49. Explain the reasons why the Crusaders lost control of Jerusalem in 1187.   6

50. Describe the Battle of Jaffa in 1192.   4

MARK

SECTION 3 — EUROPEAN AND WORLD CONTEXTS — 29 marks

Part B — "Tea and Freedom": the American Revolution, 1774–1783

Answer the following **five** questions using recalled knowledge and information from the sources where appropriate.

51. To what extent were Britain's attempts at raising revenue from the colonies the main reason why the American Wars of Independence broke out in 1775?   9

    (Use recalled knowledge to introduce, then present a **balanced assessment** of the influence of different factors and come to a **reasoned conclusion**.)

52. Explain the reasons why some colonists remained loyal to Britain during the war.   6

Source A is about the condition of the American army in 1777.

Source A

> The Revolutionary War was waged by small armies on both sides. The American forces were often led by inefficient, even incompetent, commanders who fought muddled campaigns. The men gathering in Boston were very enthusiastic. They were however badly armed and lacking supplies. The American commander, George Washington, could rely on no more than 5,000 regular soldiers. Most men were part-time and served for only a few months at a time. Britain's professional army was larger but not large enough to subdue the Americans.

53. How fully does **Source A** describe the condition of the American army in 1777? (Use the source and recall to reach a judgement.)   6

MARKS

54. Describe the events leading up to the British surrender at Saratoga in 1777.   **4**

Sources B and **C** are about the events of the Battle of Yorktown, 1781.

Source B

> In 1781, Cornwallis moved into Virginia and began to build a base at Yorktown. By late summer, Cornwallis's position at Yorktown was deteriorating fast. While American forces prevented him from moving inland, a large French fleet carrying 3,000 troops had sailed up to join the siege. The fate of Cornwallis was sealed when the French defeated the British fleet in Chesapeake Bay. On 19 October, Cornwallis surrendered his entire army of 7,000 men.

Source C

> To launch his campaign in Virginia, Cornwallis's army carried out raids, harassing the American forces wherever he could. In August 1781, Cornwallis's British forces set up camp at Yorktown. Yorktown however turned out to be a poor position and his situation became more serious. American troops moved quickly into the area to surround him and keep him there. The British could not help Cornwallis's army to escape, or bring in reinforcements.

55. Compare the views of **Sources B** and **C** about the events of the Battle of Yorktown. (Compare the sources overall and/or in detail.)   **4**

MARKS

SECTION 3 — EUROPEAN AND WORLD CONTEXTS — 29 marks

Part C — USA, 1850–1880

Answer the following **five** questions using recalled knowledge and information from the sources where appropriate.

56. Explain the reasons why settlers moved West after 1850.   6

Source A is about the events that led to the outbreak of the Civil War.

Source A

> The Compromise of 1850 was created by Henry Clay and others to deal with the balance between slave and free states. The Kansas-Nebraska Act of 1854, however, increased tensions. This allowed continued expansion to the West. The real issue occurred in Kansas. Pro-slavery people of Missouri began to pour into Kansas to help force it to be a slave state. The fight over slavery even erupted on the floor of the Senate. Anti-slavery campaigner Charles Sumner was beat over the head by South Carolina's pro-slavery Senator Preston Brooks.

57. How fully does **Source A** describe the events that led to the outbreak of the Civil War? (Use the source and recall to reach a judgement.)   6

58. Describe the work of the Freedmen's Bureau after 1865.   4

MARKS

Sources **B** and **C** are about what happened during Reconstruction.

Source B

> Many school houses were burned down. Hostility was shown to the school teachers like me who taught in schools for blacks. Two school board directors were warned to leave the Board. One of them did. They came at night and gave these warnings. I asked them while they were whipping me what I had done. They said I wanted to make these blacks equal to the white men; that this was a white man's country.

Source C

> The violence that the whites committed was directed not only at black people but anyone who furthered their cause. Teachers in schools for black Americans became key figures so they were frequently intimidated. These attacks usually took place at night: leaving behind a burning cross they whipped, mutilated and murdered black people. Black Americans were reluctant to resist as they wanted to be seen by others as peaceful and law-abiding.

59. Compare the views of **Sources B** and **C** about what happened during Reconstruction. (Compare the sources overall and/or in detail.)   **4**

60. To what extent was the discovery of gold the main reason for growing tension between the Native Americans and the white settlers?   **9**

(Use recalled knowledge to introduce, then present a **balanced assessment** of the influence of different factors and come to a **reasoned conclusion**.)

MARK

SECTION 3 — EUROPEAN AND WORLD CONTEXTS — 29 marks

Part D — Hitler and Nazi Germany, 1919–1939

Answer the following **five** questions using recalled knowledge and information from the sources where appropriate.

61. Describe the events of the Beer Hall Putsch of 1923.   4

62. To what extent was discontent with the Weimar Republic the main reason for the Nazi rise to power by January 1933?   9

    (Use recalled knowledge to introduce, then present a **balanced assessment** of the influence of different factors and come to a **reasoned conclusion**.)

Sources **A** and **B** are about the Nazi views on race.

Source A

> The Nazi theory of racial superiority was not original even though Hitler had stated, in *Mein Kampf*, that differences between the races was a matter of scientific fact. There could be no argument that the Aryan people of northern Europe were superior in every way. This was not just a matter of physical superiority but also of intellectual strength. It was logical that superior people like this should be in control of all other races.

Source B

> The stereotype of the blond haired and blue-eyed warrior took a powerful hold on many young Germans who were taught that the Aryans of Germany and Scandinavia were the Master Race. According to Nazi propaganda, which continually stressed the importance of "pure blood", biological research had shown that there was a distinction between races. This gave these superior races the authority to rule over the peoples of the world.

63. Compare the views of **Sources A** and **B** about Nazi views on race. (Compare the sources overall and/or in detail.)   4

64. Explain the reasons why it was so difficult to oppose the Nazi Government after 1933.   6

MARKS

Source C is about changes to education in Nazi Germany.

Source C

> There were many changes at school. Some were barely noticed, others were introduced as though with a great fanfare of trumpets. None questioned the introduction of new Nazi textbooks. In line with National Socialist education policies, the number of PE periods was increased at the expense of religious education. When competitive field games were added to the curriculum our teacher spelled it out to us, "It is what the Führer wants for you". At the start of class we had to raise our arms in the "Heil Hitler!" salute.

65. How fully does **Source C** describe the changes to education in Nazi Germany? (Use the source and recall to reach a judgement.)   6

MARK!

SECTION 3 — EUROPEAN AND WORLD CONTEXTS — 29 marks

Part E — Red Flag: Lenin and the Russian Revolution, 1894—1921

Answer the following **five** questions using recalled knowledge and information from the sources where appropriate.

66. Describe the methods used by the Tsar to control Russia before 1905.   4

67. Explain the reasons why there was a revolution in Russia in January 1905.   6

Source A is about the reforms introduced in Russia after the 1905 Revolution.

Source A

> With the growing unrest threatening his authority, the Tsar gave in and agreed to introduce reforms. The October Manifesto established a parliament or Duma elected by the people. It also allowed the Russian people basic rights, such as freedom of speech. This helped the Tsar regain control of the country. In 1906 the Tsar appointed Peter Stolypin as Prime Minister. His land reforms allowed peasants to become owners of their own land. He also set up a peasants' bank to provide loans to help them buy the land.

68. How fully does **Source A** describe the reforms introduced in Russia after the 1905 Revolution? (Use the source and recall to reach a judgement.)   6

MARKS

Sources **B** and **C** describe the effects of the First World War on the Russian people.

Source B

> The workers are not in a patriotic mood. The high cost of living and barbaric government policies have turned the masses against the war. There are more and more strikes all over the country. Prices have gone up and people are discontented. Food is hard to get. They blame the Tsar and say "he does not care we might starve". People hate the war now and want it to end.

Source C

> Throughout much of the war, Russian cities suffered from a shortage of food. This was due to a series of bad harvests. The loss of large areas of rich farmland to the Germans did not help. The shortages meant that food prices went up and, although workers' wages increased, they did not keep pace with rising inflation. By 1917, urban workers faced terrible starvation which they blamed on the Tsar.

69. Compare the views of **Sources B** and **C** about effects of the First World War on the Russian people. (Compare the sources overall and/or in detail.)   4

70. To what extent was the leadership of Trotsky the main reason for the Reds' victory in the Civil War?   9

    (Use recalled knowledge to introduce, then present a **balanced assessment** of the influence of different factors and come to a **reasoned conclusion**.)

MARKS

SECTION 3 — EUROPEAN AND WORLD CONTEXTS — 29 marks

Part F — Mussolini and Fascist Italy, 1919–1939

Answer the following **five** questions using recalled knowledge and information from the sources where appropriate.

Sources A and **B** are about why Mussolini was able to seize power in 1922.

Source A

> The Fascist squads had a reputation for ruthless violence. This put Mussolini in the position to challenge the government, which he did in what became known as the famous "March on Rome". The government decided to send in the army to try and stop Mussolini. The King, Victor Emmanuel III, however instead of using the army, decided to give in to Mussolini's demands. He therefore appointed him head of a new Italian government.

Source B

> The Socialists and Communists launched an anti-Fascist general strike but the people failed to support them. After the strike, Mussolini decided to seize the government when he and his followers marched on the capital, Rome. Before he resigned, the prime minister called out the army when the Fascists surrounded Rome. However, the pressure proved too much for the Italian King who refused to use the military to squash Mussolini's "march".

71. Compare the views of **Sources A** and **B** about the events which led to Mussolini's seizure of power in Italy in 1922. (Compare the sources overall and/or in detail.)   4

Source **C** is about the cult of Il Duce in Fascist Italy.

Source **C**

> The leadership cult in Fascist Italy started almost as soon as Mussolini came to power in 1922. By the end of 1925, his role as Duce of Fascism and Head of the Government had been secured by changes to the law. The nature of Mussolini's leadership and, above all, the quality of his political judgement, has been hotly debated. Mussolini had undoubted charisma and political intelligence with which to maintain his power over Fascism and the Italian people. However, his main talents lay in the areas of acting and propaganda.

72. How fully does **Source C** describe the cult of Il Duce in Fascist Italy? (Use the source and recall to reach a judgement.)

    6

73. Explain the reasons why many Italians were unhappy with Mussolini's economic policies.

    6

74. Describe the aims of Fascist foreign policy.

    4

75. To what extent was fear the main reason why Mussolini was able to overcome opposition in Fascist Italy?

    9

    (Use recalled knowledge to introduce, then present a **balanced assessment** of the influence of different factors and come to a **reasoned conclusion**.)

MARK*

SECTION 3 — EUROPEAN AND WORLD CONTEXTS — 29 marks

Part G — Free at Last? Civil Rights in the USA, 1918–1968

Answer the following **five** questions using recalled knowledge and information from the sources where appropriate.

76. To what extent was fear of revolution the main reason why many Americans' attitude towards immigration changed after 1918?   9

    (Use recalled knowledge to introduce, then present a **balanced assessment** of the influence of different factors and come to a **reasoned conclusion**.)

Sources A and **B** are about the experience of immigrants in the USA in the 1920s.

Source A

> Italians didn't want to buy land. Few planned to stay in America for long, but wanted to return to Italy some day. They headed for the great cities where there was a far better prospect of finding employment. Italian Americans succeeded in jobs requiring little formal education, such as small business ownership. However, like other immigrants, they found other ways of making a living. Politics and sports were ladders for upward mobility.

Source B

> My family lived in the city of Chicago. When I was 14 years old I started dodging school and so didn't get much formal education. Around this time I turned to stealing. Then we joined an older gang because although they were only around 20 years old they were in the big money and drove around in fancy automobiles. My father came from Monfalcone in Italy and always hoped to return there.

77. Compare the views of **Sources A** and **B** about the experience of immigrants in the USA during the 1920s. (Compare the sources overall and/or in detail.)   4

78. Describe how the Jim Crow laws affected black Americans.   4

79. Explain the reasons why there was a growth in the civil rights movement between 1945 and 1968.   6

MARKS

Source C is about the appeal of the Black Panthers to many black Americans.

Source C

> The name 'Black Panther' was chosen because the panther is a strong fighter when it is cornered. They urged that it was now time to defend black Americans against this white aggression. When Huey Newton said things like "The police have never been our protectors", he voiced the distrust many black Americans felt towards the police. Little credit or publicity was given to the self-help programmes organised by the Black Panthers. In addition they also had a ten-point programme which included demands for better housing and education.

80. How fully does **Source C** describe the appeal of the Black Panthers to many black Americans? (Use the source and recall to reach a judgement.)   6

MARK<

SECTION 3 — EUROPEAN AND WORLD CONTEXTS — 29 marks

Part H — Appeasement and the Road to War, 1918–1939

Answer the following **five** questions using recalled knowledge and information from the sources where appropriate.

81. Explain the reasons why Germany hated the terms of the Treaty of Versailles.   6

Sources A and **B** are about the work of the League of Nations.

Source A

> Wilson had been the driving force behind the League of Nations. The refusal of the USA to join the League however greatly weakened its ability to succeed. In the years after the war, the League did a great deal of useful humanitarian work. The League did manage to settle disputes between smaller nations who could be leaned on. When disputes involved larger countries, the League however often failed to act.

Source B

> The Covenant was the document which outlined how the League would work. Actions against larger nations who challenged the League were inadequate and frequently half-hearted. Many members were not willing to use sanctions, which weakened the League. The League however did achieve some success in solving arguments between lesser countries. The failure of several big powers, including the USA , to join the League badly damaged its effectiveness.

82. Compare the views of **Sources A** and **B** about the work of the League of Nations. (Compare the sources overall and/or in detail.)   4

83. Describe the aims of Nazi foreign policy.   4

84. To what extent were military concerns the main reason why Chamberlain followed a policy of appeasement?   9

    (Use recalled knowledge to introduce, then present a **balanced assessment** of the influence of different factors and come to a **reasoned conclusion**.)

Source C is about the events that led to the outbreak of war between Britain and Germany in 1939.

Source C

> The loss of the Sudetenland to Germany in October 1938 left the rest of Czechoslovakia weak and vulnerable to attack. In March 1939, German troops marched into Czechoslovakia. This action broke the Munich Agreement. Slovakia broke away and became a pro-German 'puppet state'. Bohemia and Moravia became a German protectorate. Up to this point Hitler had justified his demands in terms of self-determination. This was impossible after his actions in March 1939. Germany's aggression led to Great Britain and France abandoning the policy of appeasement.

85. How fully does **Source C** describe the events in 1939 leading to the outbreak of war between Britain and Germany? (Use the source and recall to reach a judgement.)   6

MARKS

SECTION 3 — EUROPEAN AND WORLD CONTEXTS — 29 marks

Part I — World War II, 1939–1945

Answer the following **five** questions using recalled knowledge and information from the sources where appropriate.

86. Explain the reasons why Hitler ordered the invasion of Russia in June 1941.   **6**

87. Describe the Battle of Midway in June 1942.   **4**

Sources A and **B** are about the work of the French Resistance.

Source A

> Resistance movements in occupied countries carried on the fight against Germany's armed forces. Their methods included sabotage of the German rail network. They also distributed anti-German propaganda. This resistance took place in all countries occupied by the Germans. The help they gave the Allies was extremely important. Some historians believe without their help the Allies would have been defeated. If members of the Resistance were caught they would almost certainly be tortured and executed.

Source B

> As a result of the German invasion in 1940 a resistance movement grew in France. Over the course of the war, the French Resistance scored key victories against the German occupation forces. Resistance members organised themselves in secret groups. They destroyed trains carrying German troops and military equipment. These accomplishments carried a heavy price as many members of the Resistance paid for their bravery with their lives.

88. Compare the views of **Sources A** and **B** about the work of the French Resistance. (Compare the sources overall and/or in detail.)   **4**

89. To what extent were German mistakes the main reason for the Allied success at Normandy in 1944?   **9**

    (Use recalled knowledge to introduce, then present a **balanced assessment** of the influence of different factors and come to a **reasoned conclusion**.)

Source C is about the fall of Berlin.

Source C

> Friday 20th April was Hitler's birthday. The Soviets sent him a birthday present in the form of an artillery barrage right into the heart of Berlin. The Western Allies launched a massive air raid. The radio announced Hitler had come out of his bomb-proof bunker. He spoke to young boys who had 'volunteered' to join the SS and die for their Führer in defence of Berlin. What a cruel lie! They didn't volunteer, but had no choice. Boys who were found hiding were hanged as traitors by the SS.

90. How fully does **Source C** describe events leading to the fall of Berlin? (Use the source and recall to reach a judgement.)   6

MARK

SECTION 3 — EUROPEAN AND WORLD CONTEXTS — 29 marks

Part J — The Cold War, 1945–1989

Answer the following **five** questions using recalled knowledge and information from the sources where appropriate.

Sources A and **B** are about why a Cold War broke out between the superpowers.

Source A

> Once World War Two was over, relations between the two allies deteriorated, to be replaced by a climate of suspicion between America and the Soviet Union. Soviet and American leaders held opposing ideological views and attempted to spread their beliefs to other countries. Tensions continued to grow over the next few years. America's decision to develop and use the atomic bomb against the Japanese without consulting the Soviets placed further strain on relations.

Source B

> As soon as the war ended, the Soviet Union and the Americans developed open hostility towards each other. The meetings at Yalta and Potsdam did little to improve relations between the two countries. The new American President Truman and Soviet leader Stalin seemed hostile to one another, and this emphasised their ideological divisions. The tension at Potsdam was increased by America's use of the atomic bomb against Japan.

91. Compare the views of **Sources A** and **B** about the reasons why a Cold War broke out between the Soviet Union and the USA. (Compare the sources overall and/or in detail.)

4

MARKS

Source C is about the events which led to the crisis in Berlin in 1961.

Source C

> By 1960 the situation in East Berlin was very dangerous. A new East German labour law, which stopped workers from going on strike, had led to growing unrest in the factories. Agriculture reforms had led to higher prices and food shortages. All of this led to a massive increase in the numbers of refugees fleeing to the West. At a meeting of the Warsaw Pact states, Khrushchev had been informed about the situation. In the six months up to June 1961, 103,000 East Germans had fled through Berlin.

92. How fully does **Source C** describe the events which led to the crisis in Berlin in 1961? (Use the source and recall to reach a judgement.)   6

93. Explain the reasons why the USA became involved in a crisis over Cuba in 1962.   6

94. To what extent were Vietcong tactics the main reason for their success in winning the war in Vietnam?   9

    (Use recalled knowledge to introduce, then present a **balanced assessment** of the influence of different factors and come to a **reasoned conclusion**.)

95. Describe the steps taken to reduce tension between the USA and the USSR between 1968 and 1989.   4

[BLANK PAGE]

DO NOT WRITE ON THIS PAGE

NATIONAL 5

Answers

NATIONAL 5 HISTORY
2016

Section 1, Context A, The Wars of Independence, 1286–1328

1. *Candidates can be credited in a number of ways up to a maximum of 6 marks.*

Candidates must show a causal relationship between events.

Up to a maximum of **6 marks** in total, **1 mark** should be given for each accurate, relevant reason, and a **second mark** should be given for reasons that are developed. Candidates may achieve full marks by providing six straightforward reasons, three developed reasons, or a combination of these.

Possible reasons may include:
1. he was inexperienced in Scottish affairs/he was essentially an English noble
2. had to accept Edward as Overlord of Scotland/he had paid homage to Edward which made him unpopular
3. Edward insisted on treating him like an English noble/not as a king
4. Edward undermined him by summoning him to appear at court/before his parliament
5. Edward undermined his authority by hearing Scottish legal cases
6. Edward forced him to appoint an Englishman as his Chancellor, further humiliating him
7. not supported by the Scottish nobles/the twelve Guardians challenged his authority
8. made an Alliance with France which provoked Edward and other Scottish nobles loyal to him
9. the powerful Bruce family resented his kingship and did not support him
10. his army was defeated by Edward at Dunbar
11. he was publicly stripped of his kingship by Edward/taken from Scotland to the Tower of London as Edward's prisoner

2. *Candidates can be credited in a number of ways up to a maximum of 6 marks.*

Candidates must make a judgement about the usefulness of the source and support this by making evaluative comments on identified aspects of the source.

1 mark should be given for each relevant comment made, up to a **maximum of 6 marks in total.**

• A maximum of **4 marks** can be given for evaluative comments relating to the author, type of source, purpose and timing.
• A maximum of **2 marks** may be given for comments relating to the content of the source.
• A maximum of **2 marks** may be given for comments relating to points of significant omission.
• Examples of aspects of the source and relevant comments:

Examples of aspects of the source and relevant comments:

Aspect of the source	Possible comment
Author: Wallace and Murray (Moray)	Useful as it is a first-hand account
Type of Source: Letter	Useful as it is an official document
Purpose: To persuade	Less useful as it exaggerates the level of stability in Scotland
Timing: 1297	Useful as it is from the time when Wallace was Guardian

Content	Possible comment
The kingdom has been freed by war from the power of the English	Useful as it accurately states (the hope that) Scotland is free again
Merchants...may safely trade their goods to all ports in the kingdom of Scotland	Useful as it accurately states (the hope that) Scotland is open for business again
Our merchants will bring their trade to you	Useful as it accurately shows Scots looking out to Europe as they did before war

Possible points of significant omission may include:
1. Wallace made Guardian because of victory at Stirling Bridge
2. only a temporary respite for Scotland
3. Wallace resigned as Guardian after his defeat at Falkirk
4. Wallace went to Europe to negotiate Balliol's release
5. Wallace needed to trade for iron for the army

3. *Candidates can be credited in a number of ways up to a maximum of 8 marks.*

Candidates must use knowledge to present a balanced assessment of the influence of different possible factors and come to a reasoned conclusion. **Up to 5 marks** are allocated for relevant points of knowledge used to support factors (but one mark should be deducted if the process is not clear in at least two factors).

1 mark should be given for each relevant, factual key point of knowledge used to support a factor. **If only one factor is presented, a maximum of 3 marks should be given for relevant points of knowledge.**

Possible factors may include:	Relevant, factual, key points of knowledge to support this factor may include:
Defeated Scottish enemies	1. Had killed his main rival – John Comyn 2. Had destroyed the Comyns in the north 3. Had defeated the MacDougalls at the Pass of Brander 4. He defeated the Earl of Buchan at Inverurie
Defeated English opponents	5. Successfully used guerrilla tactics to defeat English forces 6. Defeated English troops at Loudoun Hill 7. Won back control of Scottish castles from the English 8. Destroyed captured castles to prevent their use against him in the future
Defeated Edward II	9. Defeated superior English army at Bannockburn 10. Humiliated Edward II by Bannockburn defeat and by raiding into Northumbria
Some opposition remained	11. Edward II still would not accept Bruce as king/still claimed to be overlord 12. Failed to convince the Pope to lift his excommunication 13. Forced nobles to choose between their Scottish or English lands/titles – alienated some nobles by this (eg Edward) Balliol/Soules – created the "Disinherited" 14. English had captured and imprisoned Bruce's family
	15. Any other valid point.

Up to 3 marks should be given for presenting the answer in a structured way, leading to a conclusion which addresses the question, as follows:

1 mark for the answer being presented in a structured way, with knowledge being organised in support of different factors.

1 mark for a conclusion with a valid judgement or overall summary.

1 mark for a reason being provided in support of the judgement.

Section 1, Context B, Mary Queen of Scots, and the Scottish Reformation, 1542–1587

4. *Candidates can be credited in a number of ways up to a maximum of 6 marks.*

Candidates must show a causal relationship between events.

Up to a **maximum of 6 marks in total**, **1 mark** should be given for each accurate, relevant reason, and a **second mark** should be given for reasons that are developed. Candidates may achieve full marks by providing six straightforward reasons, three developed reasons, or a combination of these.

Possible reasons may include:

1. some Scots began to question the teachings of the Catholic Church
2. resentment at churchmen who were wealthy while everyone else worked hard
3. criticisms of the wealth of the Church in Scotland and its concerns with money (eg Pluralism)
4. shortages of parish priests and poor quality of rest drew criticism
5. criticisms of the lack of spirituality among some members of the Catholic Church (eg monks and nuns not leading holy lives)
6. criticisms of abuse of responsibilities by some members of the Church (eg local priests charging money for important ceremonies such as christenings and funerals/or employing others to perform ceremonies for them)
7. resentment of French Catholic influence on Scotland/resentment at Mary of Guise who had persecuted Protestants
8. Protestant Lords of the Congregation used Protestant religion to attack French influence
9. presence of Protestant preachers from England widespread (eg John Knox)
10. criticism of the severity of treatment of some Protestant preachers (eg Wishart who was burned at the stake for being a heretic in 1546)
11. Protestantism was appealing to many as the style of worship meant people could be more involved/congregation allowed to sing psalms and say prayers
12. English translations of the New Testament were being distributed in Scotland during the period of the 'Rough Wooing'/the Good and Godly Ballads spread Protestant ideas
13. resentment over money spent to decorate Roman Catholic churches

5. *Candidates can be credited in a number of ways up to a maximum of 8 marks.*

Candidates must use knowledge to present a balanced assessment of the influence of different possible factors and come to a reasoned conclusion. **Up to 5 marks** are allocated for relevant points of knowledge used to support factors (but one mark should be deducted if the process is not clear in at least two factors). **1 mark** should be given for each relevant, factual key point of knowledge used to support a factor. **If only one factor is presented, a maximum of 3 marks should be given for relevant points of knowledge.**

Possible factors may include:	Relevant, factual, key points of knowledge to support this factor may include:
Mary's marriage to Darnley	1. Darnley was unpopular with many Scots/Mary ignored warnings about him 2. Darnley discredited Mary with his behaviour (eg excessive drinking/gambling) 3. Darnley insulted James Stewart and most of the important Scottish nobles which lost Mary support 4. Most of Mary's trusted officials resigned and rebelled against him (Chaseabout Raid), which weakened her Government 5. Darnley was involved in the murder of Riccio which reflected badly on Mary 6. Darnley was murdered and Mary was assumed to be involved/led to Mary's imprisonment and abdication
Mary's relationship with Bothwell	7. Mary was blamed for having a relationship with Bothwell before Darnley's murder 8. Mary married Bothwell who was assumed to be Darnley's murderer which made her a co-conspirator 9. Mary allowed Bothwell to prevent a fair inquiry into Darnley's death
Religious reasons	10. Many Scots did not want to have a Catholic as a ruler 11. Protestants did not trust her for being pro-French 12. Attitude of Knox and the Kirk who criticised Mary 13. Bothwell was a Protestant and the marriage turned some Catholics against her
Other factors	14. any other valid point

Up to 3 marks should be given for presenting the answer in a structured way, leading to a conclusion which addresses the question, as follows:

1 mark for the answer being presented in a structured way, with knowledge being organised in support of different factors.

1 mark for a conclusion with a valid judgement or overall summary.

1 mark for a reason being provided in support of the judgement.

6. *Candidates can be credited in a number of ways up to a maximum of 6 marks.*

Candidates must make a judgement about the usefulness of the source and support this by making evaluative comments on identified aspects of the source.

1 mark should be given for each relevant comment made, up to a maximum of **6 marks** in total.

A maximum of **4 marks** can be given for evaluative comments relating to the author, type of source, purpose and timing.

A maximum of **2 marks** may be given for comments relating to the content of the source.

A maximum of **2 marks** may be given for comments relating to points of significant omission.

Examples of aspects of the source and relevant comments:

Aspect of the source	Possible comment
Author: Mary Queen of Scots	Useful as it is a first-hand account (directly implicates her as co-operating with the plotters)
Type of Source: Letter	Useful as personal/secret communication so may be less guarded
Purpose: To persuade	Useful as it shows Mary was directly involved in plotting to escape
Timing: 1586	Useful as it is from the time leading up to Mary's execution

Content	Possible comment
When everything is prepared and the forces are ready both in this country and abroad, then you must set the six gentlemen to work	Useful as it accurately shows Mary's knowledge of the plot
Give orders that when the act is done, they get me away from here	Useful as accurately shows Mary giving orders to be released from her captivity/ may refer to plans to kill Elizabeth
At the same time get all your forces into battle order to protect me while we wait for help from abroad	Useful as accurately indicates Mary's intent to seek foreign assistance

Possible points of significant omission may include:
1. Sir Francis Walsingham added an extra section where he forged Mary's request for the names of the men who would kill Elizabeth
2. English Parliament had already voted that Mary would be executed should there be any more plots against Elizabeth discovered
3. Mary was denied legal counsel at her trial

Section 1, Context C, The Treaty of Union, 1689–1715

7. *Candidates can be credited in a number of ways up to a maximum of 8 marks.*

Candidates must use knowledge to present a balanced assessment of the influence of different possible factors and come to a reasoned conclusion. **Up to 5 marks** are allocated for relevant points of knowledge used to support

factors (but one mark should be deducted if the process is not clear in at least two factors). **1 mark** should be given for each relevant, factual key point of knowledge used to support a factor. **If only one factor is presented, a maximum of 3 marks should be given for relevant points of knowledge.**

Possible factors may include:	Relevant, factual, key points of knowledge to support this factor may include:
Anger over the Darien Scheme	1. King William wanted to remain on good terms with the Spanish and so deliberately sabotaged the colony 2. English officials prevented investment in the Darien Scheme 3. English colonies, including Jamaica, Barbados and New York, were forbidden by William to offer assistance to Scots at Darien 4. William worried that success for Darien would encourage independence for the American colonies 5. A huge number of Scots had invested in the Darien Scheme 6. many Scots believed that only the successful establishment of colonies could make Scotland a prosperous nation
Anger over the poor state of the Scottish economy strained relations	7. many in Scotland were angry that the Navigation Acts prevented Scotland trading with English colonies 8. there was a feeling that the English had not done enough to help Scotland during the "ill years" of the 1690s 9. the Worcester Incident where some of the English crew were hanged
Many Scots were unhappy over the operation of the Union of Crowns	10. belief that since the Union of Crowns Scotland had been unable to operate independently 11. William took little interest in Scotland. 12. Darien had shown Scotland had a King who acted against her interests 13. Anne declared herself to be "entirely English" 14. Scottish trade had been disrupted by England's wars and there was no recompense in the peace treaties
Problems arose over the succession	15. Scots were angry that the English Parliament passed the succession to Sophia of Hanover without consulting them 16. Scots reacted by passing the Act of Security which annoyed the English
Other factors	17. any other valid point

Up to 3 marks should be given for presenting the answer in a structured way, leading to a conclusion which addresses the question, as follows:

1 mark for the answer being presented in a structured way, with knowledge being organised in support of different factors.

1 mark for a conclusion with a valid judgement or overall summary.

1 mark for a reason being provided in support of the judgement.

8. *Candidates can be credited in a number of ways up to a maximum of 6 marks.*

Candidates must make a judgement about the usefulness of the source and support this by making evaluative comments on identified aspects of the source.

1 mark should be given for each relevant comment made, up to a **maximum of 6 marks in total**.
- A maximum of **4 marks** can be given for evaluative comments relating to the author, type of source, purpose and timing.
- A maximum of **2 marks** may be given for comments relating to the content of the source.
- A maximum of **2 marks** may be given for comments relating to points of significant omission.

Examples of aspects of the source and relevant comments:

Aspect of the source	Possible comment
Author: Stirling town council	Useful as it is a first-hand account of the concerns of a royal burgh/ typical of the concerns of other burghs
Type of Source: A petition	Useful as it shows that many people opposed the Union
Purpose: To persuade	Useful as the majority of petitions were against the Union
Timing: November 1706	Useful as it is written at the time of Union

Content	Possible comment
Union will bring a high burden of taxation upon this land	Useful as it accurately reflects a widespread concern
The English may discourage our trade (if they think it will be in competition with their own)	Useful as it accurately states a common view expressed by those who were anti-Treaty
The Union will ruin our industry, our religion, laws and liberties	Useful as it accurately states a common view expressed by those who were anti-Treaty

Possible points of significant omission may include:
1. Scotland had always been an independent nation and its identity would be subsumed if there was a new united Parliament/a dislike of merging with 'The Auld Enemy'
2. there were already fears that English foreign policy was operating against Scottish interests, eg anger in Scotland over failure of English to consult before entry into Spanish War of Succession
3. public opinion in Scotland was against a union
4. some Scots would have preferred a Federal Union
5. Episcopalians in Scotland opposed union as it would secure the Hanoverian succession and only a return to the Stuart dynasty could restore episcopacy to the Scottish church/Union guaranteed the position of the Presbyterian Church

9. *Candidates can be credited in a number of ways up to a maximum of 6 marks.*

Candidates must show a causal relationship between events.

Up to a **maximum of 6 marks in total**, **1 mark** should be given for each accurate, relevant reason, and a **second mark** should be given for reasons that are developed. Candidates may achieve full marks by providing six straightforward reasons, three developed reasons, or a combination of these.

Possible reasons may include:
1. Act of Security for the Kirk was vital in securing Presbyterian support for Union (in the aftermath of its passage Presbyterian ministers preached in favour of Union)
2. fear of English invasion if Union was rejected (during the Union negotiations English troops were stationed on the border with Scotland)
3. opponents of Union were unable to unite because of their differences (eg Catholics and extreme Presbyterians hated each other)
4. the Duke of Hamilton proved to be a very ineffective leader of the anti-Union cause
5. many Scots were worried that the Aliens Act would come into effect if they voted against Union. Scots would have lost land which they owned in England
6. many Scots were attracted by the possibility of trade with England's colonies (the Scots economy had gone through a very bad time in the 1690s and the prospect of full access to England's colonies seemed too good an opportunity to miss)
7. many were attracted by the prospect of compensation for Darien
8. the role of the Squadrone Volante was vital in ensuring Union was accepted (some motivated by their moderate Presbyterianism, others by belief they would control distribution of the Equivalent)
9. some Scottish nobles were offered English titles (which meant an automatic seat in the House of Lords) if they voted for Union
10. other inducements (money, trading privileges) were offered to others in the Scottish Parliament in return for their vote
11. fear of withdrawal of royal favour (and even loss of expenses claims and salary) if they did not vote for Union

Section 1, Context D, Migration and Empire, 1830–1939

10. *Candidates can be credited in a number of ways up to a maximum of 8 marks.*

Candidates must use knowledge to present a balanced assessment of the influence of different possible factors and come to a reasoned conclusion. Up to 5 marks are allocated for relevant points of knowledge used to support factors (but one mark should be deducted if the process is not clear in at least two factors). **1 mark** should be given for each relevant, factual key point of knowledge used to support a factor. **If only one factor is presented, a maximum of 3 marks should be given for relevant points of knowledge**

Possible factors may include:	Relevant, factual, key points of knowledge to support this factor may include:
Clearances	1. many landlords no longer lived in the Highlands and needed additional income to fund their new lifestyles 2. landlords would make more money letting land to sheep farmers/ creating hunting estates 3. tenants had no security of tenure so could easily be evicted/made homeless 4. whole districts were brutally cleared (eg Strathconon in 1850, South Uist and Barra in 1851, Knoydart in 1853) 5. some landlords assisted tenants by paying their passage if they agreed to leave 6. forced clearances ended after Crofters' Holdings Act 1886
Difficulties of earning a living	7. collapse of kelp industry/fall in demand for black cattle 8. overpopulation led to subdivision of holdings/not enough land to support a family or pay rent 9. poor stony soils – primitive equipment (cas chrom)/poor climate – short growing season 10. failure of potato crop in 1846 – blight and famine 11. loss of market for herring after Russian Revolution 12. few employment opportunities for ambitious young people/limited number of professional posts for well educated 13. deer forests and shooting estates employed few people 14. little land made available to returning servicemen after the war
Poor standard of living	15. 19th century blackhouses shared with animals/blackhouses often had no chimneys/roofs leaked 16. houses often lacked basic amenities (eg bathrooms/toilets, electricity in 1920s and 30s) 17. limited access to medical care/ shops/entertainment
Pull factors	18. the promise of cheap land 19. employment opportunities/higher wages 20. encouragement from relatives/friends
Other factors	21. any other valid point

Up to 3 marks should be given for presenting the answer in a structured way, leading to a conclusion which addresses the question, as follows:

1 mark for the answer being presented in a structured way, with knowledge being organised in support of different factors.

1 mark for a conclusion with a valid judgement or overall summary.

1 mark for a reason being provided in support of the judgement.

11. *Candidates can be credited in a number of ways up to a maximum of 6 marks.*

Candidates must show a causal relationship between events.

Up to a **maximum of 6 marks in total**, **1 mark** should be given for each accurate, relevant reason, and a **second mark** should be given for reasons that are developed. Candidates may achieve full marks by providing six straightforward reasons, three developed reasons, or a combination of these.

Possible reasons may include:
1. close to Ireland so only a short journey – important for people with little money to have only a short time when they could not earn
2. fares to Scotland from Ireland were very cheap so it was a more affordable destination/adverts encouraged immigration
3. Catholic Church offered assistance with finding jobs and housing
4. Scotland was involved early in the Industrial Revolution so there was a wide range of jobs available (eg coal mines, textile factories, sugar refineries, construction, railway building etc which used existing skills or were suitable for unskilled workers)
5. some jobs (eg coal mining, had tied housing available to workers/housing available in growing towns and cities)
6. wages in Scotland were consistently higher than they were in Ireland
7. it became cheaper for migrants from Europe to sail to America from Glasgow instead of direct from Europe; many stayed in Scotland rather than move on
8. there were existing communities of Jews, Irish, Italians which made it easy for others to settle in/Protestant Irish found it very easy to settle in Scottish society
9. Italians were able to set up small family businesses such as cafes and fish and chip shops all over Scotland, as few others were doing this and the Scots enjoyed the products
10. Scotland did not persecute religious minorities which made it attractive to Jewish immigrants fleeing from Russia

12. *Candidates can be credited in a number of ways up to a maximum of 6 marks.*

Candidates must make a judgement about the usefulness of the source and support this by making evaluative comments on identified aspects of the source.

1 mark should be given for each relevant comment made, up to a **maximum of 6 marks in total**.
- A maximum of 4 marks can be given for evaluative comments relating to the author, type of source, purpose and timing.
- A maximum of 2 marks may be given for comments relating to the content of the source.
- A maximum of 2 marks may be given for comments relating to points of significant omission.

Examples of aspects of the source and relevant comments:

Aspect of the source	Possible comment
Author: Scottish emigrant	Useful as he experienced emigration for himself
Type of Source: Song	Less useful as it may be exaggerated for emotional effect
Purpose: To inform	Less useful as his feelings may not be representative of others' experiences/useful because many immigrants shared these feelings
Timing: 1920s	Useful as at a time after the war when many Scots emigrated to Canada

Content	Possible comment
I see only bleak empty prairie, There's no sound of waves breaking on the shore/The winter night is long for me.	Useful as it accurately states new physical environment very unfamiliar for many emigrants/ were unused to long Canadian winter
In the evening darkness My spirit sinks with homesickness	Useful as it accurately states many Scots experienced homesickness
No ceilidh on the prairie	Useful as it accurately states what many immigrants felt or less useful as may be a purely personal response to the situation/feeling of isolation/loneliness

Possible points of significant omission may include:

1. many Scots successfully formed close-knit communities
2. many Scots were attracted by the grants of prairie land and prospered there
3. many Scots kept their traditions going with Caledonian societies, Burns Clubs, Highland dancing, pipe bands, etc.
4. many Scots became very successful in Canada and other new countries (eg Andrew Carnegie, John A MacDonald, Robert Dunsmuir)
5. some Scots did not settle and returned to Scotland
6. some Scots prospered and returned wealthy to Scotland

Section 1, Context E, The Era of the Great War, 1900–1928

13. *Candidates can be credited in a number of ways up to a maximum of 6 marks.*

Candidates must show a causal relationship between events.

Up to a **maximum of 6 marks in total**, **1 mark** should be given for each accurate, relevant reason, and a **second mark** should be given for reasons that are developed. Candidates may achieve full marks by providing six straightforward reasons, three developed reasons, or a combination of these.

Possible reasons may include:

Patriotism/Martial Tradition
1. Patriotic appeal of slogans/people were carried away by a wave of patriotism
2. Scotland already had a proud military/martial tradition

Xenophobia
3. Scots affected by stories of spies and "Belgian Atrocities" of German Army

Local Loyalties
4. the Cameronians recruited largely from Glasgow and Lanarkshire. The Royal Scots tended to attract men from Edinburgh
5. after 13 Hearts players signed up, 600 Hearts supporters in six days also joined the 16th Royal Scots which became known as McCrae's Battalion

Adventure
6. opportunity to see new places and countries and perform heroic deeds – and/or quite possibly to leave behind a boring or difficult job
7. the attraction of setting out on this great adventure with your friends was possible by the formation of "pals" battalions'

Peer Pressure
8. peer pressure from family, friends and wider society/sense of duty

9. women were encouraged to press men into service eg white feather campaign

Economic Necessity
10. fear of unemployment was probably an important factor in joining up/recruitment in high unemployment areas more successful than in low
11. Earl of Wemyss threatened to dismiss any employee who failed to join up

Propaganda
Posters/Newspapers/Government propaganda

14. *Candidates can be credited in a number of ways up to a maximum of 8 marks.*

Candidates must use knowledge to present a balanced assessment of the influence of different possible factors and come to a reasoned conclusion. **Up to 5 marks** are allocated for relevant points of knowledge used to support factors (but one mark should be deducted if the process is not clear in at least two factors). **1 mark** should be given for each relevant, factual key point of knowledge used to support a factor. **If only one factor is presented, a maximum of 3 marks should be given for relevant points of knowledge.**

Possible factors may include:	Relevant, factual, key points of knowledge to support this factor may include:
Food Shortages	1. Voluntary rationing had little impact/ posters discouraged people from wasting food 2. People started to keep an allotment to grow food 3. The contribution of the Women's Land Army 4. Conscientious Objectors were used to produce food 5. Parks and tennis courts turned into vegetable plots 6. Rationing introduced for certain foodstuff from 1917 7. Substitute foods were used/standard loaves made using powdered potato flour and beans 8. Rationing had some health benefits
	9. Game such as rabbit was eaten- especially by country dwellers 10. Black market existed for those who could afford it 11. People had to queue for some foods/on occasion food lorries hijacked
DORA	12. Blackouts 13. Restrictions to pub opening hours/ watering down of alcohol 14. Censorship 15. Conscription
Loss of loved ones	16. Mourning huge numbers of soldiers killed
Changing role of women	17. Women became head of household 18. Difficulties experienced balancing work with looking after the children 19. More women working than ever before 20. Details about Land Army/Munitions factories/nursing etc 21. Experienced more freedom/equality
Other factors	22. any other valid point (including more details of DORA restrictions)

Up to 3 marks should be given for presenting the answer in a structured way, leading to a conclusion which addresses the question, as follows:

1 mark for the answer being presented in a structured way, with knowledge being organised in support of different factors.

1 mark for a conclusion with a valid judgement or overall summary.

1 mark for a reason being provided in support of the judgement.

15. *Candidates can be credited in a number of ways **up to a maximum of 6 marks**.*

Candidates must make a judgement about the usefulness of the source and support this by making evaluative comments on identified aspects of the source.

1 mark should be given for each relevant comment made, up to a **maximum of 6 marks in total**.
- A maximum of **4 marks** can be given for evaluative comments relating to the author, type of source, purpose and timing.
- A maximum of **2 marks** may be given for comments relating to the content of the source.
- A maximum of **2 marks** may be given for comments relating to points of significant omission.

Examples of aspects of the source and relevant comments:

Aspect of the source	Possible comment
Author: Historian John Kerr	Useful as he is a well-informed expert/will have researched the issue (using a variety of primary sources)
Type of Source: Book	Useful because it is a factual viewpoint on the extension on the right to vote
Purpose: To inform	Useful as it is balanced/no evidence of historical bias
Timing: 2010	Useful as it is a secondary source written with the benefit of hindsight

Content	Possible comment
The 1918 Representation of the People Act gave some women over 30 the vote in national elections	Useful as it accurately states that the franchise was restricted to "some" women.
They had to be either: householders or the wives of householders, occupiers of property with an annual rent of £5, graduates of British universities	Useful as it accurately explains the qualifications required for women to get the vote.
The electorate increased to about 21 million, of which 8.4 million were women	Useful as it accurately gives the statistical evidence of the increase in the franchise.

Possible points of significant omission may include:
1. it gave the right to vote to all men over 21
2. women still did not have the vote on the same terms as men
3. 19 if they had been on active service in the armed forces
4. women now made up 40% of the total voters

Section 2, Context A, The Creation of the Medieval Kingdoms, 1066–1406

16. *Candidates can be credited in a number of ways **up to a maximum of 5 marks**.*

Candidates must show a causal relationship between events.

Up to a **maximum of 5 marks in total**, **1 mark** should be given for each accurate, relevant reason, and a **second mark** should be given for reasons that are developed. Candidates may achieve full marks by providing five straightforward reasons, three developed reasons, or a combination of these.

Possible reasons may include:
1. William was related to Edward the Confessor through marriage
2. William claimed Edward had promised him the throne
3. William had supported Edward during rebellion in England/had supplied Edward with soldiers to put down the revolt
4. Harold Godwinson had sworn an oath to accept William as the rightful heir
5. Harold had seized the throne/broken his oath/this made him unworthy to be king
6. William had also received the support of the Pope before his invasion
7. William felt God was on his side after his victory at Hastings

17. *Candidates can be credited in a number of ways **up to a maximum of 4 marks**.*

Candidates must make direct comparisons of the two sources, either overall or in detail. A simple comparison will indicate what points of detail or overall viewpoint they agree or disagree about and should be given **1 mark**.

A developed comparison of the points of detail or overall viewpoint should be given **2 marks**. Candidates may achieve full marks by making four simple comparisons, two developed comparisons or by a combination of these.

Possible points of comparison may include:

Overall: The sources agree about the way William dealt with rebellion	
Source A	**Source B**
Every home and farmland was burnt and all livestock destroyed	Crops were set on fire, herds of animals were slaughtered and supplies of food ruined
So many people were massacred that their bodies filled the streets	Hundreds of people were slaughtered
The few who had survived now faced starvation	Whole families died of hunger

18. *Candidates can be credited in a number of ways **up to a maximum of 5 marks**.*

They may take different perspectives on the events and may describe a variety of different aspects of the events.

1 mark should be given for each accurate relevant key point of knowledge. A **second mark** should be given for each point that is developed, up to a maximum of **5 marks**. Candidates may achieve full marks by providing five straightforward points, by making three developed points, or a combination of these.

Possible points of knowledge may include:
1. Henry knocked down any castles built illegally by the barons
2. Henry sent the barons' armies home
3. Henry introduced the exchequer (eg Nigel of Ely)
4. Henry introduced new laws to deal with crime (eg The Assize of Clarendon/Northampton)
5. Henry introduced new laws to deal with land (eg The Novel Disseisin)

6. Henry introduced the jury system/trial by ordeal
7. Henry sacked corrupt sheriffs
8. Henry prevented barons from becoming sheriffs
9. Henry introduced key officials (eg Justices in Eyre)
10. Henry appointed his sons to control other parts of his kingdom

19. *Candidates can be credited in a number of ways **up to a maximum of 6 marks.***

Candidates must make an overall judgement about how fully the source explains the events. **1 mark** may be given for each valid point from the source or each valid point of significant omission provided.

A maximum of 2 marks may be given for answers in which no judgement has been made or which refer only to the source.

Possible points which may be identified in the source include:
1. offered support and comfort in difficult times/ encouraged people not to give up
2. taught people how to be good Christians
3. heard confessions/issued penance
4. controlled the way people behaved

Possible points of significant omission may include:
5. carried out key ceremonies (eg baptism/marriage/funeral)
6. performed last rites for the dying
7. kept tithes for villages in case of harvest failure
8. identified holidays
9. educated boys/trained them for a career in the Church
10. was part of the feudal system/owed service to the king
11. was active politically (eg clergy often acted as advisors to the king)
12. employed large number of people from the community

Section 2, Context B, War of the Three Kingdoms, 1603–1651

20. *Candidates can be credited in a number of ways **up to a maximum of 4 marks.***

Candidates must make direct comparisons of the two sources, either overall or in detail. A simple comparison will indicate what points of detail or overall viewpoint they agree or disagree about and should be given **1 mark**.

A developed comparison of the points of detail or overall viewpoint should be given **2 marks**. Candidates may achieve full marks by making four simple comparisons, two developed comparisons or by a combination of these.

Possible points of comparison may include:

Overall: The sources agree that the reign of Charles was unpopular	
Source A	**Source B**
The reign of Charles I began with an unpopular friendship with the Duke of Buckingham/Buckingham was assassinated in 1628	Charles also angered many by having favourites at court, particularly the Duke of Buckingham/In 1628 Buckingham was assassinated
There was ongoing tension with Parliament over money (made worse by the costs of war abroad)	Charles also angered many with the methods he used to raise money
Religious tensions led to further resentment of Charles I as he preferred Anglican forms of worship which made Puritans suspicious	Charles I was a very religious man who enjoyed Anglican church services full of ritual, and this led to clashes with Puritans who preferred plain and simple services

21. *Candidates can be credited in a number of ways **up to a maximum of 5 marks.***

Candidates must show a causal relationship between events.

Up to a **maximum of 5 marks in total**, **1 mark** should be given for each accurate, relevant reason, and a **second mark** should be given for reasons that are developed. Candidates may achieve full marks by providing five straightforward reasons, three developed reasons, or a combination of these.

Possible reasons may include:
1. ship money – only to be collected in times of war and from coastal areas – Charles began to collect it from inland areas, in times of peace and on a yearly basis
2. forest fines imposed on people living in areas that had been forests in the distant past (14th century)
3. distraint of Knighthood fines – fining people if they did not accept knighthoods (Knights had to provide loans to the Crown)
4. nuisances – in London people who had built outside of the original walls were forced to buy a licence to 'commit a nuisance'
5. monopolies – reappeared in different forms, the most resented being the soap monopoly
6. Court of Wards – the much disliked Court of Wards doubled its income (to £76,000)
7. plantations – 1632 City of London was fined for failing to push forward the plantation of Ulster (finding Protestant families to take over land in Ireland)
8. customs farmers – customs farmers gave the Crown a larger sum in exchange for the right to collect the customs, these extra dues were passed on to the merchants to pay
9. many disliked new taxation caused by King and court's love of luxury (eg banquets, clothes, foreign dynastic wars)

22. *Candidates can be credited in a number of ways **up to a maximum of 5 marks.***

They may take different perspectives on the events and may describe a variety of different aspects of the events.

1 mark should be given for each accurate relevant key point of knowledge. A **second mark** should be given for each point that is developed, up to a maximum of 5 **marks**. Candidates may achieve full marks by providing five straightforward points, by making three developed points, or a combination of these.

Possible points of knowledge may include:
1. riot in St. Giles Cathedral saw men and women assault the Dean of St. Giles whilst reading from the New Prayer Book
2. other potential violence in the north as Bishop of Brechin threatened his congregation with two loaded pistols as he read from the new service
3. emergency body was formed to organise opposition to the New Prayer Book – "The Tables" members were chosen from the Scottish Parliament
4. Petitions organised and sent to Charles
5. National Covenant for the Defence of True religion was drawn up in 1638
6. General Assembly of the Kirk banned the New Prayer Book in 1638
7. Charles decided to use force against the Scots in 1638 (First Bishops' War), caused further opposition

23. *Candidates can be credited in a number of ways **up to a maximum of 6 marks.***

Candidates must make an overall judgement about how fully the source explains the events. **1 mark** may be given for each valid point interpreted from the source or each valid point of significant omission provided

A maximum of 2 marks may be given for answers in which no judgement has been made or which refer only to the source.

Possible points which may be identified in the source include:
1. the King ordered his army to occupy the high ridge on Edgehill, hoping that the Parliamentarian army would be forced to attack uphill
2. Parliament arranged their army on flat ground
3. Essex decided to wait for the King to make the first move
4. Essex's decision to wait forced the King to take action/the King moved his army down off the ridge and attacked

Possible points of significant omission may include:
5. Royalist cavalry on the right wing charged into Parliamentarian cavalry causing them to flee
6. Royalist cavalry pursued the Parliamentarians to village of Kineton/3 miles away
7. Royalist left wing cavalry scattered by right wing of Parliamentarian army
8. Parliamentarians now had the only effective cavalry left on the field
9. Royalist cavalry drifted back from Kineton to find the situation had altered greatly
10. night came and exhausted soldiers stopped fighting
11. 3000 men had died, many wounded or fled
12. battle ended in a draw – both sides moved towards London the next day
13. Charles' army was prevented from capturing London

Section 2, Context C, The Atlantic Slave Trade, 1770–1807

24. *Candidates can be credited in a number of ways up to a maximum of 6 marks.*

Candidates must make an overall judgement about how fully the source explains the events. **1 mark** may be given for each valid point interpreted from the source or each valid point of significant omission provided.

A maximum of 2 marks may be given for answers in which no judgement has been made or which refer only to the source.

Possible points which may be identified in the source include:
1. slaves were often tightly packed below deck for the journey across the Atlantic ocean
2. conditions below deck were horrendous and slaves were denied basic sanitation
3. disease was common/and many died (from conditions such as dysentery)
4. the food was unfamiliar and many slaves simply refused to eat

Possible points of significant omission may include:
5. slaves were sometimes held below deck using a loose pack system/men usually kept shackled
6. lack of fresh air – slaves held for long periods below deck/terrible smell below deck
7. floor in hold became covered in blood, mucus, vomit and faeces
8. some slaves had to be force fed to keep them alive
9. crew were often cruel towards slaves
10. female slaves often suffered sexual abuse from crew
11. slaves taken above deck and whipped to make them exercise/made to dance

25. *Candidates can be credited in a number of ways up to a maximum of 5 marks.*

Candidates must show a causal relationship between events.

Up to a **maximum of 5 marks in total**, **1 mark** should be given for each accurate, relevant reason, and a **second mark** should be given for reasons that are developed. Candidates may achieve full marks by providing five straightforward reasons, three developed reasons, or a combination of these.

Possible reasons may include:
1. the slave trade brought great wealth to British cities
2. the slave trade provided employment for many people (eg jobs for sailors, dock workers, rope makers)
3. manufactured goods made in Britain were traded in Africa or exported to the plantations
4. the slave trade provided a boost to shipbuilding/led to expansion of docks
5. the port cities (eg Liverpool or Glasgow) grew in size and power through its involvement in the transportation of slaves
6. Glasgow made great profits from the trade in tobacco and sugar
7. many great buildings were built from the profits of the slave trade
8. led to the growth of banking and insurance industries (eg in London)
9. Bristol became wealthy through its involvement in the sugar trade
10. British cotton mills relied on supplies of slave produced cotton

26. *Candidates can be credited in a number of ways up to a maximum of 4 marks.*

Candidates must make direct comparisons of the two sources, either overall or in detail. A simple comparison will indicate what points of detail or overall viewpoint they agree or disagree about and should be given **1 mark**.

A developed comparison of the points of detail or overall viewpoint should be given **2 marks**. Candidates may achieve full marks by making four simple comparisons, two developed comparisons or by a combination of these.

Possible points of comparison may include:

Source B	Source C
Overall: The sources agree about resistance on the plantations.	
They sabotaged their owners by working slowly and inefficiently	The mildest forms of resistance were doing a job slowly or badly.
They were harshly punished for such behaviour/ whipping, slaves had their ears, noses and limbs cut off	The punishments for slaves who resisted were very harsh/punishments such as hanging, mutilation or lashing were common
Many slaves attempted to run away	Slaves ran away when they saw a chance

27. *Candidates can be credited in a number of ways up to a maximum of 5 marks.*

Candidates must show a causal relationship between events.

Up to a **maximum of 5 marks in total**, **1 mark** should be given for each accurate, relevant reason, and a **second mark** should be given for reasons that are developed. Candidates may achieve full marks by providing five straightforward reasons, three developed reasons, or a combination of these.

Possible reasons may include:
1. abolitionists formed The Society for the Abolition of the Slave Trade to campaign against the Slave Trade
2. Thomas Clarkson visited ports such as Liverpool and Bristol to collect evidence/collected artefacts such as manacles and thumbscrews to show people the horrors of the trade
3. Equiano highlighted his experience of slavery
4. a diagram of a slave ship, the Brookes, was also published/other pamphlets and posters were produced
5. the society produced evidence that hundreds of British seamen involved in the trade died every year
6. William Wilberforce tried to influence the prime minister and Prince of Wales to support the abolition of the slave trade/MPs were routinely petitioned
7. Wilberforce presented a bill to Parliament on numerous occasions to end the slave trade
8. John Newton, a former slave ship captain, preached against slavery
9. Newton wrote the hymn "Amazing Grace"
10. Granville Sharp challenged slavery in the courts
11. anti-slavery petitions were signed
12. Wedgwood produced goods with the slogan "Am I not a man and a brother?"
13. people boycotted goods such as sugar

Section 2, Context D, Changing Britain, 1760–1914

28. *Candidates can be credited in a number of ways up to a maximum of 4 marks.*

Candidates must make direct comparisons of the two sources, either overall or in detail. A simple comparison will indicate what points of detail or overall viewpoint they agree or disagree about and should be given **1 mark.**

A developed comparison of the points of detail or overall viewpoint should be given **2 marks.** Candidates may achieve full marks by making four simple comparisons, two developed comparisons or by a combination of these.

Possible points of comparison may include:

Overall: Sources mostly agree about the events of the massacre	
Source B	**Source C**
People had gathered from all over Lancashire in St Peter's Fields	I saw a large crowd that had gathered from miles around and was moving towards St Peter's Fields
The magistrates wrongly believed that people had been marching and drilling like soldiers in preparation	(I laughed at the fears of the magistrates as) the so-called "marching" protest was actually a procession of men with their wives, sisters and children
11 people were killed and hundreds injured	I could see that many people had been hurt/I will always be haunted by the sight of those trampled bodies.

29. *Candidates can be credited in a number of ways up to a maximum of 5 marks.*

Candidates must show a causal relationship between events.

Up to a **maximum of 5 marks in total, 1 mark** should be given for each accurate, relevant reason, and a **second mark** should be given for reasons that are developed. Candidates may achieve full marks by providing five straightforward reasons, three developed reasons, or a combination of these.

Possible reasons may include:
1. hot temperatures led to exhaustion/poor health/made accidents more likely
2. long hours (12 to 18 hour days) led to exhaustion/poor health/made accidents more likely
3. few breaks led to exhaustion/made accidents more likely
4. lack of ventilation made it hard to breathe
5. harmful dust particles and fibres in the air led to a high rate of lung disease (TB)
6. noise of machinery often damaged hearing
7. open lavatory buckets smelly and unhygienic
8. machines were not fenced, so accidents were frequent
9. workers often had to work and eat during short breaks which led to accidents being more likely
10. children often had to climb beneath machinery to clean, causing accidents
11. child workers prone to rickets due to lack of sunlight and poor quality of food
12. workers became deformed/stomach pains due to long hours bending over machines
13. varicose veins common from workers spending long hours on feet
14. workers were often badly treated or beaten by overseers
15. before 1830s no laws to regulate working conditions/protect health
16. difficult to enforce laws passed/not enough factory inspectors

30. *Candidates can be credited in a number of ways up to a maximum of 6 marks.*

Candidates must make an overall judgement about how fully the source explains the events. **1 mark** may be given for each valid point interpreted from the source or each valid point of significant omission provided.

A maximum of 2 marks may be given for answers in which no judgement has been made or which refer only to the source.

Possible points which may be identified in the source include:
1. even the most remote country areas were brought into contact with towns and cities
2. industries benefited greatly from being able to transport their raw materials and goods quickly/cheaply
3. farmers were able to sell their fresh produce over greater distances
4. faster travel meant that people could live further from their jobs/towns spread as suburbs were built

Possible points of significant omission may include:
5. many jobs created (eg to build or run the railways)
6. daily national newspapers now possible
7. improved postal services
8. cheap fares/day trips and holidays for working class possible
9. Parliamentary trains meant railway travel was accessible to all
10. MPs could travel quickly between constituencies and London
11. political parties able to campaign nationwide
12. enabled growth of trade union movement
13. standardised time across Britain (GMT/Railway time)
14. enabled national sporting leagues to develop
15. perishable foods more widely available, so diet improved

31. *Candidates can be credited in a number of ways **up to a maximum of 5 marks.***

They may take different perspectives on the events and may describe a variety of different aspects of the events.

1 mark should be given for each accurate relevant key point of knowledge. A **second mark** should be given for each point that is developed, up to a maximum of **5 marks**. Candidates may achieve full marks by providing five straightforward points, by making three developed points, or a combination of these.

Possible points of knowledge may include:

1832 Reform Act:
1. seats were distributed more fairly (eg industrial towns gained MPs)
2. pocket/rotten boroughs lost their MPs
3. boroughs with less than 4,000 inhabitants lost one MP each
4. more seats were awarded to the counties
5. Scotland was awarded extra seats/Ireland was given extra seats
6. some people lost the right to vote (eg working men in 'potwalloper' burghs)
7. 1 in 6 adult men now had the vote/1 in 8 in Scotland, 1 in 5 in England.
8. electorate increased by about 60%/from 435,000 to 652,000
9. in Scotland the electorate increased from 4,500 to 65,000
10. in burghs the franchise was standardised/all male householders paying £10 per annum rent got the vote
11. in counties the franchise was extended to 40 shilling (£2)freeholders/£10 copyholders/£50 tenants
12. this meant that middle-class men now had the vote (eg small landowners, tenant farmers and shopkeepers)
13. voter registration introduced/duration of polling limited to two days

1867 Reform Act:
14. enfranchised 1.25 million men/effectively doubled the electorate/1 in 3 men now had vote
15. all male householders/lodgers in burghs who paid rent of £10 per annum got the vote (enfranchised skilled working men in towns)
16. business owners who paid rates of £12 per annum got the vote
17. seats were redistributed from small towns to the growing industrial towns or counties(eg Liverpool got an extra MP/Edinburgh from two to four MPs)
18. the University of London was also given a seat/two seats given to Scottish universities

Section 2, Context E, The Making of Modern Britain, 1880–1951

32. *Candidates can be credited in a number of ways **up to a maximum of 5 marks.***

They may take different perspectives on the events and may describe a variety of different aspects of the events.

1 mark should be given for each accurate relevant key point of knowledge. A **second mark** should be given for each point that is developed, up to a maximum of **5 marks**. Candidates may achieve full marks by providing five straightforward points, by making three developed points, or a combination of these.

Possible points of knowledge may include:
1. poor housing (eg dampness, vermin, shared outside toilets)
2. poor health/lack of affordable health-care.
3. overcrowding – often leading to health problems (eg TB)
4. malnutrition led to health problems (eg Rickets)
5. low wages/few benefits
6. Unemployment/employment often cyclical or seasonal
7. dependence on charity/voluntary organisations (eg no pensions until 1908)
8. fear/stigma of workhouse/poorhouse (splitting up of families in workhouse)
9. destitution/homelessness
10. high death rates – especially of young children/vulnerable people
11. lack of sympathy – due to laissez-faire attitudes
12. lack of education
13. excessive drunkenness/gambling

33. *Candidates can be credited in a number of ways **up to a maximum of 6 marks.***

Candidates must make an overall judgement about how fully the source explains the events. **1 mark** may be given for each valid point interpreted from the source or each valid point of significant omission provided.

A maximum of 2 marks may be given for answers in which no judgement has been made or which refer only to the source.

Possible points which may be identified in the source include:
1. other parties were afraid that they might lose votes to Labour if they did not show that they wanted to help the poor
2. most working class men now had the vote, so it was possible that they could vote for Labour
3. Trade unions put pressure on the Liberals and Conservatives, to do more to help the poor
4. society was beginning to accept that some people became poor through no fault of their own

Possible points of significant omission may include:
5. Booth's survey revealed high levels of poverty in London.
6. Rowntree's survey revealed that the problem was not confined to London – provincial cities like York affected too.
7. concerns over fitness of recruits during Boer War led to desire to improve health by tackling poverty.
8. concerns over national efficiency/worries about Britain's future workforce led to desire to tackle poverty and poor health
9. other countries beginning to challenge Britain's position (eg Germany and the USA)
10. "New Liberals" accepted that government had to intervene more in the lives of the people to help the poor
11. politicians such as David Lloyd George came from a working class background and had genuine concern for the poor
12. the Germans had introduced some welfare reforms already and the "German Model" was studied and copied by the British/David Lloyd George had visited Germany for this purpose

34. *Candidates can be credited in a number of ways **up to a maximum of 5 marks.***

Candidates must show a causal relationship between events.

Up to a maximum of **5 marks** in total, **1 mark** should be given for each accurate, relevant reason, and a **second mark** should be given for reasons that are developed. Candidates may achieve full marks by providing five straightforward reasons, three developed reasons, or a combination of these.

Possible reasons may include:
1. Liberals had no overall plan for social reform
2. reforms were selective/only helped some groups/ deserving poor
3. benefit levels were ungenerous/often below subsistence level (eg pensions)
4. many of the reforms were voluntary/optional/control given to local authorities (eg school meals only made compulsory in 1914)
5. unemployment benefit only paid for short-term (15 weeks), so did not tackle long-term unemployment
6. unemployment insurance only for certain trades
7. problems with pensions (eg payable at 70 – well above average life-expectancy)
8. medical inspections did not provide treatment (until 1912 when school clinics introduced)
9. health insurance did not cover most hospital treatment
10. families of workers not covered by health insurance
11. housing not tackled at all
12. Education barely tackled (apart from some scholarships in 1907/8 Education Act)

35. *Candidates can be credited in a number of ways up to a maximum of 4 marks.*

Candidates must make direct comparisons of the two sources, either overall or in detail. A simple comparison will indicate what points of detail or overall viewpoint they agree or disagree about and should be given **1 mark.**

A developed comparison of the points of detail or overall viewpoint should be given **2 marks.** Candidates may achieve full marks by making four simple comparisons, two developed comparisons or by a combination of these

Possible points of comparison may include:

Overall: The Sources disagree about the success of the Labour reforms

Source B	Source C
Their record of success is difficult to argue with	Their reputation … is not entirely deserved
The National Health Service was the greatest achievement of the Labour welfare state, giving free medical and dental treatment to all	By 1951, charges had to be introduced (for some dentaled treatment, spectacles and prescriptions) meaning that the NHS was not an entirely free service.
Considerable progress was made in tackling the housing shortage/between 1948 and 1951, around 200,000 homes were built per year	Labour's record on house building is poor (when compared to that of the previous governments of the 1930s)

Section 3, Context A, The Cross and the Crescent; the Crusades, 1071–1192

36. *Candidates can be credited in a number of ways up to a maximum of 5 marks.*

They may take different perspectives on the events and may describe a variety of different aspects of the events.

1 mark should be given for each accurate relevant key point of knowledge. A **second mark** should be given for each point that is developed, up to a maximum of **5 marks.** Candidates may achieve full marks by providing five straightforward points, by making three developed points, or a combination of these.

Possible points of knowledge may include:
1. knights were expected to fight for the king
2. knights were expected to carry out castle guard duty
3. knights were expected to fight for the Church/protect the clergy
4. orders of knights protected pilgrims (eg the Knights Templar)
5. knights were expected to protect the weak and vulnerable in society (eg elderly, children)
6. knights were part of the feudal system providing land for peasants to cultivate
7. knights enforced law and order/were members of a jury in some countries
8. knights were expected to be role models/to live by the Code of Chivalry

37. *Candidates can be credited in a number of ways up to a maximum of 5 marks.*

Candidates must show a causal relationship between events.

Up to a **maximum of 5 marks in total**, **1 mark** should be given for each accurate, relevant reason, and a **second mark** should be given for reasons that are developed. Candidates may achieve full marks by providing five straightforward reasons, three developed reasons, or a combination of these.

Possible reasons may include:
1. Peter the Hermit was a poor military leader
2. belief in the righteousness of their cause made them overconfident
3. the peasants were not trained soldiers/accompanied by wives, children, even the elderly
4. the peasants had few weapons
5. the peasants ran out of supplies/money whilst travelling across Europe
6. the peasants were ill-disciplined on their journey (eg treatment of the Jews making communities unwilling to help them)
7. the peasants ignored Emperor Alexius' advice to wait for the main Crusader army
8. the peasants split into different groups and elected their own leaders/Peter the Hermit was cast aside
9. peasants were lured into an ambush by spies
10. the peasants were defeated by Muslim forces/most were killed/supplies lost

38. *Candidates can be credited in a number of ways up to a maximum of 5 marks.*

Candidates must make an overall judgement about how fully the source explains the events. **1 mark** may be given for each valid point interpreted from the source or each valid point of significant omission provided

A maximum of 2 marks may be given for answers in which no judgement has been made or which refer only to the source.

Possible points which may be identified in the source include:
1. Muslim communities did not attack Crusaders/gave them money to keep the peace
2. refused to join together and thought only of their own land
3. Seljuk Turks had been defeated by Egyptian forces and lost the city
4. Egyptians asked for help but no Muslim armies came to their aid

Possible points of significant omission may include:
5. the Crusaders captured Nicaea because Kilij Arslan was away fighting other Muslims (eg The Danishmends)

6. at Antioch the Crusaders bribed a Muslim who let them into the city eg Firouz
7. Kerbogha arrived late to Antioch because he spent time trying to protect his own land first (eg attacked Edessa)
8. Muslim forces refused to attack together at Antioch (eg Ridwan of Aleppo/Duqaq of Damascus)
9. Kerbogha's men fled the battlefield at Antioch
10. Turks did not attempt to recapture Jerusalem because they had land disputes to settle with other Muslim groups elsewhere.

39. *Candidates can be credited in a number of ways up to a maximum of 5 marks.*

Candidates must make a judgement about the usefulness of the source and support this by making evaluative comments on identified aspects of the source.

1 mark should be given for each relevant comment made, up to a **maximum of 5 marks in total.**
- A maximum of **4 marks** can be given for evaluative comments relating to the author, type of source, purpose and timing.
- A maximum of **2 marks** may be given for comments relating to the content of the source.
- A maximum of **2 marks** may be given for comments relating to points of significant omission.

Examples of aspects of the source and relevant comments:

Aspect of the source	Possible comment
Author: A Crusader	Useful because he has first-hand experience/eyewitness
Type of Source: Chronicle	Useful because it was a well-researched record of events in the East
Purpose: To record/blame King Guy for the defeat	Useful because it provides a detailed account of the battle/less useful as it may be biased
Timing: 1187	Useful because it was written at the time of the Battle of Hattin

Content	Possible comment
Crusaders constantly attacked by Saladin's army	Useful because it accurately explains why the Crusaders tired
King Guy made a terrible mistake and made camp near Hattin	Useful because it accurately describes the error made by the Crusaders
Saladin's army surrounded the Crusaders' camp and slaughtered nearly all those inside	Useful because it accurately describes what happened in the battle.

Possible points of significant omission may include:
1. Saladin's army set fire to the grass around the Crusaders' camp
2. not all Crusaders agreed with the march to Tiberias (eg Roland of Tripoli)
3. Saladin's army captured some Crusaders as prisoners
4. Saladin's army captured a shard of the True Cross
5. Saladin spared the life of King Guy and some other Christian lords
6. repeated charges by mounted Crusaders against Muslim lines failed

Section 3, Context B, "Tea and Freedom": the American Revolution, 1774–83

40. *Candidates can be credited in a number of ways up to a maximum of 5 marks.*

Candidates must show a causal relationship between events.

Up to a **maximum of 5 marks in total**, 1 mark should be given for each accurate, relevant reason, and a **second mark** should be given for reasons that are developed. Candidates may achieve full marks by providing five straightforward reasons, three developed reasons, or a combination of these.

Possible reasons may include:
1. the colonists were unhappy with the imposition of laws and taxes which were seen as unjust (eg the passing of the Stamp Act and Townshend Act in the 1760s had been very unpopular measures)
2. they resented being taxed without representation in the British parliament
3. events such as the Boston Tea Party led to an increase in anti-British feeling among colonists/unhappiness at high-handed actions of British government
4. the colonists were unhappy with the continuing presence of British soldiers in the colonies
5. some colonists were frustrated that the British were stopping them from moving West
6. some colonists felt that the policies of the British government were damaging trade

41. *Candidates can be credited in a number of ways up to a maximum of 5 marks.*

They may take different perspectives on the events and may describe a variety of different aspects of the events.

1 mark should be given for each accurate relevant key point of knowledge. A **second mark** should be given for each point that is developed, up to a maximum of **5 marks.** Candidates may achieve full marks by providing five straightforward points, by making three developed points, or a combination of these.

Possible points of knowledge may include:
1. Colonists secured high ground at Bunker Hill overlooking British forces
2. British Navy opened fire on the colonists' position (but shells fell short)
3. Prescott told the colonists, "Don't fire until you see the whites of their eyes!" (to save much needed ammunition)
4. British charged the hill three times before the colonists were driven away/ran out of ammunition
5. British soldiers were exposed to American musket fire as they made their way up the hill
6. Bright uniforms of British soldiers made them easy targets
7. British suffered around 1,000 casualties (226 killed, 828 wounded)
8. Colonists suffered less than half of British casualties (around 100-400 killed and 300 wounded)
9. British were victorious/Colonists achieved confidence boost for future battles against British forces

42. *Candidates can be credited in a number of ways up to a maximum of 5 marks.*

Candidates must make an overall judgement about how fully the source explains the events. **1 mark** may be given for each valid point interpreted from the source or each valid point of significant omission provided.

A maximum of 2 marks may be given for answers in which no judgement has been made or which refer only to the source.

Possible points which may be identified in the source include:
1. British soldiers were dispatched to seize the supplies
2. when the British arrived at Lexington they were confronted by a group of minutemen
3. shots were fired and several colonists were killed
4. the British then marched on to Concord where they destroyed any remaining supplies.

Possible points of significant omission may include:
1. the Sons of Liberty had discovered that the British were planning to march on Concord.
2. Paul Revere and other riders sounded the alarm
3. church bells roused the minutemen from their beds.
4. the British soldiers were attacked by angry colonists as they tried to make their way back to Boston.
5. many British soldiers were killed and injured.
6. Colonists in Massachusetts continued to attack the British forces.

43. *Candidates can be credited in a number of ways up to a maximum of 5 marks.*

Candidates must make a judgement about the usefulness of the source and support this by making evaluative comments on identified aspects of the source.

1 mark should be given for each relevant comment made, up to a **maximum of 5 marks in total**.
- A maximum of **4 marks** can be given for evaluative comments relating to the author, type of source, purpose and timing.
- A maximum of **2 marks** may be given for comments relating to the content of the source.
- A maximum of **2 marks** may be given for comments relating to points of significant omission.

Examples of aspects of the source and relevant comments:

Aspect of the source	Possible comment
Author: American army officer	Useful as he is an eyewitness/first-hand experience
Type of Source: Diary entry	Useful as it is more likely to reveal his true opinion/feelings
Purpose: To record	Useful as it is a private record and is less likely to be biased on the poor condition of the American army
Timing: 1777	Useful because it was written during the Wars of Independence

Content	Possible comment
The army now continues to grow sickly from the exhaustion they have suffered in this campaign	Useful as it accurately shows the true condition of the army
Poor food/cold weather/nasty clothes/nasty cooking	Useful as it accurately shows the extent of suffering of the army
The men still show a spirit	Useful as it accurately shows that the morale of the American army remained high

Possible points of significant omission may include:
1. the American forces had endured a number of military setbacks in 1777
2. the Army was small in number/lacked experienced leadership/few professional soldiers
3. Washington used the difficult winter of 1777 to train and discipline his soldiers into a much more effective force

Section 3, Context C, USA 1850–1880

44. *Candidates can be credited in a number of ways up to a maximum of 5 marks.*

They may take different perspectives on the events and may describe a variety of different aspects of the events.

1 mark should be given for each accurate relevant key point of knowledge. A **second mark** should be given for each point that is developed, up to a maximum of **5 marks**. Candidates may achieve full marks by providing five straightforward points, by making three developed points, or a combination of these.

Possible points of knowledge may include:
1. problems of trying to cross mountains and rivers
2. difficulties with wagons (eg broken wheels)
3. had to be timed to complete journey before winter struck
4. dangers of weather – possibility of being stuck in snow
5. had to cross deserts and plains/lack of water
6. navigating the terrain was challenging
7. problems of supplies lasting for the whole journey/lack of fuel in treeless plains
8. threats of attack from Native Americans
9. problems of disease (eg cholera killed many)
10. attacks by wild animals

45. *Candidates can be credited in a number of ways up to a maximum of 5 marks.*

Candidates must show a causal relationship between events.

Up to a **maximum of 5 marks in total**, **1 mark** should be given for each accurate, relevant reason, and a **second mark** should be given for reasons that are developed. Candidates may achieve full marks by providing five straightforward reasons, three developed reasons, or a combination of these.

Possible reasons may include:
1. failure to resolve slavery as an issue between the states
2. failure to resolve disputes over tariffs
3. growth of abolitionism in North
4. Dred Scott Case upset Northern States and abolitionists
5. Kansas – Nebraska Act led to "Bleeding Kansas"
6. growing tension between North and South (eg incidents such as John Brown/Harpers Ferry)
7. south felt it was being blocked from expansion in new western territories
8. growing industry/wealth and immigrant population of North was at odds with plantation life of South
9. growth of Republican Party which favoured Northern interests/North increasingly dominating politics
10. south felt it was being marginalised/losing influence election of Lincoln in 1860 angered Southern states who saw it as an attack upon them

46. *Candidates can be credited in a number of ways up to a maximum of 5 marks.*

Candidates must make a judgement about the usefulness of the source and support this by making evaluative comments on identified aspects of the source.

1 mark should be given for each relevant comment made, up to a **maximum of 5 marks in total.**

- A maximum of 4 marks can be given for evaluative comments relating to the author, type of source, purpose and timing.
- A maximum of 2 marks may be given for comments relating to the content of the source.
- A maximum of 2 marks may be given for comments relating to points of significant omission.

Examples of aspects of the source and relevant comments:

Aspect of the source	Possible comment
Author: George Fitzhugh	Useful as he was an eyewitness/ first-hand experience
Type of Source: Letter	Useful as it gives his own honest opinion
Purpose: To persuade	Less useful as it presents a biased view of slavery
Timing: 1857	Useful as it was written at the time when slavery existed

Content	Possible comment
The children, the aged and the sick do not work at all	Less useful as not true of all plantations
They have all the comforts and necessaries of life provided for them such as food and housing	Less useful as false impression given is of caring owners
The slave men and boys do not work more than nine hours a day in good weather/the slave women do little hard work	Less useful as slaves worked very long hours in all weathers

Possible points of significant omission may include:
1. no mention of punishments
2. no mention of particular mistreatment of female slaves
3. no mention of splitting of slave families
4. no mention of slaves as property
5. no mention of slaves running away
6. no mention of Abolitionist viewpoints

47. *Candidates can be credited in a number of ways **up to a maximum of 5 marks.***

Candidates must make an overall judgement about how fully the source explains the events. **1 mark** may be given for each valid point interpreted from the source or each valid point of significant omission provided.

A maximum of 2 marks may be given for answers in which no judgement has been made or which refer only to the source.

Possible points which may be identified in the source include:
1. slaves were made free in 1865
2. the right of citizenship granted in the Fourteenth Amendment is practically a mockery/is ignored
3. the right to vote, provided for in the Fifteenth Amendment, is under attack/is ignored
4. the old ruling class is victorious today/the newly freed slaves are little better off than they were before

Possible points of significant omission may include:
5. Carpetbaggers and Scalawags exploited opportunities in South
6. Freedman's Bureau helped freed slaves with their needs (eg jobs)
7. Sharecroppers little better off after 1865
8. Black Codes restricted the rights of black Americans eg could not leave employment without permission
9. KKK and other groups used violence to attack freed slaves
10. Jim Crow Laws began to be passed after 1877 (eg separate facilities)

Section 3, Context D, Hitler and Nazi Germany, 1919–1939

48. *Candidates can be credited in a number of ways **up to a maximum of 5 marks.***

Candidates must show a causal relationship between events.

Up to a **maximum of 5 marks in total**, **1 mark** should be given for each accurate, relevant reason, and a **second mark** should be given for reasons that are developed. Candidates may achieve full marks by providing five straightforward reasons, three developed reasons, or a combination of these.

Possible reasons may include:
1. Germany got no say in the Treaty/called it a "DIKTAT" a dictated peace
2. Germany blamed for starting the war (War Guilt Clause)
3. felt it humiliated Germany/was unacceptable/too harsh
4. Germans resented having to pay reparations
5. with the Kaiser gone Germans did not believe they should be punished
6. not based on Wilson's 14 points eg no self determination
7. Germany lost land eg people living under foreign rule
8. loss of colonies felt to be unfair
9. Armed forces reduced increasing unemployment/leaving them vulnerable to attack

49. *Candidates can be credited in a number of ways **up to a maximum of 5 marks.***

They may take different perspectives on the events and may describe a variety of different aspects of the events.

1 mark should be given for each accurate relevant key point of knowledge. A **second mark** should be given for each point that is developed, up to a maximum of **5 marks**. Candidates may achieve full marks by providing five straightforward points, by making three developed points, or a combination of these.

Possible points of knowledge may include:
1. Anti-Jewish propaganda: blamed for World War One/ Communism/economic ruin/contaminating the "Master Race"
2. Jews were often abused or beaten up in the streets
3. Anti-Semitic education: pupils taught to be hostile to Jews; teachers humiliated Jewish children
4. from 1933 Anti-Jewish Laws/boycott of Jewish shops/ doctors/lawyers/lecturers dismissed
5. Law for the Restoration of the Professional Civil Service banned Jews from government jobs
6. 1935: Jews forbidden to join the Army; restrictions on opportunities for employment, education; Civil Liberties restricted; Anti-Jewish signs displayed in shops/ restaurants/cafes

7. 1935 Nuremburg Laws for protection of German blood and honour (eg ban on marriage between Jews and non-Jews)
8. Sexual relations between Jews and non-Jews outside marriage – criminal offence
9. 1935 National Law of Citizenship meant Jews lost citizenship – no vote/rights
10. 1938 Government contracts only for Aryan firms
11. 1938 only Aryan doctors were allowed to treat Aryan patients
12. 1938 all Jews had to take new first name: Israel and Sarah: adding to signatures/passport stamped with letter "J"
13. 1938 Kristallnacht – massive anti-Semitic campaign: Jewish homes/shops/synagogues destroyed; 100 killed/2000 arrested
14. Many Jews sent to concentration camps/murdered

50. *Candidates can be credited in a number of ways **up to a maximum of 5 marks.***

Candidates must make a judgement about the usefulness of the source and support this by making evaluative comments on identified aspects of the source.

1 mark should be given for each relevant comment made, up to a **maximum of 5 marks in total.**

- A maximum of **4 marks** can be given for evaluative comments relating to the author, type of source, purpose and timing.
- A maximum of **2 marks** may be given for comments relating to the content of the source.
- A maximum of **2 marks** may be given for comments relating to points of significant omission.

Examples of aspects of the source and relevant comments:

Aspect of the source	Possible comment
Author: Ernst Thalmann	Useful as it is from someone who has first-hand experience of Nazi intimidation
Type of Source: Diary	Useful as it is an honest personal account
Purpose: To inform	Useful as it provides a balanced (and detailed) account of the use of intimidation by the Nazis
Timing: 1933	Useful as it is from the time that the Nazis were routinely intimidating their opponents

Content	Possible comment
Every cruel method of blackmail was used against me	Useful as it accurately describes how the Nazis threatened prisoners families to extract confessions
I was then assaulted and in the process had four teeth knocked out/a Gestapo officer with a whip in his hand then beat me with measured strokes	Useful as it accurately describes methods used by Gestapo
They tried hypnosis which was also ineffective	Useful as it accurately describes methods used by Gestapo

Possible points of significant omission may include:
1. the SS also very intimidating
2. fear of concentration camps intimidating
3. use of Gestapo informers/other spying systems intimidated people public executions acted as a warning to others
4. public executions acted as a warning to others

51. *Candidates can be credited in a number of ways **up to a maximum of 5 marks.***

Candidates must make an overall judgement about how fully the source explains the events. **1 mark** may be given for each valid point interpreted from the source or each valid point of significant omission provided.

A maximum of 2 marks may be given for answers in which no judgement has been made or which refer only to the source.

Possible points which may be identified in the source include:
1. boys learned military skills such as practising with weapons
2. to toughen them up, they were taken on cross country hikes and runs
3. boys were also tested on their knowledge of Nazism
4. however they did not all enjoy the endless marching

Possible points of significant omission may include:
5. details on "military athletics" (Wehrsport) (eg bayonet drill, grenade throwing, trench digging, map reading, gas defence, use of dugouts, how to get under barbed wire and pistol shooting)
6. compulsory gymnastics/other sporting activities like football/handball
7. competitive boxing matches (where the rules were not as important as beating your opponent)
8. camping trips
9. played musical instruments/learned Nazi songs parades/pageants
10. parades/pageants

Section 3, Context E, Red Flag: Lenin and the Russian Revolution, 1894–1921

52. *Candidates can be credited in a number of ways **up to a maximum of 5 marks.***

Candidates must make an overall judgement about how fully the source explains the events. **1 mark** may be given for each valid point interpreted from the source or each valid point of significant omission provided.

A maximum of 2 marks may be given for answers in which no judgement has been made or which refer only to the source.

Possible points which may be identified in the source include:
1. police brutality is steadily growing
2. many workers are now imprisoned along with political prisoners
3. millions of peasants...become poorer every year
4. famine is now normal throughout the country

Possible points of significant omission may include:
5. redemption payments and high taxes meant peasants struggle
6. shortage of land/the majority of land owned by nobility
7. backward agricultural techniques led to poor output
8. poor living conditions for peasants (eg one room huts)
9. workers have poor working conditions/many accidents in factories
10. low pay/rising cost of food and fuel
11. workers have poor living conditions/many live in overcrowded conditions
12. lacked basic freedoms (eg free speech, democratic elections)
13. constant fear of arrest by Okhrana

53. *Candidates can be credited in a number of ways up to a maximum of 5 marks.*

They may take different perspectives on the events and may describe a variety of different aspects of the events.

1 mark should be given for each accurate relevant key point of knowledge. A **second mark** should be given for each point that is developed, up to a maximum of **5 marks**. Candidates may achieve full marks by providing five straightforward points, by making three developed points, or a combination of these.

Possible points of knowledge may include:
1. Stolypin Reforms introduced to improve agriculture
2. ended redemption payments
3. allowed peasant families to leave the commune or Mir
4. encouraging peasants to group their strips of land into larger fields/changed the rules of inheritance
5. created the Kulak class
6. Duma was set up/the October Manifesto introduced greater freedoms
7. Trade unions legalised
8. National insurance scheme introduced for industrial workers
9. education extended to increase literacy
10. armed forces modernised

54. *Candidates can be credited in a number of ways up to a maximum of 5 marks.*

Candidates must show a causal relationship between events.

Up to a **maximum of 5 marks in total**, **1 mark** should be given for each accurate, relevant reason, and a **second mark** should be given for reasons that are developed. Candidates may achieve full marks by providing five straightforward reasons, three developed reasons, or a combination of these.

Possible reasons may include:
1. dual power had weakened authority of Provisional Government
2. Provisional Government losing support due to problems caused by war (eg failure to tackle inflation and shortages)
3. Provisional Government losing support due to failure to tackle the land issue
4. Provisional Government losing support for continuing the war despite military defeats
5. failure to hold quick elections to the Constituent Assembly made it unpopular
6. Provisional Government appeared weak due to Kornilov Revolt
7. Kornilov Revolt had resulted in the arming of Bolshevik Red Guards
8. Bolshevik slogan "Peace, Bread and Land" gained popular support
9. Bolsheviks had been gaining control in the Petrograd Soviet/increasingly Soviets taking charge
10. leadership of Lenin/Trotsky was decisive
11. Military Revolutionary Council set up by Bolsheviks to control army units
12. only Women's Battalion of Death and a few others still defending Government in Winter Palace/seized Winter Palace with little opposition
13. seizure of communication centres prevented help being summoned
14. blocking of transport links prevented help being summoned

55. *Candidates can be credited in a number of ways up to a maximum of 5 marks.*

Candidates must make a judgement about the usefulness of the source and support this by making evaluative comments on identified aspects of the source.

1 mark should be given for each relevant comment made, up to a **maximum of 5 marks in total**.
- A maximum of **4 marks** can be given for evaluative comments relating to the author, type of source, purpose and timing.
- A maximum of **2 marks** may be given for comments relating to the content of the source.
- A maximum of **2 marks** may be given for comments relating to points of significant omission.

Examples of aspects of the source and relevant comments:

Aspect of the source	Possible comment
Author: Leon Trotsky	Useful as he had first-hand experience/was the commander of the Red Army and therefore well informed
Type of Source: Diary	Useful as it is an honest personal account
Purpose: To record	Less useful as may be limited to his perspective
Timing: 1921	Useful as it written at the time of the Civil War

Content	Possible comment
Formed an army out of peasants, workers and refugees	Useful as it accurately describes groups who supported Bolsheviks
What was needed were good commanders and a few experienced fighters	Useful as it accurately describes how Red Army improved leadership
The mob would fight as long as they had boots for the barefooted, a bathhouse, food, underwear, tobacco/a dozen or so Communists ready to inspire them	Useful as it accurately describes some methods used to improve morale

Possible points of significant omission may include:
1. fear of Cheka
2. Red Terror forced obedience
3. fear of Commissars/using former Tsarist officers by holding families
4. strict discipline within Red Army
5. lack of cooperation between White armies
6. Whites lacked widespread support (eg land issue)
7. Red Army controlled a compact central area/White armies were scattered
8. Reds controlled key industries/transport
9. unpopularity of foreign intervention/Bolshevik propaganda

Section 3, Context F, Mussolini and Fascist Italy, 1919–1939

56. *Candidates can be credited in a number of ways up to a maximum of 5 marks.*

Candidates must show a causal relationship between events.

Up to a **maximum of 5 marks in total**, **1 mark** should be given for each accurate, relevant reason, and a **second mark** should be given for reasons that are developed. Candidates may achieve full marks by providing five straightforward reasons, three developed reasons, or a combination of these.

Possible reasons may include:
1. Mussolini exploited weaknesses of other groups by use of his newspaper "Il Popolo D'Italia"
2. by 1921 fascism was anti-communist, anti-trade union, anti-socialist and pro-nationalism and thus became attractive to the middle and upper classes
3. fascism became pro-conservative, appealed to family values, supported church and monarchy
4. promised to work within the accepted political system (this made fascism more respectable and appealing to both the monarchy and the papacy)
5. violence showed fascism was strong and ruthless (it appealed to many ex-soldiers)
6. middle class frightened by Communism/fascists appeared to be only ones prepared to stand up to Communists
7. fascists promised strong government. This was attractive after a period of extreme instability
8. Mussolini attracted many with his powerful oratory. Mussolini manipulated his image, kept out of violence himself but exploited the violence of others
9. Parliamentary government was weak – informal "liberal" coalitions. Corruption was commonplace (transformismo)
10. the Acerbo law was used to secure a Fascist parliamentary majority
11. the King gave in to Fascist pressure during the March on Rome. He failed to call Mussolini's bluff
12. after the Aventine Secession the King was unwilling to dismiss Mussolini
13. Mussolini's political opponents were divided and this weakened them
14. Mussolini's Blackshirts terrorised the cities and provinces causing fear with tactics such as force-feeding with toads and castor oil
15. destruction of opposition press severely weakened them

57. *Candidates can be credited in a number of ways up to a maximum of 5 marks.*

They may take different perspectives on the events and may describe a variety of different aspects of the events.

1 mark should be given for each accurate relevant key point of knowledge. **A second mark** should be given for each point that is developed, up to a maximum of **5 marks.** Candidates may achieve full marks by providing five straightforward points, by making three developed points, or a combination of these.

Possible points of knowledge may include:
1. from 1925 teachers with suspect political views could be dismissed
2. from 1929 all teachers were required to take an oath of loyalty to the regime
3. in 1931 a Fascist Teachers Association was set up to regulate the profession. Membership was compulsory by 1937
4. in schools, the cult of personality was heavily promoted (the Duce's portrait had to be hung alongside that of the King)
5. teachers were ordered to stress the genius and strength of Mussolini
6. children were taught the importance of obedience in the Fascist state/textbooks were altered
7. in history children were taught that Italy had been the cradle of European civilisation and that Italians had always been at the forefront of events. Italy's role in the First World War was exaggerated
8. The Fascist Youth movement, the Opera Nazionale Balliala (ONB) was set up to control young people's leisure activities
9. The Ballila and Avanguardista provided military and ideological training as well as sports and fitness training for boys

10. in the Piccole Italiane and Giovani Italiane, girls were prepared for a traditional role by being taught sewing and child care
11. at university level, the Gruppi Universitari Fascisti (GUF) provided further sporting and military training/students had to join to further careers

58. *Candidates can be credited in a number of ways up to a maximum of 5 marks.*

Candidates must make an overall judgement about how fully the source explains the events. **1 mark** may be given for each valid point interpreted from the source or each valid point of significant omission provided.

A maximum of 2 marks may be given for answers in which no judgement has been made or which refer only to the source.

Possible points which may be identified in the source include:
1. media played an important role in establishing the cult of "Il Duce"
2. the cult was intended to build popular support for the dictator and to secure support for the government
3. Benito Mussolini was shown as a man chosen by destiny to save Italy and its people from Communism and Socialism
4. he was the new Caesar/a man of genius/a man of action

Possible points of significant omission may include:
5. Mussolini started a new calendar with Year 1 beginning in 1922
6. the regime made propagandist feature films
7. the Duce was shown as a great athlete and musician
8. always uniformed to portray strength and aggression
9. the newspapers suggested that Mussolini was infallible
10. an image of youthfulness was portrayed by not referring to Mussolini's age or the fact he wore glasses
11. it was said that Mussolini worked 16 hour days. His light was left on after he had gone to bed to maintain this fiction
12. indoctrination of children into "cult" (eg school textbooks/fascist youth groups)

59. *Candidates can be credited in a number of ways up to a maximum of 5 marks.*

Candidates must make a judgement about the usefulness of the source and support this by making evaluative comments on identified aspects of the source.

1 mark should be given for each relevant comment made, up to a **maximum of 5 marks in total.**
- A maximum of 4 marks can be given for evaluative comments relating to the author, type of source, purpose and timing.
- A maximum of 2 marks may be given for comments relating to the content of the source.
- A maximum of 2 marks may be given for comments relating to points of significant omission.

Examples of aspects of the source and relevant comments:

Aspect of the source	Possible comment
Author: Mussolini	Useful as he was in charge of Fascist foreign policy/first-hand experience
Type of Source: A speech	Less useful as Mussolini might exaggerate as this is intended for public consumption.
Purpose: To persuade	Less useful as Mussolini would be keen to justify military action/offers a one-sided view
Timing: 1922	Useful as Mussolini was in power with responsibility for Fascist foreign policy

Content	Possible comment
Perfect unity in Italy cannot be spoken of until Fiume and Dalmatia and other territories have come back to us	Useful as it is accurate/ Mussolini did target Fiume (which became an Italian possession in 1924)
Violence may have to be used	Useful as it is accurate/ Fascist ideology did glorify the use of violence
Italy, in order to become a Mediterranean power, must have control over the Adriatic sea	Useful as it is accurate/ Mussolini was obsessed with making the Mediterranean an "Italian lake"

Possible points of significant omission may include:
1. Mussolini aimed to make Italy a great power/new Roman Empire
2. he wanted to expand Italy's colonial empire in Africa
3. he wanted to increase Italian influence in the Balkans
4. in early years of power he aimed to appear as peaceful statesman (eg Locarno 1925)
5. he wanted to reverse Italy's humiliation at Versailles (eg bombardment of Corfu)
6. wanted to act to stop German expansion after 1933 (eg in Austria/Stresa Front)
7. he wanted to encourage friendly regimes abroad and discourage Socialism/Communism, eg in Spain
8. latterly he wanted to adopt a more aggressive foreign policy to distract public attention away from problems at home
9. Axis/Pact of Steel – Italian foreign policy in conjunction with Germany eg Munich Conference
10. played crucial role as mediator at Munich Conference Sept 1938/tried to appear as a moderate

Section 3, Context G, Free at Last? Civil Rights in the USA, 1918–1968

60. *Candidates can be credited in a number of ways up to a maximum of 5 marks.*

They may take different perspectives on the events and may describe a variety of different aspects of the events.

1 mark should be given for each accurate relevant key point of knowledge. A **second mark** should be given for each point that is developed, up to a maximum of **5 marks**. Candidates may achieve full marks by providing five straightforward points, by making three developed points, or a combination of these.

Possible points of knowledge may include:
1. separate restaurants
2. separate schools
3. separate toilets, drinking fountains and restrooms
4. separate carriages on busses/trains
5. separate entrances and wards in hospitals
6. separate graveyards
7. separate leisure and sporting facilities
8. in some states marriage between whites and blacks was forbidden

61. *Candidates can be credited in a number of ways up to a maximum of 5 marks.*

Candidates must show a causal relationship between events.

Up to a **maximum of 5 marks in total**, **1 mark** should be given for each accurate, relevant reason, and a **second mark** should be given for reasons that are developed. Candidates may achieve full marks by providing five straightforward reasons, three developed reasons, or a combination of these.

Possible reasons may include:
1. unemployment increased after the war/immigrants were accused of taking jobs from Americans
2. concern that immigrant workers were forcing wages down by working for less
3. concern that immigrants would be used by employers to break strikes
4. WASPs feared "inferior" immigrants from south and east Europe would threaten their way of life/new immigrants had different religions
5. concern that immigrants would create pressure on scarce housing
6. feeling that new immigrants who were uneducated and illiterate had little to contribute to American life/spoke different languages
7. immigrants were often blamed for crime, disease, alcoholism and other social problems in cities
8. new immigrants often settled amongst people from their own countries leading to a perception that they were unwilling to mix with other Americans
9. fear of political unrest from communist and socialist immigrants

62. *Candidates can be credited in a number of ways up to a maximum of 5 marks.*

Candidates must make an overall judgement about how fully the source explains the events. **1 mark** may be given for each valid point interpreted from the source or each valid point of significant omission provided.

A maximum of 2 marks may be given for answers in which no judgement has been made or which refer only to the source.

Possible points which may be identified in the source include:
1. wearing white robes and pointed hats
2. during elections, the Klan would wait outside the voting place to beat up blacks if they came near
3. a divorced woman in Texas was tarred and feathered for remarrying
4. a massive march in Washington DC in 1925

Possible points of significant omission may include:
5. the Klan held elaborate ceremonies and used a coded language
6. the Klan were intimidating (eg burned large crosses on hillsides and near the homes of people they wished to frighten)
7. the Klan brutally assaulted many blacks/night raids on black households
8. the Klan lynched many blacks
9. the Klan bombed and burned churches, schools and other meeting places used by black people
10. use of propaganda/advertised to gain larger membership
11. influenced all aspects of local authority (eg courts, police departments)

63. *Candidates can be credited in a number of ways up to a maximum of 5 marks.*

Candidates must make a judgement about the usefulness of the source and support this by making evaluative comments on identified aspects of the source.

1 mark should be given for each relevant comment made, up to a **maximum of 5 marks in total**.
- A maximum of **4 marks** can be given for evaluative comments relating to the author, type of source, purpose and timing.
- A maximum of **2 marks** may be given for comments relating to the content of the source.
- A maximum of **2 marks** may be given for comments relating to points of significant omission.

Examples of aspects of the source and relevant comments:

Aspect of the source	Possible comment
Author: A black American taxi driver	Useful as he eyewitness/first-hand experience of Malcolm X/a member of the black American community
Type of Source: Newspaper interview	Useful as it contains an honest opinion/may be less useful as possibility of bias
Purpose: To inform	Useful as the interview provides several reasons for supporting Malcolm X
Timing: 1961	Useful as it is from the time when Malcolm X was a leading figure

Content	Possible comment
I can believe in a leader who comes from the street, Malcolm is one of us	Useful as it is accurate/many black Americans did relate to a leader who had grown up in a predominantly black neighbourhood
Malcolm isn't afraid to stand up to the FBI and the cops	Useful as it is accurate/police harassment and brutality was a common complaint amongst black Americans
Those black Muslims make more sense than the NAACP and all of the rest of them put together, you don't see Malcolm tip-toeing around the whites like he's scared of them	Useful as it is accurate/many did support Malcolm X's belief that blacks had the right to defend themselves with the use of violence

Possible points of significant omission may include:
1. Malcolm X was a charismatic figure and speaker who gained support from his public speeches and his appearances on television
2. many agreed with Malcolm X that white Americans were inherently racist and blacks could only gain true equality if they separated from white society
3. Malcolm X encouraged blacks to be proud of the colour of their skin and their African American culture – this appealed to many

Section 3, Context H, Appeasement and the Road to War, 1918–1939

64. *Candidates can be credited in a number of ways **up to a maximum of 5 marks.***

They may take different perspectives on the events and may describe a variety of different aspects of the events.

1 mark should be given for each accurate relevant key point of knowledge. A **second mark** should be given for each point that is developed, up to a maximum of **5 marks**. Candidates may achieve full marks by providing five straightforward points, by making three developed points, or a combination of these.

Possible points of knowledge may include:
1. Hitler instructed industry to begin the secret production of new tanks, aircraft and other weapons
2. by 1934, Hitler had doubled the size of the German army
3. Hitler built up an air force of 2000 planes by the end of 1934
4. Hitler introduced conscription to the German army/ greatly expanded the office corps
5. by the end of 1935 the German army totalled over 500,000 men

6. the Anglo-German Naval agreement was signed giving Germany permission to build up its navy to a level that was 35% of Britain's naval strength

65. *Candidates can be credited in a number of ways **up to a maximum of 5 marks.***

Candidates must make a judgement about the usefulness of the source and support this by making evaluative comments on identified aspects of the source.

1 mark should be given for each relevant comment made, up to a **maximum of 5 marks in total**.
- A maximum of **4 marks** can be given for evaluative comments relating to the author, type of source, purpose and timing.
- A maximum of **2 marks** may be given for comments relating to the content of the source.
- A maximum of **2 marks** may be given for comments relating to points of significant omission.

Examples of aspects of the source and relevant comments:

Aspect of the source	Possible comment
Author: Historian	Useful as it is written by a well-informed expert
Type of Source: Article (from a modern history journal)	Useful as it will have been well-researched
Purpose: To inform	Useful as it gives a balanced insight in to the consequences of the Anschluss
Timing: 2008	Useful as it was written with the benefit of hindsight

Content	Possible comment
It marked the beginning of Germany's territorial expansion, starting a chain of events which continued with the occupation of the Sudetenland	Useful as it is accurate/ Germany did gain control of the Sudetenland by October 1938
The lack of meaningful opposition from Britain and France underlined again for Hitler that he could do as he pleased	Useful as it is accurate/ Hitler's aggressive actions over Czechoslovakia and Poland did suggest that he did not believe Britain and France would take action against him
The persecution of Jews was greatly intensified following the Anschluss, especially in Austria	Useful as it is accurate/ persecution of Jews did start immediately after German troops entered Austria

Possible points of significant omission may include:
1. Germany added 100,000 Austrian troops to the German army
2. Germany gained useful economic resources such as iron, steel and other raw materials
3. Czechoslovakia was under threat as it was now surrounded on three fronts by Germany
4. lack of action against Germany encouraged Hitler further
5. enhanced Hitler's popularity

66. *Candidates can be credited in a number of ways **up to a maximum of 5 marks.***

Candidates must make an overall judgement about how fully the source explains the events. **1 mark** may be given for each valid point interpreted from the source or each valid point of significant omission provided.

A maximum of 2 marks may be given for answers in which no judgement has been made or which refer only to the source.

Possible points which may be identified in the source include:

1. a belief that given the harsh treatment of Germany at Versailles, Hitler's demands were not unreasonable
2. the British public were still haunted by memories of World War One and unwilling to back military action
3. Chiefs of the armed forces advised that that the British military was unprepared for war
4. the Treasury meanwhile warned against the financial consequences of war

Possible points of significant omission may include:

5. Germany had rearmed with a powerful army, navy and air force
6. by appeasing Hitler, Britain bought itself time to re-arm and strengthen the military
7. there was fear of war due to the likely destruction caused by bombing from the air
8. lack of allies – Empire countries unwilling, USA isolationist and France not trusted
9. Britain wanted a stronger Germany to prevent Communist expansion
10. fear of war and its impact on the British Empire

67. *Candidates can be credited in a number of ways **up to a maximum of 5 marks.***

Candidates must show a causal relationship between events.

Up to a **maximum of 5 marks in total**, **1 mark** should be given for each accurate, relevant reason, and a **second mark** should be given for reasons that are developed. Candidates may achieve full marks by providing five straightforward reasons, three developed reasons, or a combination of these.

Possible reasons may include:

1. Germany had a grievance over land lost to Poland at the end of World War One
2. millions of Germans were forced to live under Polish rule
3. Danzig, a German town and free city under the League, was run to suit the Poles
4. The "Polish Corridor" divided East Prussia from the rest of Germany
5. A successful invasion of Poland would be popular/provide land for Lebensraum
6. Hitler regarded the Poles as inferior (untermenschen)
7. The Nazi-Soviet Pact meant that Russia would not protect Poland
8. The Pact of Steel had assured Germany of Italy's support
9. Hitler did not believe that Britain would help Poland in the event of war

Section 3, Context I, World War II, 1939–1945

68. *Candidates can be credited in a number of ways **up to a maximum of 5 marks.***

Candidates must show a causal relationship between events.

Up to a **maximum of 5 marks in total**, **1 mark** should be given for each accurate, relevant reason, and a **second mark** should be given for reasons that are developed. Candidates may achieve full marks by providing five straightforward reasons, three developed reasons, or a combination of these.

Possible reasons may include:

1. Hitler hated the Communist ideals of the USSR/thought Communism was a threat to Germany

2. Hitler believed in the expansion rights of the Master Race and wanted Russian land as Lebensraum (living space)/declared plans to invade in Mein Kampf
3. Hitler believed the Russian army would be easily defeated due to Russia's failure in the Finnish war/as well as by purge of Red army
4. believed USSR would be an easy target/fall in 6 to 8 weeks
5. Hitler wanted to enslave the Russian people (untermenschen) to work for the German Master Race
6. Hitler wanted valuable resources contained in Russia eg grain, oil, iron ore/Germany was running short of vital raw materials by 1940
7. Hitler believed Russia to be a threat to Germany's interests in the Balkans and Scandinavia
8. Stalin had resisted joining Germany, Italy and Japan in the Tripartite Pact of 1940
9. Nazi–Soviet Pact of 1939 was only an alliance of convenience so that Hitler could successfully invade Poland/Hitler did not trust Stalin
10. conquest of Russia would force Britain to surrender

69. *Candidates can be credited in a number of ways **up to a maximum of 5 marks.***

They may take different perspectives on the events and may describe a variety of different aspects of the events.

1 mark should be given for each accurate relevant key point of knowledge. A **second mark** should be given for each point that is developed, up to a maximum of **5 marks**. Candidates may achieve full marks by providing five straightforward points, by making three developed points, or a combination of these.

Possible points of knowledge may include:

1. surprise attack on the morning of December 7th 1941
2. Japanese bombers, fighter and torpedo planes were launched from six aircraft carriers in the Pacific
3. attack came in two waves and lasted around 2 hours
4. Japanese attacked US battleships and airfields
5. USS Arizona exploded when a bomb hit the ship's magazine, killing approximately 1,100 men
6. USS Oklahoma was torpedoed and listed so badly that it turned upside down
7. Japanese sent in 5 midget subs to aid the air force/Americans sunk 4 of the midget subs and captured the 5th
8. all battleships stationed at Pearl Harbour were sunk or damaged
9. over 2,400 Americans were dead/21 ships had been sunk or damaged/over 188 US aircraft destroyed
10. Japanese lost only 29 aircraft and 65 killed
11. Japanese missed main targets as American aircraft carriers at sea

70. *Candidates can be credited in a number of ways **up to a maximum of 5 marks.***

Candidates must make an overall judgement about how fully the source explains the events. **1 mark** may be given for each valid point interpreted from the source or each valid point of significant omission provided.

A maximum of 2 marks may be given for answers in which no judgement has been made or which refer only to the source.

Possible points which may be identified in the source include:

1. preparations began in 1943 under the overall command of General Eisenhower of the United States
2. Normandy was chosen as the site for the landings because of its open beaches that were not as well defended as those at Calais

3. Normandy was also chosen because it had a fairly large port, Cherbourg
4. it was also opposite the main ports of southern England

Possible points of significant omission may include:

5. deception plans intended to fool Germans into believing an attack would come at Pas de Calais or Norway/Allies had decoded German messages which gave the Allies an advantage
6. imaginary army units/rubber tanks/inflatable aircraft were stationed at areas around the Kent coast (opposite Calais)
7. double agents operated to pass false information to Germans (Garbo)
8. massive drive to manufacture equipment including transport ships, landing craft, amphibious tanks, etc.
9. floating harbours constructed on Clydeside (Mulberry Harbours)
10. pipe-line laid under the channel to transport fuel (Pluto)
11. large numbers of soldiers trained in Devon and on Scottish coasts, amongst other places/mobilised in secret to Southern England
12. prior to invasion, Allied air forces targeted the railways and bridges of northern France to stop any counter-attack
13. coordination with French Resistance

71. *Candidates can be credited in a number of ways up to a maximum of 5 marks.*

Candidates must make a judgement about the usefulness of the source and support this by making evaluative comments on identified aspects of the source.

1 mark should be given for each relevant comment made, up to a **maximum of 5 marks in total.**
- A maximum of 4 marks can be given for evaluative comments relating to the author, type of source, purpose and timing.
- A maximum of 2 marks may be given for comments relating to the content of the source.
- A maximum of 2 marks may be given for comments relating to points of significant omission.

Examples of aspects of the source and relevant comments:

Aspect of the source	Possible comment
Author: US Government	Useful as it is a first-hand account
Type of Source: Leaflet	Less useful as it is a propaganda leaflet
Purpose: To persuade	Useful as it is an attempt to frighten the Japanese into surrendering
Timing: 16 August 1945	Useful as this leaflet comes from the time atomic bombs were dropped over Japan

Content	Possible comment
In possession of the most destructive explosive devised by man	Useful as it is accurate/the US were first to design the bomb
We have just begun to use this weapon against your country/ask what happened to Hiroshima	Useful as it is accurate/the first bomb had already been dropped on Hiroshima
Take steps now to surrender. Otherwise we shall use this bomb again to promptly and forcefully end the war	Useful as it is accurate/the US did threaten to drop a second bomb unless Japan surrendered

Possible points of significant omission may include:

1. US used atomic bombs to avoid losing men in an invasion of Japan
2. Hiroshima bombed using the uranium bomb "Little Boy"
3. bomb killed 70–80,000 people immediately (70,000 were to die of after effects)
4. Hiroshima chosen to be completely destroyed as an entire city/was not a military target
5. 3 days after the first bomb on Hiroshima, Nagasaki was attacked with the second bomb "Fat Man"
6. 40% of Nagasaki was destroyed, approximately 70,000 died by the end of the year
7. effects of bombing: instant vaporisation, severe burns, radiation poisoning/sickness
8. led to Japan formally surrendering

Section 3, Context J, The Cold War, 1945–1989

72. *Candidates can be credited in a number of ways up to a maximum of 5 marks.*

Candidates must make a judgement about the usefulness of the source and support this by making evaluative comments on identified aspects of the source.

1 mark should be given for each relevant comment made, up to a maximum of 5 marks in total.
- A maximum of 4 marks can be given for evaluative comments relating to the author, type of source, purpose and timing.
- A maximum of 2 marks may be given for comments relating to the content of the source.
- A maximum of 2 marks may be given for comments relating to points of significant omission.

Examples of aspects of the source and relevant comments:

Aspect of the source	Possible comment
Author: East German government	Useful as it is a first-hand account
Type of Source: Leaflet	Useful as it is an attempt to justify the building of the Berlin Wall
Purpose: To persuade	Less useful as it is a propaganda leaflet
Timing: 1962	Useful as it is from the time that the Wall was built

Content	Possible comment
We could no longer stand by and see so many of our doctors, engineers and skilled workers persuaded by corrupt methods to work in West Germany or West Berlin	Useful as it is accurate (East Germany was concerned about losing population)
These dirty tricks cost East Germany annual losses amounting to 3.5 thousand million marks	Useful as it is accurate (East Germany was concerned about economic damage)
But we prevented something much more important with the Wall – West Berlin could have become the starting point for military conflict.	Useful as it is accurate (East Germany was concerned about military escalation)

Possible points of significant omission may include:
1. West Berlin/Germany was attractive because it was more prosperous than the East
2. West Berlin/Germany was attractive because it had more democratic freedoms than the East
3. East Germans feared that open border in Berlin enabled the West to spy more easily
4. food shortages in 1960 in the East (following enforced collectivisation) added to the urge to leave
5. departures from the East made Communism look bad.
6. fear of what would happen in other East European states if exodus continued

73. *Candidates can be credited in a number of ways up to a maximum of 5 marks.*

Candidates must make an overall judgement about how fully the source explains the events. **1 mark** may be given for each valid point interpreted from the source or each valid point of significant omission provided.

A **maximum of 2 marks** may be given for answers in which no judgement has been made or which refer only to the source.

Possible points which may be identified in the source include:
1. crisis in Cuba because by the early 1960s the USA and the Soviet Union were bitter rivals
2. many in the United States believed that the Soviet actions in Cuba provided proof of a determination to spread Communism all around the world
3. Cuba was very close to the American mainland and this explains why Americans were so concerned by events there
4. both sides were afraid to back down in case they lost face

Possible points of significant omission may include:
5. Cuban leader Castro had formed a close alliance with the Soviet Union which alarmed the USA
6. Castro had angered American businesses by nationalising key industries
7. American spy planes revealed evidence of missile bases being constructed in Cuba
8. Soviet convoys carrying missiles to Cuba caused alarm
9. American public opinion would not accept the threat posed by Soviet missiles on the island.
10. fear in America that their country was falling behind in the Cold War
11. Kennedy was looking for an opportunity to take revenge after the failed Bay of Pigs invasion

74. *Candidates can be credited in a number of ways up to a maximum of 5 marks.*

They may take different perspectives on the events and may describe a variety of different aspects of the events.

1 mark should be given for each accurate relevant key point of knowledge. **A second mark** should be given for each point that is developed, up to a maximum of **5 marks**. Candidates may achieve full marks by providing five straightforward points, by making three developed points, or a combination of these.

Possible points of knowledge may include:
1. many supported it as they believed America was defending freedom and democracy
2. many supported it as they believed it was the job of America to fight Communism
3. many supported it because of fear of the domino theory
4. many supported it as they believed it was a response to North Vietnamese aggression in the Gulf of Tonkin
5. unpopularity of the draft/the draft was disproportionate in taking poor Blacks
6. opposition to the war grew because of the media coverage of high casualties, lack of success, etc.
7. evidence of atrocities such as the My Lai massacre weakened support
8. anti-war protests and demonstrations grew
9. cost of the war led to growing opposition
10. some were concerned that the war was preventing social progress in America (eg Martin Luther King)

75. *Candidates can be credited in a number of ways up to a maximum of 5 marks.*

Candidates must show a causal relationship between events.

Up to a **maximum of 5 marks in total**, 1 mark should be given for each accurate, relevant reason, and a **second mark** should be given for reasons that are developed. Candidates may achieve full marks by providing five straightforward reasons, three developed reasons, or a combination of these.

Possible reasons may include:
1. in the 1960s they came to the brink of nuclear war and wanted to avoid similar crises
2. Brezhnev felt the economic burden of the nuclear arms race was too great
3. the American economy was in financial trouble as a result of the Vietnam war/growing social unrest called for a reassessment of spending priorities
4. the Soviets hoped for better relations with Western Europe, perhaps detaching them from the USA
5. the Soviet leadership was terrified of a possible Sino-American alliance
6. both sides had achieved rough parity in nuclear arms so continuing an arms race seemed pointless
7. a state of mutually assured destruction (MAD) had been reached
9. both Brezhnev and Nixon thought that it would boost their domestic popularity
10. Brezhnev was intent on using a period of détente to prepare for Soviet expansion in the 1980s

NATIONAL 5 HISTORY 2017

Section 1, Context A, The Wars of Independence, 1286–1328

1. *Candidates can be credited in a number of ways up to a maximum of 5 marks.*

Candidates must show a causal relationship between events.

Up to a **maximum of 5 marks in total**, **1 mark** should be given for each accurate, relevant reason, and a **second mark** should be given for reasons that are developed. Candidates may achieve full marks by providing five straightforward reasons, three developed reasons, or a combination of these.

Possible reasons may include:
1. she was a girl – people did not believe females were suitable to be monarchs so were not happy to accept her as queen
2. as a female she would not be able to lead an army in battle so would not fulfil her role as monarch/defend her realm which worried people
3. she was a small child so would need someone else to rule on her behalf – people knew this could cause rivalries among the nobles for this role so they were worried
4. she could be kidnapped by an unscrupulous noble in order to gain control over the country so her safety caused concern
5. she would not be able to control powerful nobles so a danger of civil war would remain which made many very unhappy
6. she would have to marry and a Scottish husband would lead to rivalry among the nobles
7. choosing a foreign husband would lead to Scotland being ruled by a foreigner
8. she herself was foreign and she was living far away in Norway, which some found unacceptable
9. there would have to be negotiations with her father before she could come to Scotland/about her future marriage – this would involve foreign interest which worried many Scots
10. nobles such as Bruce felt that they had a better claim so did not want her to be queen

2. *Candidates can be credited in a number of ways up to a maximum of 5 marks.*

Candidates must make a judgement about the usefulness of the source and support this by making evaluative comments on identified aspects of the source.

1 mark should be given for each relevant comment made, up to a **maximum of 5 marks in total.**
- A maximum of **4 marks** can be given for evaluative comments relating to the author, type of source, purpose and timing.
- A maximum of **2 marks** may be given for comments relating to the content of the source.
- A maximum of **2 marks** may be given for comments relating to points of significant omission.

Examples of aspects of the source and relevant comments:

Aspect of the source	Possible comment
Author: Modern historian	Useful because he has expert knowledge/has studied a range of relevant sources
Type of Source: Textbook	Useful because it contains straightforward factual information without bias/well researched
Purpose: To inform	Useful because it provides detailed information
Timing: 2009	Useful because it has the benefit of hindsight

Content	Possible comment
King Edward called for a parliament to be held in May 1291 to settle the future of the Scottish crown	Useful as it is accurate (Edward was in charge of the event rather than the Scots)
The location he chose was Norham Castle on the English side of the Tweed	Useful as it is accurate (Edward's intention was to disadvantage the Scots)
He said that the proceedings would not start until the Guardians and the claimants to the throne had acknowledged his position as overlord of Scotland.	Useful as it is accurate (Edward did want to be the ruler of Scotland)

Possible points of significant omission may include:
1. Scottish nobles/representatives did not think they could make such an agreement – only a king could do so
2. some claimants agreed very quickly (eg Bruce) and made it difficult for others to refuse (eg Balliol)
3. Civil war a possibility due to rival factions/13 claimants in all including Edward
4. Edward brought an army with him to Norham to intimidate the Scots

3. *Candidates can be credited in a number of ways up to a maximum of 5 marks.*

Candidates may take different perspectives on the events and may describe a variety of different aspects of the events. **1 mark** should be given for each accurate relevant key point of knowledge. A **second mark** should be given for each point that is developed, up to a maximum of **5 marks**. Candidates may achieve full marks by providing five straightforward points, by making three developed points, or a combination of these.

Possible points of knowledge may include:
1. sacked Berwick
2. slaughtered the townspeople as a warning against resistance
3. defeated Scots noble-led army at Dunbar
4. marched his army throughout Scotland from Dunbar as far as Elgin and back
5. took control of Scottish castles eg Stirling, Edinburgh, Perth
6. dethroned Balliol/stripped Balliol of his king's insignia
7. took Balliol to London as his prisoner/took other hostages to ensure loyalty
8. made important Scots sign allegiance to him/Ragman Rolls
9. took away the Stone of Scone to England to stop another king being crowned
10. took away important Scottish legal documents/Black Rood of St Margaret

4. *Candidates can be credited in a number of ways **up to a maximum of 5 marks**.*

Candidates must make an overall judgement about how fully the source explains the events. **1 mark** may be given for each valid point interpreted from the source or each valid point of significant omission provided.

Up to **3 marks** should be given for their identification of points from the source that supports their judgement. Candidates should be given up to **4 marks** for their identification of points of significant omission, based on their own knowledge, that support their judgement.

A maximum of 2 marks may be given for answers in which no judgement has been made.

Possible points which may be identified in the source include:
1. Wallace left Scotland
2. he travelled to France as part of his campaign to free John Balliol
3. Wallace planned to visit the Pope to get him on Balliol's side
4. Wallace was back in Scotland well before 1305 where he continued to fight against Edward's rule

Possible points of significant omission may include:
5. resigned as Guardian of Scotland in 1298
6. declared an outlaw by Scottish parliament (in March 1305 at Edward's behest)
7. handed over to English by John Menteith in August 1305
8. taken to London and tried for treason
9. executed by being hanged, drawn and quartered

Section 1, Context B, Mary Queen of Scots, and the Scottish Reformation, 1542–1587

5. *Candidates can be credited in a number of ways **up to a maximum of 5 marks**.*

Candidates must show a causal relationship between events.

Up to a **maximum of 5 marks in total**, **1 mark** should be given for each accurate, relevant reason, and a **second mark** should be given for reasons that are developed. Candidates may achieve full marks by providing five straightforward reasons, three developed reasons, or a combination of these.

Possible reasons may include:
1. Scotland broke the Treaty of Greenwich with England (promise for Mary to marry Henry VIII's son) so Mary would have been in danger from the English ('Rough Wooing')
2. Mary had to be moved around the country many times so it was becoming difficult to keep her safe from the attacking English
3. a plan was developed to smuggle Mary out of Scotland to France because the English continued to try and enforce the treaty even after Henry VIII had died (1547)
4. the French wanted Mary to marry the heir to the French throne so Mary had to leave Scotland to live in France
5. in August 1548 Mary set sail for France because Scotland and France had signed the Treaty of Haddington which promised Mary in marriage to the French heir to the throne
6. moving Mary to France was a precondition for French military aid against the English

6. *Candidates can be credited in a number of ways **up to a maximum of 5 marks**.*

Candidates may provide a number of straightforward points or a smaller number of developed points, or a combination of these. Up to a maximum of **5 marks**, **1 mark** should be given for each accurate relevant point of knowledge, and a **second mark** should be given for any point that is developed. Candidates may achieve full marks by providing five straightforward points, by making three developed points, or a combination of these.

Possible points of knowledge may include:
1. some Scots began to question the teachings of the Catholic Church
2. criticism of the wealth of the Catholic Church in Scotland
3. English translations of the Bible were distributed
4. religious pamphlets were brought over from abroad
5. Protestant preachers like John Knox started preaching/returned to Scotland in 1559
6. resentment of French/Catholic influence over Scotland
7. criticism of how some Protestant preachers were treated eg Wishart
8. death of Catholic Queen Mary of Guise in 1560
9. Parliament in August abolished the mass, ended the authority of the Pope and adopted the Protestant Confession of Faith

7. *Candidates can be credited in a number of ways **up to a maximum of 5 marks**.*

Candidates must make a judgement about the usefulness of the source and support this by making evaluative comments on identified aspects of the source.

1 mark should be given for each relevant comment made, up to a **maximum of 5 marks in total**.
- A maximum of **4 marks** can be given for evaluative comments relating to the author, type of source, purpose and timing.
- A maximum of **2 marks** may be given for comments relating to the content of the source.
- A maximum of **2 marks** may be given for comments relating to points of significant omission.

Examples of aspects of the source and relevant comments:

Aspect of the source	Possible comment
Author: Historian	Useful because he has expert knowledge/has studied a range of relevant sources
Type of Source: Textbook	Useful because it contains straightforward factual information without bias/well researched
Purpose: To inform	Useful because it provides detailed information
Timing: 2013	Useful because it has the benefit of hindsight

Content	Possible comment
Deafening noise shook the entire area	Useful because it is accurate (the explosion was heard by many)
Mary thought they were under attack	Useful because it is accurate (Mary appeared not to know about the plot to kill Darnley)
Darnley's house reduced to a pile of rubble	Useful because it is accurate (Darnley's house did suffer extensive damage)

Possible points of significant omission may include:
1. Darnley's naked body was found in another area away from the explosion along with a servant/without any marks that would indicate that he was in an explosion
2. beside Darnley's body were found a cloak, a dagger, a chair and a coat
3. witnesses say they saw men running from the scene before the explosion
4. Mary's political enemies accused her of being involved in a plot to kill Darnley

8. *Candidates can be credited in a number of ways **up to a maximum of 5 marks**.*

Candidates must make an overall judgement about how fully the source explains the events. **1 mark** may be given for each valid point interpreted from the source or each valid point of significant omission provided.

A maximum of 2 marks may be given for answers which refer only to the source.

Possible points which may be identified in the source include:
1. Scottish nobles, outraged at Mary's marriage to Bothwell, decided to rebel against Mary and Bothwell
2. the Protestant nobles raised an army and so did Mary and her new husband
3. the nobles said they would withdraw if Mary gave up Bothwell but she refused
4. Bothwell escaped and Mary surrendered to the Scottish nobles

Possible points of significant omission may include:
5. the nobles then imprisoned Mary in Loch Leven Castle
6. the nobles forced Mary to abdicate (July 1567)
7. in July Mary miscarried twins
8. Mary's son James was to be King
9. Earl of Moray ruled as King Regent

Section 1, Context C, The Treaty of Union, 1689–1715

9. *Candidates can be credited in a number of ways **up to a maximum of 5 marks**.*

Candidates must make an overall judgement about how fully the source explains the events. **1 mark** may be given for each valid point interpreted from the source or each valid point of significant omission provided.

A maximum of 2 marks may be given for answers which refer only to the source.

Possible points which may be identified in the source include:
1. in England there was a lot of resentment at the level of support for the Jacobites in Scotland
2. the Scots were angry at not being consulted by the English over the Act of Settlement of 1701
3. as the smaller partner in the union of crowns the Scots felt their interests were ignored
4. the Scots were also annoyed that they had not been consulted over entry into the war of Spanish Succession

Possible points of significant omission may include:
5. Scots were angry at the role of England in the failure of the Darien scheme
6. England's wars with France had worsened Scotland's economic problems, especially hitting towns such as Ayr which imported French goods
7. the English were annoyed when Scots passed the Act Anent Peace and War

8. the Scottish parliament angered Westminster by appointing a Protestant successor to Queen Anne without consulting them
9. the Scots regarded the Aliens Act as an attempt to bully them
10. The Worcester Affair (execution of English captain for piracy) angered the English

10. *Candidates can be credited in a number of ways **up to a maximum of 5 marks**.*

They may take different perspectives on the events and may describe a variety of different aspects of the events.

1 mark should be given for each accurate relevant key point of knowledge. A **second mark** should be given for each point that is developed, up to a maximum of 5 marks. Candidates may achieve full marks by providing five straightforward points, by making three developed points, or a combination of these.

Possible points of knowledge may include:
1. Union would lead to a rise in taxes in Scotland
2. the Scottish MPs would be outnumbered in a new British parliament
3. Union would end Scotland's identity as an independent nation (eg currency and laws)
4. Union would threaten the independence of the Scottish church
5. Scotland would be unable to compete with the more developed English industry (at home or abroad)
6. fears that English trading interests would be prioritised

11. *Candidates can be credited in a number of ways **up to a maximum of 5 marks**.*

Candidates must show a causal relationship between events.

Up to a **maximum of 5 marks in total**, **1 mark** should be given for each accurate, relevant reason, and a **second mark** should be given for reasons that are developed. Candidates may achieve full marks by providing five straightforward reasons, three developed reasons, or a combination of these.

Possible reasons may include:
1. Protestants were happy that Union would guarantee the Protestant Succession
2. if Scotland failed to agree to Union, England might invade and enforce a worse settlement
3. Union would give the Scots access to England and her colonies and so enrich the country
4. Scotland would be more secure as they would gain English military protection
5. Many Scots were swayed by promises of temporary tax exemptions
6. the Union would give Scots greater standing in Europe
7. Scotland and England shared a similar language, religion and trade traditions

12. *Candidates can be credited in a number of ways **up to a maximum of 5 marks**.*

Candidates must make a judgement about the usefulness of the source and support this by making evaluative comments on identified aspects of the source.

1 mark should be given for each relevant comment made, up to a **maximum of 5 marks in total**.
- A **maximum of 4 marks** can be given for evaluative comments relating to the author, type of source, purpose and timing.
- A **maximum of 2 marks** may be given for comments relating to the content of the source.
- A **maximum of 2 marks** may be given for comments relating to points of significant omission.

Examples of aspects of the source and relevant comments:

Aspect of the source	Possible comment
Author: Modern historian	Useful because he has expert knowledge/has studied a range of relevant sources
Type of Source: Textbook	Useful because it contains straightforward factual information without bias/ well researched
Purpose: To inform on views towards the Union	Useful because it provides detailed information
Timing: 1996	Useful because it has the benefit of hindsight

Content	Possible comment
But when Parliament passed an Act for the Security of the Kirk many of them changed their tune.	Useful as it is accurate (the Kirk was satisfied by the passing of this Act)
The Equivalent was the biggest incentive for many as it led to the sum of over three hundred thousand pounds sterling to be sent in cash to Scotland	Useful as it is accurate (the Equivalent did succeed as an incentive)
English guarantees over the independence of the Scots legal system also soothed most fears within the Scottish legal profession	Useful as it is accurate (the legal profession was satisfied by these guarantees)

Possible points of significant omission may include:
1. the Earl of Glasgow distributed £20,000 amongst the supporters of Union
2. the Squadrone Volante backed Union as they believed they would get control of the distribution of the Equivalent
3. Government pensions, promotions and job positions were offered to those who voted for Union

Section 1, Context D, Migration and Empire, 1830–1939

13. *Candidates can be credited in a number of ways **up to a maximum of 5 marks.***

They may take different perspectives on the events and may describe a variety of different aspects of the events.

1 mark should be given for each accurate relevant key point of knowledge. A **second mark** should be given for each point that is developed, up to a maximum of **5 marks**. Candidates may achieve full marks by providing five straightforward points, by making three developed points, or a combination of these.

Possible points of knowledge may include:
1. wealth of cities such as Glasgow increased and cities grew/ population 1 million by 1911
2. built environment benefited from investment of profits made from Empire investment – fine public buildings, mansions for successful entrepreneurs
3. many jobs were created in Scotland in manufacturing goods for export to the Empire (eg railway locomotives, ships)
4. raw materials from the Empire (eg jute, sugar) were processed in Scotland
5. Empire cultures introduced into Scotland (eg food, music)

6. some investment capital went overseas instead of into developing new Scottish industries
7. immigrant workers provided a cheap labour force and kept wages down
8. large available cheap labour force discouraged investment in new mechanisation (eg in mining, shipbuilding)
9. created many opportunities for Scots within the Empire (eg armed forces, civil service)

14. *Candidates can be credited in a number of ways **up to a maximum of 5 marks.***

Candidates must make an overall judgement about how fully the source explains the events. **1 mark** may be given for each valid point interpreted from the source or each valid point of significant omission provided.

A maximum of 2 marks may be given for answers which refer only to the source.

Possible points which may be identified in the source include:
1. the church enabled them to keep their religious identity in Scotland through worshipping in their traditional way
2. it was the centre of social life for many Irish immigrants/ offered a friendly environment where people could meet and be made welcome
3. the church also established youth groups
4. the church also attempted to tackle some of the issues Scottish society faced, such as the problem of poverty

Possible points of significant omission may include:
5. parish priests helped with writing letters, finding work and accommodation etc
6. church ran charities to help poor immigrants (eg St Vincent de Paul Society)
7. church set up and supervised schools for Catholic children
8. church set up sports organisations such as Celtic FC and Hibernian FC
9. immigrants from the north of Ireland were often Protestants so the Catholic Church did not play a part in their lives

15. *Candidates can be credited in a number of ways **up to a maximum of 5 marks.***

Candidates must make a judgement about the usefulness of the source and support this by making evaluative comments on identified aspects of the source.

1 mark should be given for each relevant comment made, up to a **maximum of 5 marks in total.**
- A maximum of **4 marks** can be given for evaluative comments relating to the author, type of source, purpose and timing.
- A maximum of **2 marks** may be given for comments relating to the content of the source.
- A maximum of **2 marks** may be given for comments relating to points of significant omission.

Examples of aspects of the source and relevant comments:

Aspect of the source	Possible comment
Author: Modern Historian	Useful because he has expert knowledge/has studied a range of relevant sources
Type of Source: Textbook	Useful because it contains straightforward factual information without bias/well researched
Purpose: To inform	Useful because it provides detailed information
Timing: 2007	Useful because it has the benefit of hindsight

Content	Possible comment
They supplied goods and services/brought their skills with them from their native lands	Useful as it is accurate (Jews did not tend to work in Scotland's traditional industries)
Many worked in the clothing industry	Useful as it is accurate (the clothing industry did employ many Jewish immigrants)
Many made a living selling door-to-door or running small shops	Useful as it is accurate (Jewish immigrants did often set up their own businesses)

Possible points of significant omission may include:
1. worked in the tobacco trade/making cigarettes
2. worked in the jewellery trade
3. many other immigrants worked in agriculture
4. many other immigrants did work in heavy industries (eg coalmining)

16. *Candidates can be credited in a number of ways **up to a maximum of 5 marks.***

Candidates must show a causal relationship between events.

Up to a **maximum of 5 marks in total, 1 mark** should be given for each accurate, relevant reason, and a **second mark** should be given for reasons that are developed. Candidates may achieve full marks by providing five straightforward reasons, three developed reasons, or a combination of these.

Possible reasons may include:
1. improved transport – steam ships and railways – encouraged Scots to move because they would not be without earnings for long/could return if necessary
2. some felt compelled to do missionary work/spread Christianity in the Empire
3. established Scots communities abroad were attractive to new emigrants who would feel more comfortable with their familiar culture
4. some countries offered free or cheap land (eg Canada) which attracted Scots farmers and crofters
5. land in New Zealand and the USA was known to be fertile and better than the land in Scotland so farmers were attracted there
6. agents for Empire countries held information meetings to encourage Scots to emigrate by showing the positive side of emigration
7. family and friends who had emigrated wrote letters home encouraging others to join them as they were doing well/helped with the cost of fares
8. higher wages for skilled Scots encouraged both permanent and temporary emigration
9. wide range of work available in trades that Scots were experienced in (eg farming, mining, engineering) so they could find work easily
10. administrative empire jobs with high status were attractive to well-educated Scots

Section 1, Context E, The Era of the Great War, 1900–1928

17. *Candidates can be credited in a number of ways **up to a maximum of 5 marks.***

They may take different perspectives on the events and may describe a variety of different aspects of the events.

1 mark should be given for each accurate relevant key point of knowledge. A **second mark** should be given for each point that is developed, up to a maximum of **5 marks**. Candidates may

achieve full marks by providing five straightforward points, by making three developed points, or a combination of these.

Possible points of knowledge may include:
1. the trenches were often flooded/muddy
2. the soldiers had little protection from the weather/cold in winter
3. constant strain of gunfire/explosions (eg threat of snipers, shellshock)
4. terrible smell in the trenches (eg rotting corpses, open latrines)
5. discomfort caused by lice/flies
6. problems caused by conditions such as: trench foot; trench mouth
7. danger of gas; blisters; blindness; suffocation
8. problem of rats searching for food/spreading diseases
9. difficulty of coping with seeing friends wounded or killed
10. food was monotonous/supply of food varied

18. *Candidates can be credited in a number of ways **up to a maximum of 5 marks.***

Candidates must show a causal relationship between events.

Up to a **maximum of 5 marks in total, 1 mark** should be given for each accurate, relevant reason, and a **second mark** should be given for reasons that are developed. Candidates may achieve full marks by providing five straightforward reasons, three developed reasons, or a combination of these.

Possible reasons may include:
1. health was being affected by lack of food/malnutrition
2. some people were starving
3. soldiers took priority therefore there was less food on the Home Front
4. vital war workers needed fed adequately to produce weapons etc
5. U-boats sank many supply ships which reduced the amount of food available
6. there was a limit to what civilians could grow (especially in cities)
7. food became expensive/prices of goods rose faster than peoples' wages
8. farm production affected by recruitment of labourers/requisitioning of horses
9. failure of propaganda campaigns to limit food waste
10. rationing introduced to maintain a fair supply of food/necessary to maintain high morale on the Home Front

19. *Candidates can be credited in a number of ways **up to a maximum of 5 marks.***

Candidates must make an overall judgement about how fully the source explains the events. **1 mark** may be given for each valid point interpreted from the source or each valid point of significant omission provided.

A maximum of 2 marks may be given for answers which refer only to the source.

Possible points which may be identified in the source include:
1. it gave women an opportunity to prove themselves in a male-dominated society (doing more than cleaning the house and tending to the children)
2. (with so many men going to war there was a large gap in employment and) women responded by replacing men in the workplace
3. Women's Royal Air Force was created/women worked on planes as mechanics
4. less well known roles of women in the war included selling war bonds

Possible points of significant omission may include:
5. they worked in heavy industry
6. they worked in public transport (eg railways, trams, buses)
7. in farming and forestry/Land Army
8. they joined the newly formed women's police force
9. they joined the women's WRENS, WAACS/further details about the WRAF
10. many women worked in munitions
11. greater responsibility/promotion (eg supervisors)

20. *Candidates can be credited in a number of ways up to a maximum of 5 marks.*

Candidates must make a judgement about the usefulness of the source and support this by making evaluative comments on identified aspects of the source.

1 mark should be given for each relevant comment made, up to a **maximum of 5 marks in total.**
- A maximum of **4 marks** can be given for evaluative comments relating to the author, type of source, purpose and timing.
- A maximum of **2 marks** may be given for comments relating to the content of the source.
- A maximum of **2 marks** may be given for comments relating to points of significant omission.

Examples of aspects of the source and relevant comments:

Aspect of the source	Possible comment
Author: Modern Historian	Useful because he has expert knowledge/has studied a range of relevant sources
Type of Source: A text book/history book	Useful because it contains straightforward factual information without bias/well researched
Purpose: To inform	Useful because it provides detailed information
Timing: 1989	Useful because it has the benefit of hindsight

Content	Possible comment
the hundreds of fishing boats that had been working for the Royal Navy were free again to go fishing	Useful as it is accurate (wartime restrictions were lifted and fishing grounds reopened)
It meant there were far more boats chasing the same amount of fish/many boats could not make enough money to stay in business	Useful as it is accurate (many boats did go out of business)
On top of that it was far more difficult to sell fish. (Before the war most of the herring that were caught were sold to Germany and Russia)	Useful as it is accurate (Germany and Russia were both in chaos after the war)

Possible points of significant omission may include:
1. many industries received a boost during the war (eg shipbuilding, jute)
2. people at home were eating a lot less fish which decreased demand/European countries started to compete strongly with Scottish fleets and in 1920 the government removed the guaranteed price for herring
3. some fishing boats were in poor condition after wartime so not as productive
4. many industries declined after the war due to lack of wartime demand (eg agriculture, coal, jute)

Section 2, Context A, The Creation of the Medieval Kingdoms, 1066–1406

21. *Candidates can be credited in a number of ways up to a maximum of 6 marks.*

Candidates must show a causal relationship between events.

Up to a **maximum of 6 marks in total**, **1 mark** should be given for each accurate, relevant reason, and a **second mark** should be given for reasons that are developed. Candidates may achieve full marks by providing six straightforward reasons, three developed reasons, or a combination of these.

Possible reasons may include:
1. David's mother Margaret was English/from a Saxon family which experienced Norman rule
2. David's sister was married to the King of England, Henry I
3. David spent part of his childhood in the royal court in England
4. David was married to an Anglo-Norman heiress (Matilda of Huntingdon)
5. David took part in Anglo-Norman ceremonies (eg was made a knight by Henry I)
6. David had many friends who were Anglo-Norman barons
7. David had land in England (eg Northampton/Huntingdon/Bedford)

22. Specific marking instructions for this question

Candidates can be credited in a number of ways up to a maximum of 8 marks.

Candidates must use knowledge to present a balanced assessment of the influence of different possible factors and come to a reasoned conclusion. **Up to 5 marks** are allocated for relevant points of knowledge used to support factors (but one mark should be deducted if the process is not clear in at least two factors). **1 mark** should be given for each relevant, factual key point of knowledge used to support a factor. **If only one factor is presented, a maximum of 3 marks should be given for relevant points of knowledge.**

Possible factors may include:	Relevant, factual, key points of knowledge to support this factor may include:
Illegal castles	1. Barons had built illegal castles without royal permission during the civil war
2. some Barons refused to hand the castles over to Henry (eg The Earl of York/Scarborough castle)
Illegal armies	3. Barons had hired mercenaries to fight for them/protect their land
4. illegal armies threatened Henry's control
Corrupt sheriffs	5. some sheriffs had been keeping fines paid by criminals instead of paying them to the king
6. some sheriffs had been accepting bribes from criminals
No common law	7. the law was different in every area across Henry's kingdom
8. Barons decided the law in their own area and as a result were very powerful
Land theft	9. some Barons were stealing land from their weaker neighbours
10. some Barons forged documents making false claims that they were the rightful heir to land
Large empire	11. Henry had a large empire (eg Scotland to the Pyrenees and could not be everywhere at once)
12. Henry's empire did not share many customs or traditions making it difficult to govern

Up to 3 marks should be given for presenting the answer in a structured way, leading to a conclusion which addresses the question, as follows:

1 mark for the answer being presented in a structured way, with knowledge being organised in support of different factors.

1 mark given for a conclusion with a valid judgement or overall summary.

1 mark given for a reason being provided in support of the judgement.

23. *Candidates can be credited in a number of ways **up to a maximum of 6 marks**.*

Candidates must make a judgement about the usefulness of the source and support this by making evaluative comments on identified aspects of the source.

1 mark should be given for each relevant comment made, up to a **maximum of 6 marks in total.**
- A maximum of **4 marks** can be given for evaluative comments relating to the author, type of source, purpose and timing.
- A maximum of **2 marks** may be given for comments relating to the content of the source.
- A maximum of **2 marks** may be given for comments relating to points of significant omission.

Examples of aspects of the source and relevant comments:

Aspect of the source	Possible comment
Author: Monk	Useful because he would have been well placed to receive information/perhaps less useful because he is not an eyewitness
Type of Source: Chronicle	Useful because it was a detailed record of events
Purpose: To inform	Useful because it was written to inform us about the king's role in ending the Peasants' Revolt/perhaps less useful because it is biased in favour of the king
Timing: 1381	Useful because it was written at the time of the Peasants' Revolt

Content	Possible comment
The peasants' leader, Wat Tyler was killed	Useful because it is accurate (Wat Tyler did die during the Peasants' Revolt)
The king rode toward them (peasants) and persuaded them to put their weapons away	Useful because it is accurate (the king was successful in getting the peasants to lay down their arms)
The king promised the peasants that they would be treated fairly and so they agreed to go home	Useful because it is accurate (the king did manage to persuade the peasants to disperse)

Possible points of significant omission may include:
1. the king did agree to the peasants' demands
2. peasants ambushed by the king's army and arrested
3. leaders of the rebellion hanged

Section 2, Context B, War of the Three Kingdoms, 1603–1651

24. *Candidates can be credited in a number of ways **up to a maximum of 6 marks**.*

Candidates must make a judgement about the usefulness of the source and support this by making evaluative comments on identified aspects of the source.

1 mark should be given for each relevant comment made, up to a **maximum of 6 marks in total.**
- A maximum of **4 marks** can be given for evaluative comments relating to the author, type of source, purpose and timing.
- A maximum of **2 marks** may be given for comments relating to the content of the source.
- A maximum of **2 marks** may be given for comments relating to points of significant omission.

Examples of aspects of the source and relevant comments:

Aspect of the source	Possible comment
Author: House of Commons	Useful because it is from eyewitnesses who were in dispute with the king
Type of Source: Official statement	Useful because it is an official government statement which outlines the concerns of parliament and will therefore be truthful/perhaps less useful as it may be biased
Purpose: To persuade	Useful because it attempts to justify the position of Parliament/perhaps less useful as it is not balanced
Timing: 1621	Useful because it is a primary source from the time when there were disputes between King James VI and I and Parliament

Content	Possible comment
Privileges of Parliament are our ancient birth right	Useful because it is accurate (Parliament was concerned that the king was trying to limit its power)
Matters concerning the king, state, defence, the church and the making of laws are for debating in Parliament only	Useful because it is accurate (Parliament did want to retain the right to debate certain state matters which the king opposed)
If any of its members are questioned for anything said or done in Parliament, the same is to be applied to the king	Useful because it is accurate (Parliament did believe the king should be accountable to Parliament as much as they were to him)

Possible points of significant omission may include:
1. James formally deleted the Protestation from the journals of Parliament
2. James dissolved Parliament demonstrating he did not agree with their protests
3. James and Parliament argued over the rights of the King with the King stressing his 'divine right' to rule
4. other issues that Parliament and the King argued over (eg the Spanish match/war in Europe)

25. *Candidates can be credited in a number of ways up to a maximum of 6 marks.*

Candidates must show a causal relationship between events.

Up to a **maximum of 6 marks in total, 1 mark** should be given for each accurate, relevant reason, and a **second mark** should be given for reasons that are developed. Candidates may achieve full marks by providing five straightforward reasons, three developed reasons, or a combination of these.

Possible reasons may include:

1. there was resentment towards the Anglican High Church ceremony that was part of Charles' coronation
2. Resentment of Charles as an absentee monarch
3. Scots suspicion that Charles wanted to be an absolute monarch
4. Charles demanded that Ministers accept and use the new Prayer Book, which was unpopular amongst the Ministers
5. there was public opposition to the introduction of the new Prayer Book (eg 1637 St Giles riots)
6. the Scottish clergy opposed the requirement to wear gowns and surplices as dictated by Laud's Canons
7. resentment at the abolition of Presbyteries and the threat of dissolution
8. Charles introduced Bishops into the Scottish Church which was opposed
9. Charles ruled that the General Assembly was not allowed to meet which caused opposition
10. Charles imposed the Act of Revocation which took back church or royal property that had been alienated since 1540, this angered the Church
11. resentment towards the money raising methods of Charles (eg Ship Money)

26. *Candidates can be credited in a number of ways up to a maximum of 8 marks.*

Candidates must use knowledge to present a balanced assessment of the influence of different possible factors and come to a reasoned conclusion. **Up to 5 marks** are allocated for relevant points of knowledge used to support factors (but one mark should be deducted if the process is not clear in at least two factors). **1 mark** should be given for each relevant, factual key point of knowledge used to support a factor.
If only one factor is presented, a maximum of 3 marks should be given for relevant points of knowledge.

Possible factors may include:	Relevant, factual, key points of knowledge to support this factor may include:
Financial disputes	1. arguments over the buying of titles, rich men were persuaded to buy titles and if they refused they were fined the same sum of money it would have cost for a title
	2. in 1635 Charles ordered that everyone in the country should pay Ship Money. This tax was only meant to be paid by coastal towns but Charles insisted inland areas were also to pay, which caused resentment/led to arrests of some MPs eg Hampden
	3. April 1640 Charles called for a Parliament to grant the money needed to fight a war in Scotland. Parliament refused and cited Laud and Strafford as men who were abusing the authority that had been given to them.
Religious disputes	4. King Charles was married to Roman Catholic Henrietta Maria of France who was given free rein to practise her religion, this led to distrust over the religious loyalty of Charles
	5. Charles preferred a High Anglican form of worship with ceremonies and rituals that made some believe he was leaning towards Catholicism, this upset the Protestants and Puritans/Charles also clashed with the Scots over the issue of the new Prayer Book this angered the Scots so much that they invaded England in 1639
	6. the Appointment of Laud (who also preferred High Anglican worship) as Archbishop of Canterbury, brought about much opposition/Laud attempted to impose High Anglican forms of worship which were opposed by the Protestants eg the new Prayer Book and the wearing of vestments
Political disputes	7. in 1629 Charles refused to let Parliament meet. Members of Parliament arrived at Westminster to find that the doors had been locked with large chains and padlocks. They were locked out for eleven years
	8. Parliament also demanded that Charles get rid of the Court of Star Chamber, which Charles used to rule without Parliament
	9. in 1642, Charles went to Parliament with 300 soldiers to arrest his five biggest critics. Parliament had been tipped off and the five men had already fled to the safety of the city of London – this angered Parliament that the King was trying to deny them the right to speak out against him
King's character	10. Parliament considered Charles to be arrogant and conceited so they had a particularly bad relationship/Charles considered the poor relationships between his father and Parliament to be the fault of Parliament so did not trust them
	11. Parliament and the King clashed over Charles' strong belief in the Divine Rights of Kings.

Up to 3 marks should be given for presenting the answer in a structured way, leading to a conclusion which addresses the question, as follows:

1 mark for the answer being presented in a structured way, with knowledge being organised in support of different factors.

1 mark given for a conclusion with a valid judgement or overall summary.

1 mark given for a reason being provided in support of the judgement.

Section 2, Context C, The Atlantic Slave Trade, 1770–1807

27. *Candidates can be credited in a number of ways up to a maximum of 8 marks.*

Candidates must use knowledge to present a balanced assessment of the influence of different possible factors and come to a reasoned conclusion. **Up to 5 marks** are allocated for relevant points of knowledge used to support factors (but one mark should be deducted if the process is not clear in at least two factors). **1 mark** should be given for each relevant, factual key point of knowledge used to support a factor. **If only one factor is presented, a maximum of 3 marks should be given for relevant points of knowledge.**

Possible factors may include:	Relevant, factual, key points of knowledge to support this factor may include:
Employment (marks should be awarded for any valid job related to the slave trade)	1. jobs in construction (eg factories, homes) 2. many people relied on the slave trade for employment, (eg shipbuilding, sailors, rope-makers, sail-makers) 3. other jobs (eg banking, insurance, industrial)
Industrial benefits	4. Glasgow – tobacco trade contributed to growth of industry 5. growth of industries such as copper-smelting, sugar-refining, glass-making and textiles 6. profits from the slave trade provided the capital for the Industrial Revolution
Financial/Municipal benefits	7. individuals/cities became richer due to the slave trade (eg Liverpool, Bristol, London) 8. wealthy individuals invested profits from the trade (eg schools, colleges, libraries) 9. London – provided financial services such as insurance/ London banks provided long-term loans for slave trade
Consumer benefits	10. cotton, tobacco and sugar in high demand

Up to 3 marks should be given for presenting the answer in a structured way, leading to a conclusion which addresses the question, as follows:
- **1 mark** for the answer being presented in a structured way, with knowledge being organised in support of different factors.
- **1 mark** given for a conclusion with a valid judgement or overall summary.
- **1 mark** given for a reason being provided in support of the judgement.

28. *Candidates can be credited in a number of ways up to a maximum of 6 marks.*

Candidates must show a causal relationship between events.

Up to a **maximum of 6 marks in total, 1 mark** should be given for each accurate, relevant reason, and a **second mark** should be given for reasons that are developed. Candidates may achieve full marks by providing five straightforward reasons, three developed reasons, or a combination of these.

Possible reasons may include:
1. native populations were cleared from the islands/wiped out
2. fear of violent rebellion/Caribbean became more volatile
3. slave uprisings caused damage and destruction
4. small farms were replaced by large plantations
5. island economies stifled by slave trade (eg Jamaican economy became too reliant on sugar production)
6. natural beauty of island landscapes was damaged by the growth of plantations
7. slave trade brought racist attitudes to the Caribbean
8. new diseases were introduced to the islands

29. *Candidates can be credited in a number of ways up to a maximum of 6 marks.*

Candidates must make a judgement about the usefulness of the source and support this by making evaluative comments on identified aspects of the source.

1 mark should be given for each relevant comment made, up to a **maximum of 6 marks in total.**
- A maximum of **4 marks** can be given for evaluative comments relating to the author, type of source, purpose and timing.
- A maximum of **2 marks** may be given for comments relating to the content of the source.
- A maximum of **2 marks** may be given for comments relating to points of significant omission.

Examples of aspects of the source and relevant comments:

Aspect of the source	Possible comment
Author: William Wilberforce	Useful as it was from a well-known abolitionist who campaigned against slave trade
Type of Source: Speech	Useful as it was part of an official Parliamentary speech
Purpose: To persuade	Useful as it gives typical evidence/arguments used by abolitionists against slavery
Timing: 1789	Useful as it was delivered during the abolitionist campaign

Content	Possible comment
The right ankle of one is connected with the left ankle of another by a small iron fetter	Useful as it is accurate (slaves were chained together during the Middle Passage)
The slaves are so miserable at leaving their country, that they set sail at night	Useful as it is accurate (slave ships did leave at night due to fears held by slaves and fear of increased panic aboard slave ships)
For exercise, these miserable people, loaded down with chains and suffering from disease, are forced to dance by the terror of the whip	Useful as it is accurate (many slaves were punished if they refused to exercise on the deck/suffered from diseases)

Possible points of significant omission may include:
1. details of plantation conditions led to the boycott of sugar and slave produced goods
2. Equiano's eyewitness account of the Middle Passage in "An Interesting Narrative" highlighted harsh conditions
3. Clarkson brought examples of slave equipment/plans of slave ships to show the public which caused outrage
4. other abolitionists used moral or religious arguments against slavery

Section 2, Context D, Changing Britain, 1760–1900

30. *Candidates can be credited in a number of ways up to a maximum of 8 marks.*

Candidates must use knowledge to present a balanced assessment of the influence of different possible factors and come to a reasoned conclusion. **Up to 5 marks** are allocated for relevant points of knowledge used to support factors (but one mark should be deducted if the process is not clear in at least **two** factors). **1 mark** should be given for each relevant, factual key point of knowledge used to support a factor. **If only one factor is presented, a maximum of 3 marks should be given for relevant points of knowledge.**

Possible factors may include:	Relevant, factual, key points of knowledge to support this factor may include:
Lack of clean water	1. contaminated/unclean drinking water led to diseases such as cholera 2. typhoid was also caused by contaminated drinking water
Lack of sanitation	3. open sewers allowed bacteria to multiply/contaminated water supplies and led to the spread of disease
Lack of rubbish disposal	4. rubbish built up in the streets which attracted vermin/rats which caused disease (eg typhus)
Lack of adequate medical care/knowledge	5. poor families could not afford medical care, which meant that health problems were untreated/worsened 6. lack of knowledge/treatment meant that some conditions that are treatable now were often fatal before 1900 (eg TB) 7. vaccinations for many diseases (eg measles/polio) were not available/many of these diseases were often fatal
Overcrowding	8. overcrowding made it easier for disease to spread (eg cholera/TB)
Poor diet	9. poor diet/lack of vitamins led to conditions such as rickets 10. poor diet led to low immunity to disease/meant that people took longer to/were less likely to recover from disease
Poor housing	11. poorly constructed houses were often damp/cold which made many medical conditions (eg TB/asthma) worse 12. lack of sunlight in cellar/basement houses or cramped tenements/closes led to conditions such as rickets

Up to 3 marks should be given for presenting the answer in a structured way, leading to a conclusion which addresses the question, as follows:
- **1 mark** for the answer being presented in a structured way, with knowledge being organised in support of different factors.
- **1 mark** given for a conclusion with a valid judgement or overall summary.
- **1 mark** given for a reason being provided in support of the judgement.

31. *Candidates can be credited in a number of ways up to a maximum of 6 marks.*

Candidates must make a judgement about the usefulness of the source and support this by making evaluative comments on identified aspects of the source.

1 mark should be given for each relevant comment made, up to a **maximum of 6 marks in total.**
- A **maximum of 4 marks** can be given for evaluative comments relating to the author, type of source, purpose and timing.
- A **maximum of 2 marks** may be given for comments relating to the content of the source.
- A **maximum of 2 marks** may be given for comments relating to points of significant omission.

Examples of aspects of the source and relevant comments:

Aspect of the source	Possible comment
Author: Government	Useful as the government will have first-hand knowledge of the steps taken to improve working conditions in factories
Type of Source: Act/Law	Useful as it gives a factual/legal description of the new rules/official document
Purpose: To inform	Useful as it is intended to give a summary of the new laws that factory/mill owners have to abide by
Timing: 1833	Useful as it is from the time of improvements to working conditions in factories

Content	Possible comment
No children under the age of 9 should be employed in mills	Useful as it is accurate (the act did ban the employment of children under 9 in textile mills)
Limits to working hours (eg Children aged 9–13 must not work more than 8 hours each day/Children aged 14–18 must not work more than 12 hours each day/ Children under 18 must not work at night)	Useful as it is accurate (the act did limit the working hours of children)
Government inspectors will be given the power to demand entry to textile mills and enforce these rules	Useful as it is accurate (the act did create government factory inspectors)

Possible points of significant omission may include:
1. 1844 act stated that women and children should no longer clean moving machinery/some machinery had to be fenced
2. 1847 act introduced a ten hour working day for women and children
3. 1878 act stated that no women should work more than 60 hours per week/no children under 10 should work in factories/introduced regulations for safety, ventilation and meals
4. new technology could make working conditions better

32. *Candidates can be credited in a number of ways up to a maximum of 6 marks.*

Candidates must show a causal relationship between events.

Up to **a maximum of 6 marks in total, 1 mark** should be given for each accurate, relevant reason, and a **second mark** should be given for reasons that are developed. Candidates may achieve full marks by providing five straightforward reasons, three developed reasons, or a combination of these.

Possible reasons may include:
1. their demands (eg …) were too radical for the time
2. the economy improved/jobs returned, so support for Chartism faded
3. the government refused to talk to the Chartists/rejected their petitions
4. many of the signatures on the petitions were false, so the Chartists lost respect
5. Chartists were ridiculed in the press, so lost respect
6. other movements offered more immediate and tangible benefits which attracted support away from Chartism
7. divisions amongst the Chartists (physical force/moral force) weakened the movement
8. Chartist demonstrations were broken up, so were not effective
9. the Chartists were poorly led (by Fergus O'Connor and William Lovett)

Section 2, Context E, The Making of Modern Britain, 1880–1951

33. *Candidates can be credited in a number of ways up to a maximum of 8 marks.*

Candidates must use knowledge to present a balanced assessment of the influence of different possible factors and come to a reasoned conclusion. **Up to 5 marks** are allocated for relevant points of knowledge used to support factors (but one mark should be deducted if the process is not clear

in at least **two** factors). **1 mark** should be given for each relevant, factual key point of knowledge used to support a factor. **If only one factor is presented, a maximum of 3 marks should be given for relevant points of knowledge.**

Possible factors may include:	Relevant, factual, key points of knowledge to support this factor may include:
Booth and Rowntree	1. Booth's report showed that 30.7% of the population of London were living in poverty. This shocked the public and government/provided evidence of poverty that could not be ignored 2. Booth's report showed that poverty was not always the poor person's own fault and helped to change laissez-faire/self-help attitudes 3. Rowntree's report showed that 27.8% of the population of York were living in poverty. This shocked the public and government/provided evidence of poverty that could not be ignored 4. Rowntree's report showed that poverty wasn't just in London/something had to be done to tackle poverty across Britain 5. Rowntree's report showed that there was a cycle of poverty, so helped convince people that the poor needed help at certain times of their lives
The Boer War/ National Efficiency	6. during the Boer War 1/3 (as high as 2/3 in some areas) of recruits were unfit for service. This was often due to poor health caused by poverty - people were worried that if poverty was not tackled then Britain would not be able to defend herself in a war 7. people were concerned that Britain would not have a healthy productive workforce if poverty was not tackled
New Liberalism	8. new Liberals such as David Lloyd George and Winston Churchill wanted to pass reforms to help the poor and helped to change attitudes in the Liberal Party
The German example	9. the Germans had introduced welfare reforms already (pensions and national insurance) so the British wanted to keep up with Germany
Democracy/Trade Unions/The Threat of Labour	10. more men/the working classes could now vote so political parties had to change their policies on poverty to avoid losing votes 11. Trade unions were becoming bigger/more influential/had helped to form the Labour Party and were pushing for reforms to help the poor 12. the Labour Party was formed in 1900 and supported reforms to help the poor/The other parties had to respond, or they would lose votes to the new Labour Party

Up to 3 marks should be given for presenting the answer in a structured way, leading to a conclusion which addresses the question, as follows:

1 mark for the answer being presented in a structured way, with knowledge being organised in support of different factors.

1 mark given for a conclusion with a valid judgement or overall summary.

1 mark given for a reason being provided in support of the judgement.

34. *Candidates can be credited in a number of ways up to a maximum of 6 marks.*

Candidates must show a causal relationship between events.

Up to **a maximum of 6 marks in total**, **1 mark** should be given for each accurate, relevant reason, and a **second mark** should be given for reasons that are developed. Candidates may achieve full marks by providing six straightforward reasons, three developed reasons, or a combination of these.

Possible reasons may include:

1. free school meals made children healthier because this was the only meal that many children got in a day/parents could not afford to feed children at home
2. medical inspections at school made children healthier because they identified medical problems/later treatment was introduced
3. The Children Act/Children's Charter improved the lives of the young because they would no longer be sent to adult prisons/treated as adult criminals
4. The Children Act/Children's Charter improved the lives of the young because children could no longer be sentenced to death for committing a crime
5. Pensions improved the lives of the elderly because they helped many of the elderly poor to stay out of the workhouse/gave the elderly poor enough extra money to get by
6. National Insurance helped to make workers healthier because free medical treatment was provided for insured workers
7. National Insurance improved the lives of families because maternity grants were given after the birth of children
8. National Insurance improved the lives of workers because they could now receive free specialist medical treatment for TB
9. National Insurance improved the lives of the unemployed because some workers received unemployment benefit, helping them to stay out of poverty
10. The Workmen's Compensation Act improved the lives of workers because now they could get compensation for illness or injury caused by work
11. Labour exchanges improved the lives of the unemployed because they helped them to find a job and earn money

35. *Candidates can be credited in a number of ways up to a maximum of 6 marks.*

Candidates must make a judgement about the usefulness of the source and support this by making evaluative comments on identified aspects of the source.

1 mark should be given for each relevant comment made, up to a **maximum of 6 marks in total.**

- A maximum of **4 marks** can be given for evaluative comments relating to the author, type of source, purpose and timing.
- A maximum of **2 marks** may be given for comments relating to the content of the source.
- A maximum of **2 marks** may be given for comments relating to points of significant omission.

Examples of aspects of the source and relevant comments:

Aspect of the source	Possible comment
Author: Government	Useful as the government will have knowledge of the health service they are introducing
Type of Source: Advertisement	Useful as it will be informative/easy to understand
Purpose: To inform	Useful as it is intended to give a summary of how the NHS will work
Timing: May 1948	Useful as it is a primary source from the time that the NHS was introduced

Content	Possible comment
The new NHS starts on the 5th July	Useful as it is accurate (the NHS was launched in the summer of 1948)
Anyone can use the NHS/men, women children/no age limits	Useful as this is accurate (the NHS was available to all)
Right to use NHS does not depend on weekly payments	Useful as this is accurate (access to the NHS did not depend on contributions)

Possible points of significant omission may include:

1. the NHS provided many services – GPs, hospital treatment, specialist treatment, opticians, dentists for example
2. the NHS was introduced by Aneurin Bevan
3. the NHS was recommended in the Beveridge Report/to tackle the 'giant' of disease
4. there was a huge demand for NHS services after it was introduced

Section 3, Context A, The Cross and the Crescent; the Crusades, 1071–1192

36. *Candidates can be credited in a number of ways up to a maximum of 4 marks.*

Candidates must make direct comparisons of the two sources, either or in detail. A simple comparison will indicate what points of detail or overall viewpoint they agree or disagree about and should be given **1 mark**. A developed comparison of the points of detail or overall viewpoint should be given **2 marks**. Candidates may achieve full marks by making four simple comparisons, two developed comparisons or by a combination of these.

Possible points of comparison may include:

Source A	Source B
Overall: Sources A and B agree that the Pope called the First Crusade in 1095	
The Pope said that Jerusalem must be recaptured.	The Pope said Jerusalem was the most important city in the world and it must be taken back from the Muslims.
The Pope warned that every Christian in the west must fight or the Muslims could advance into Europe.	The Pope said a Christian army must be called to stop the Muslims before they captured every city they attacked.
He appealed to the knights to stop their violent behaviour towards each other and instead use their military skills against God's enemy in the east.	Pope Urban told the knights of Europe to stop fighting amongst each other and unite against the infidel.

37. *Candidates can be credited in a number of ways up to a maximum of 6 marks.*

Candidates must make an overall judgement about how fully the source explains the events. **1 mark** may be given for each valid point interpreted from the source or each valid point of significant omission provided.

A maximum of 2 marks may be given for answers which refer only to the source.

Possible points which may be identified in the source include:

1. the Muslims were well prepared/had strengthened the wall around the city
2. the Muslims had collected the harvest early and had enough food to last for several months/expected a long siege
3. the Muslims fought back and forced the Crusaders to retreat
4. the Crusaders did not have scaling ladders or siege machines/required supplies from Europe

Possible points of significant omission may include:

5. the Muslims had poisoned/drained the local water wells and so the Crusaders had no water
6. Christians had been expelled from the city so the Crusaders did not have any allies inside Jerusalem
7. the city was built on slopes so could not be attacked from all angles
8. the city wall was strengthened by a large citadel/David's Tower which made an attack difficult

38. *Candidates can be credited in a number of ways up to a maximum of 5 marks.*

Candidates must show a causal relationship between events.

Up to a **maximum of 5 marks in total, 1 mark** should be given for each accurate, relevant reason, and a **second mark** should be given for reasons that are developed. Candidates may achieve full marks by providing five straightforward reasons, three developed reasons, or a combination of these.

Possible reasons may include:

1. the Crusader army was small (many Crusaders had returned to Europe) and so it was difficult to defend the Crusader states/Latin states
2. the Crusaders were constantly attacked by Muslims and so lost more soldiers/supplies
3. the Crusader states/Latin States were far apart and so were difficult to defend
4. the land was infertile so it was difficult to grow crops
5. there was a lack of peasants so there was no one to farm the land
6. the Crusaders did not have key supplies eg timber and so could not build siege machines
7. the Crusaders did not have enough boats needed to capture the coastal towns
8. the Crusaders fought among themselves and so were not united against the Muslims

39. *Candidates can be credited in a number of ways up to a maximum of 5 marks.*

They may take different perspectives on the events and may describe a variety of different aspects of the events.

1 mark should be given for each accurate relevant key point of knowledge. A **second mark** should be given for each point that is developed, up to a maximum of **5 marks**. Candidates may achieve full marks by providing five straightforward points, by making three developed points, or a combination of these.

Possible points of knowledge may include:

1. the Muslims attacked the Crusaders with darts and arrows
2. the Muslims attempted to draw the Crusaders from their defensive position
3. the Crusaders held their defensive line
4. the Muslim army grew tired
5. the Crusaders charged at the Muslims
6. many Muslims were killed/high number of casualties in the Muslim army
7. the Muslim army fled
8. the Crusaders won the battle

Section 3, Context B, "Tea and Freedom,": the American Revolution, 1774–83

40. *Candidates can be credited in a number of ways up to a maximum of 5 marks.*

Candidates must show a causal relationship between events.

Up to a **maximum of 5 marks in total, 1 mark** should be given for each accurate, relevant reason, and a **second mark** should be given for reasons that are developed. Candidates may achieve full marks by providing five straightforward reasons, three developed reasons, or a combination of these.

Possible reasons may include:

1. Thomas Paine's pamphlet "Common Sense" sold 150,000 copies and persuaded many British people the American cause was just
2. radicals in Britain opposed war and supported American demands for reform (eg no taxation without representation)
3. Edmund Burke thought that using force against the colonists would be counter-productive
4. Edmund Burke argued against taxation in America to raise funds for Britain
5. radicals in Britain supported the colonists demands for reform as they wanted political reform at home

41. *Candidates can be credited in a number of ways up to a maximum of 4 marks.*

Candidates must make direct comparisons of the two sources, either overall or in detail. A simple comparison will indicate what points of detail or overall viewpoint they agree or disagree about and should be given **1 mark**. A developed comparison of the points of detail or overall viewpoint should be given **2 marks**. Candidates may achieve full marks by making four simple comparisons, two developed comparisons or by a combination of these.

Possible points of comparison may include:

Source A	Source B
Overall: The sources agree about the capabilities of the Continental Army	
The troops themselves were usually inexperienced in battle	Many of the soldiers needed practice with their weapons
Many soldiers left to return home, leaving the army without enough men	The army needed troops even more than fortifications
Washington was always short of money to buy much needed supplies or to pay his soldiers	The Continental Army was always short of ammunition/ Gunpowder was always in short supply but houses were stripped of lead for bullets.

42. *Candidates can be credited in a number of ways **up to a maximum of 5 marks**.*

They may take different perspectives on the events and may describe a variety of different aspects of the events.

1 mark should be given for each accurate relevant key point of knowledge. A **second mark** should be given for each point that is developed, up to a maximum of **5 marks**. Candidates may achieve full marks by providing five straightforward points, by making three developed points, or a combination of these.

Possible points of knowledge may include:
1. British plan was to link their two armies to defeat the colonists
2. Burgoyne's army invaded from Canada
3. General Howe had taken the main British army to Philadelphia leaving General Clinton with a small army in New York
4. Americans cut down trees and blocked the British army's progress
5. colonists had destroyed crops and burned potential food supplies
6. some Indian troops deserted the British
7. St Leger's army was defeated/he retreated
8. British eventually outnumbered by colonists
9. Burgoyne's army surrounded and unable to break out, so surrendered

43. *Candidates can be credited in a number of ways **up to a maximum of 6 marks**.*

Candidates must make an overall judgement about how fully the source explains the events. **1 mark** may be given for each valid point interpreted from the source or each valid point of significant omission provided.

A maximum of 2 marks may be given for answers which refer only to the source.

Possible points which may be identified in the source include:
1. after the British defeat at Saratoga, many in Europe were keen to take advantage of British weakness
2. France wanted revenge for loss of colonies so offered financial support
3. France also gave military assistance in the form of soldiers and gunpowder to put more pressure on Britain
4. Spain saw an opportunity to try to retake Gibraltar to distract Britain

Possible points of significant omission may include:
5. foreign intervention challenged Britain's control of the seas
6. foreign intervention made it more difficult for Britain to reinforce and supply forces in America
7. the French attacked British colonies in the Caribbean which distracted them/Britain had to divert vital troops to Europe and the West Indies
8. foreign intervention affected British morale as they had no major allies
9. formal Franco-American alliance increased pressure on Britain

Section 3, Context C, USA 1850–1880

44. *Candidates can be credited in a number of ways **up to a maximum of 4 marks**.*

Candidates must make direct comparisons of the two sources, either overall or in detail. A simple comparison will indicate what points of detail or overall viewpoint they agree or disagree about and should be given **1 mark**. A developed comparison of the points of detail or overall viewpoint should be given **2 marks**. Candidates may achieve full marks by making four simple comparisons, two developed comparisons or by a combination of these.

Possible points of comparison may include:

Source A	Source B
Overall: Both sources agree about the treatment of slaves on Southern Plantations	
Gave me meat and bread with the other slaves, which was not half enough for me to live upon	Slaves were given the absolute minimum amount of food to survive
He flogged me nearly every day/I got a severe flogging of one hundred lashes	The usual method of punishing slaves was using a system of floggings
He set me to work without any shirt in the cotton field, in a very hot sun	Some slaves were punished by being tied to trees on the plantation, often in the burning heat of the sun

45. *Candidates can be credited in a number of ways **up to a maximum of 6 marks**.*

Candidates must make an overall judgement about how fully the source explains the events. **1 mark** may be given for each valid point interpreted from the source or each valid point of significant omission provided.

A maximum of 2 marks may be given for answers which refer only to the source.

Possible points which may be identified in the source include:
1. Southern States seceded in order to escape high taxes
2. Southern States thought of themselves as a separate community
3. Southern States disliked/despised/hated/feared their northern neighbours
4. there was also a feeling in the South that there would be more advantages to secession than staying in the union

Possible points of significant omission may include:
5. Lincoln's election alarmed pro-slavery Southerners/saw him as an abolitionist
6. Southerners wanted to protect slavery for economic reasons/Southerners viewed slavery as essential to protecting their way of life
7. economic differences between the industrial North and agricultural South
8. secession down to a fear of losing states' rights

46. *Candidates can be credited in a number of ways **up to a maximum of 5 marks**.*

They may take different perspectives on the events and may describe a variety of different aspects of the events.

1 mark should be given for each accurate relevant key point of knowledge. A **second mark** should be given for each point that is developed, up to a maximum of **5 marks**. Candidates may achieve full marks by providing five straightforward points, by making three developed points, or a combination of these.

Possible points of knowledge may include:
1. the Bureau was set up to help newly freed black slaves
2. it helped to provide food for former slaves
3. helped former slaves to purchase land for farming
4. paid for the education of former slaves
5. set up hospitals for former slaves
6. helped former slaves find jobs
7. some Bureau agents were corrupt and incompetent

47. *Candidates can be credited in a number of ways up to a maximum of 5 marks.*

Candidates must show a causal relationship between events.

Up to **a maximum of 5 marks in total, 1 mark** should be given for each accurate, relevant reason, and a **second mark** should be given for reasons that are developed. Candidates may achieve full marks by providing five straightforward reasons, three developed reasons, or a combination of these.

Possible reasons may include:

1. clash of cultures – many white Americans saw Native Americans as savages/inferior (they thought westward expansion was their right)
2. Native Americans wanted freedom to roam/hunt; white Americans wanted to farm
3. treaties with the Native Americans broken – felt betrayed due to regularly broken promises
4. White settlers had a 'property attitude' towards land/Native Americans did not/believed that Great Spirit had created land for their care
5. Government grants to encourage gold prospecting alarmed Native Americans (Colorado & Montana in 1858/& the Black Hills in 1874)
6. many white Americans favoured setting up reservations/Native Americans objected to reservation life – not enough government support
7. White/Native American tension led to atrocities/massacres/wars (eg Fetterman massacre in 1866 Battle of Little Big Horn 1876)
8. hunting/sacred grounds disturbed by settlers/miners/railroads crossing Native American territory on the way to California and Oregon
9. destruction of buffalo herds brought further conflict – took away Native American means of supporting life on the Plains

Section 3, Context D, Hitler and Nazi Germany, 1919–1939

48. *Candidates can be credited in a number of ways up to a maximum of 5 marks.*

They may take different perspectives on the events and may describe a variety of different aspects of the events.

1 mark should be given for each accurate relevant key point of knowledge. A **second mark** should be given for each point that is developed, up to a maximum of **5 marks**. Candidates may achieve full marks by providing five straightforward points, by making three developed points, or a combination of these.

Possible points of knowledge may include:

1. Hitler's oratory skills (his ability to put into words the frustrations of millions of Germans)
2. Hitler gave people somebody to blame for their problems: Communists, Jews, etc
3. Hitler promised something for everyone/claimed he was the only person who could create jobs and end Depression
4. to a worried middle-class Hitler looked like the only person willing to take on the Communists
5. the SA Brownshirts seemed well organised and disciplined/made Hitler look like a strong leader
6. Hitler's uncompromising stance against the Treaty of Versailles/the Weimar Republic
7. Hitler's genius at propaganda (eg uniforms, Swastika etc) made him and Nazis stand out from other political parties/clear simple message that appealed to many

49. *Candidates can be credited in a number of ways up to a maximum of 4 marks.*

Candidates must make direct comparisons of the two sources, either overall or in detail. A simple comparison will indicate what points of detail or overall viewpoint they agree or disagree about and should be given **1 mark**. A developed comparison of the points of detail or overall viewpoint should be given **2 marks**. Candidates may achieve full marks by making four simple comparisons, two developed comparisons or by a combination of these.

Possible points of comparison may include:

Source A	Source B
Overall: Sources A and **B** agree about the events of the Night of the Long Knives	
units of the SS arrested the leaders of the SA	Members of the SS stormed a hotel where the SA had gathered, pulled Röhm and his henchmen from their beds and had them arrested
77 men were executed on charges of treason	Some were promptly executed
Röhm was shot	An SS officer shot Röhm at point blank range

50. *Candidates can be credited in a number of ways up to a maximum of 5 marks.*

Candidates must show a causal relationship between events.

Up to **a maximum of 5 marks in total, 1 mark** should be given for each accurate, relevant reason, and a **second mark** should be given for reasons that are developed. Candidates may achieve full marks by providing five straightforward reasons, three developed reasons, or a combination of these.

Possible reasons may include:

1. widespread fear of Nazi regime (eg Gestapo/informers/concentration camps)
2. opposition leaders were arrested or killed/many leaders fled Germany
3. many Germans supported Hitler/many people who did not actively support the Nazis just kept their views quiet
4. opposition groups were often infiltrated by the Nazis/the groups had to meet in secret
5. opposition faced difficulty in publicising their views/strict censorship of anything critical of the regime
6. little co-operation between opposition groups/left wing opposition/Communists and Socialists refused to cooperate
7. opposition groups such as the Edelweiss Pirates, Texas Band and Navaho were disorganised
8. most church groups agreed to co-operate with the Nazis
9. outspoken individuals (Bonhoeffer, Neimoller) were rounded up/no protection from the courts, if arrested would be severely punished
10. overseas assistance was lacking

51. *Candidates can be credited in a number of ways up to a maximum of 6 marks.*

Candidates must make an overall judgement about how fully the source explains the events. **1 mark** may be given for each valid point interpreted from the source or each valid point of significant omission provided.

A maximum of 2 marks may be given for answers which refer only to the source.

Possible points which may be identified in the source include:

1. schools tried to develop a loyal following for Hitler
2. geography taught pupils about the land Germany had taken away from her in 1919 and the need for Germany to have living space
3. the science curriculum was changed so shooting had to be studied as well as bridge building and the impact of poisonous gases
4. girls had a different curriculum as they studied domestic science and racial studies (both of these were to prepare young girls to be the perfect wife and mother)

Possible points of significant omission may include:

5. in racial studies girls were taught about the characteristics to look out for in a perfect husband
6. all teachers had to be vetted by local Nazi officials (any teacher considered disloyal was sacked)
7. history was based on the glory of Germany – a nationalistic approach was compulsory
8. biology became a study of the different races to 'prove' the Nazi belief in racial superiority
9. teachers were expected to attack the life style of the Jews (Anti-Semitic textbooks even for young children to increase bad feeling towards Jews)
10. PE became a very important part of the curriculum to increase fitness/RE was removed as Nazis disliked Christianity
11. maths had a military slant (eg sums about the amount of bombs an aircraft could carry)
12. Hitler's photo/Swastika flag in classroom as a constant reminder of Nazism

Section 3, Context E, Red Flag: Lenin and the Russian Revolution, 1894–1921

52. *Candidates can be credited in a number of ways **up to a maximum of 5 marks**.*

They may take different perspectives on the events and may describe a variety of different aspects of the events.

1 mark should be given for each accurate relevant key point of knowledge. A **second mark** should be given for each point that is developed, up to a maximum of **5 marks**. Candidates may achieve full marks by providing five straightforward points, by making three developed points, or a combination of these.

Possible points of knowledge may include:

1. striking factory workers in St Petersburg marched to the Winter Palace
2. the Tsar was not there but the palace and the streets around it were guarded by troops
3. the march was led by Father Gapon
4. the police had asked the marchers to go home/not to march
5. the workers wanted to petition the Tsar about their working conditions/long hours and low pay
6. the crowd was large (200,000) but peaceful
7. the crowd included women and children
8. marchers wore their Sunday clothes, sang hymns and carried icons and pictures of the Tsar
9. mounted Cossacks at the front charged at the marchers
10. soldiers opened fire, killing and injuring many

53. *Candidates can be credited in a number of ways **up to a maximum of 6 marks**.*

Candidates must make an overall judgement about how fully the source explains the events. **1 mark** may be given for

each valid point interpreted from the source or each valid point of significant omission provided.

A maximum of 2 marks may be given for answers which refer only to the source.

Possible points which may be identified in the source include:

1. expansion of health services
2. system of health insurance for workers introduced
3. 50,000 additional primary schools established
4. expansion of secondary and higher educational institutions

Possible points of significant omission may include:

5. increased land available for peasants to purchase
6. creation of Kulaks
7. land organisation commissions set up to supervise these reforms
8. abolition of the Mir's communal land ownership
9. gave peasants full civil equality
10. improvement of working conditions in factories
11. trade unions legalised
12. some regulation of the justice system introduced

54. *Candidates can be credited in a number of ways **up to a maximum of 5 marks**.*

Candidates must show a causal relationship between events.

Up to **a maximum of 5 marks in total, 1 mark** should be given for each accurate, relevant reason, and a **second mark** should be given for reasons that are developed. Candidates may achieve full marks by providing five straightforward reasons, three developed reasons, or a combination of these.

Possible reasons may include:

1. Tsar decided to take personal control of the army during the First World War so was seen as responsible for defeats
2. Tsar went to the Front and left the Tsarina in charge – she was not competent to take charge/Tsarina allowed Rasputin to influence her decision making
3. Tsarina was German and many people thought she was not fully loyal/rumours she was a German spy which lost the Tsar further support
4. heavy losses demoralised the army and soldiers became reluctant to fight for the Tsar/rising numbers of deserters
5. shortage of weapons and ammunition during First World War further demoralised troops
6. generals lost faith in the Tsar and encouraged him to abdicate
7. peasants resented the loss of their sons in the fighting/loss of their animals to the army
8. war effort devastated the economy and the Tsar was blamed for this
9. workers demonstrated about shortages and working conditions/protest strikes began/shortages of food and fuel in cities led to great discontent
10. Tsar tried to return to Petrograd but the train was stopped and he had no choice but to abdicate

55. *Candidates can be credited in a number of ways **up to a maximum of 4 marks**.*

Candidates must make direct comparisons of the two sources, either overall or in detail. A simple comparison will indicate what points of detail or overall viewpoint they agree or disagree about and should be given **1 mark**. A developed comparison of the points of detail or overall viewpoint should be given **2 marks**. Candidates may achieve full marks by making four simple comparisons, two developed comparisons or by a combination of these.

Possible points of comparison may include:

Source B	Source C
Overall: Both sources agree about the reasons for the Bolshevik victory in the Civil War	
The territory held by the Bolsheviks was a great advantage to them/their control of central areas meant shorter lines of supply and communication	The Bolsheviks held better territory/had access to railways for their communication and supply lines
The Bolsheviks were better prepared to mobilise their troops and acquire resources	The Bolsheviks won the Civil War largely because they were well prepared and disciplined
The Whites were disorganised in battle	The Whites were disorganised, lacking in the ability to properly mobilise and lead their troops

Section 3, Context F, Mussolini and Fascist Italy, 1919–1939

56. *Candidates can be credited in a number of ways **up to a maximum of 5 marks**.*

They may take different perspectives on the events and may describe a variety of different aspects of the events.

1 mark should be given for each accurate relevant key point of knowledge. A **second mark** should be given for each point that is developed, up to a maximum of **5 marks**. Candidates may achieve full marks by providing five straightforward points, by making three developed points, or a combination of these.

Possible points of knowledge may include:
1. Trade Unions were outlawed
2. the currency was re-valued in the "Battle for the Lira."
3. high tariffs were placed on foreign imports
4. The Battle for Grain was established
5. Battle for Land to make marshland useable for farming eg the Pontine Marshes
6. The Ministry of Corporations was established, headed by Giuseppe Bottai
7. Government investment to create employment and modernise industry eg electrification of railways, growth of car industry
8. paid national holidays were introduced in 1938

57. **Specific marking instructions for this question**

*Candidates can be credited in a number of ways **up to a maximum of 4 marks**.*

Candidates must make direct comparisons of the two sources, either overall or in detail. A simple comparison will indicate what points of detail or overall viewpoint they agree or disagree about and should be given **1 mark**. A developed comparison of the points of detail or overall viewpoint should be given **2 marks**. Candidates may achieve full marks by making four simple comparisons, two developed comparisons or by a combination of these.

Possible points of comparison may include:

Source A	Source B
Overall: The sources disagree about the effectiveness of Fascist propaganda	
Mussolini was portrayed as athletic, strong and courageous and most Italians believed this	Few Italians believed the ridiculous claims that Mussolini was a brilliant athlete and musician
The Fascist regime was very successful in controlling the output of radio and cinema	While the Fascist regime did its best to control the media, in reality Italians watched American films which certainly did not support Fascist ideas
One admirer of him was the British Foreign Secretary, Austen Chamberlain, who was widely reported as saying that Mussolini was "a wonderful man working for the greatness of his country"	Foreigners could see through the Fascists' crude propaganda attempts and in the European press Mussolini was often presented as a figure of fun

58. *Candidates can be credited in a number of ways **up to a maximum of 6 marks**.*

Candidates must make an overall judgement about how fully the source explains the events. **1 mark** may be given for each valid point interpreted from the source or each valid point of significant omission provided.

A maximum of 2 marks may be given for answers which refer only to the source.

Possible points which may be identified in the source include:
1. his main aim was to make Italy respected as a world power
2. to achieve this he wanted to build up the Italian armed forces to make Italy feared
3. Mussolini was determined that one day Italy would be the dominant power in the Mediterranean
4. he was particularly keen to extend Italian influence in the countries of the Balkans

Possible points of significant omission may include:
5. to increase Italian influence in Albania
6. to encourage the break-up of Yugoslavia
7. to encourage Fascism in Germany
8. to take over Ethiopia/to build an Italian Empire in Africa
9. to contain Hitler's influence in Austria

59. *Candidates can be credited in a number of ways **up to a maximum of 5 marks**.*

Candidates must show a causal relationship between events.

Up to **a maximum of 5 marks in total**, **1 mark** should be given for each accurate, relevant reason, and a **second mark** should be given for reasons that are developed. Candidates may achieve full marks by providing five straightforward reasons, three developed reasons, or a combination of these.

Possible reasons may include:
1. opposition groups were weakened by their inability to unite on a common platform
2. opposition parties banned after 1926

3. opponents were afraid of imprisonment in concentration camps
4. Mussolini was popular amongst many people
5. opposition received relatively little publicity as loyal journalists received extra pay in the form of government grants
6. the regime was able to portray opposition as unpatriotic
7. people were afraid of the Blackshirts/secret police and this ensured Italians obeyed Mussolini
8. Lateran Treaty neutralised opposition from RC Church and its members

Section 3, Context G, Free at Last? Civil Rights in the USA, 1918–1968

60. *Candidates can be credited in a number of ways **up to a maximum of 4 marks**.*

Candidates must make direct comparisons of the two sources, either overall or in detail. A simple comparison will indicate what points of detail or overall viewpoint they agree or disagree about and should be given **1 mark**. A developed comparison of the points of detail or overall viewpoint should be given **2 marks**. Candidates may achieve full marks by making four simple comparisons, two developed comparisons or by a combination of these.

Possible points of comparison may include:

Source A	Source B
Overall: The sources agree about the activities of the Ku Klux Klan	
Dressed in their white hoods the Klan were very frightening – they looked like ghosts!	As far as I could see they were all disguised, with white sheets pulled over their heads
They sneaked around at night when us blacks were in our beds	The Klan came to my house about ten o'clock. I was in bed at that time fast asleep
The Klansmen tied up the blacks that they caught and beat them/They left their victims with their hands tied in the air and the blood streaming out of their wounds	They took me out into the yard they struck me three times over the head with a pistol

61. *Candidates can be credited in a number of ways **up to a maximum of 6 marks**.*

Candidates must make an overall judgement about how fully the source explains the events. **1 mark** may be given for each valid point interpreted from the source or each valid point of significant omission provided.

A maximum of 2 marks may be given for answers which refer only to the source.

Possible points which may be identified in the source include:
1. soldiers in World War II experienced life in a more equal society when abroad and were determined to fight against discrimination when they returned
2. black Americans were better educated than previous generations and therefore better equipped to challenge discrimination
3. the success of the Montgomery Bus Boycott encouraged others to become involved in the fight for civil rights

4. the leadership of civil rights campaigner Martin Luther King inspired others to join the civil rights campaign

Possible points of significant omission may include:
5. World War II had been fought against the racism of Nazi Germany for the supposed freedom of all Americans, leading to a growth in support for civil rights for black Americans
6. influence of 'Double V' campaign encouraged greater demands for civil rights
7. organisations such as the NAACP were effective in highlighting the discrimination faced by black Americans and in attracting the support of black and white Americans in the movement for black civil rights
8. the support of federal government in ending segregation, such as at Central High School in Little Rock, encouraged black Americans to believe that their demands would not be ignored
9. civil rights campaigns, such as at the Marches on Birmingham and Washington, attracted great media publicity/further fuelled demands for change

62. *Candidates can be credited in a number of ways **up to a maximum of 5 marks**.*

They may take different perspectives on the events and may describe a variety of different aspects of the events.

1 mark should be given for each accurate relevant key point of knowledge. A **second mark** should be given for each point that is developed, up to a maximum of **5 marks**. Candidates may achieve full marks by providing five straightforward points, by making three developed points, or a combination of these.

Possible points of knowledge may include:
1. nine black students were encouraged to enrol at Central High School by the NAACP
2. The Governor of Arkansas, Orval Faubus, was strongly opposed to desegregation and sent State troopers to the school to prevent the black students from entering
3. a mob of white people also gathered outside awaiting the arrival of the black students
4. the first black student to attempt to enter the building was Elizabeth Eckford/she was faced with verbal abuse from white protestors outside the school
5. President Eisenhower ordered Governor Faubus to remove the State troopers
6. President Eisenhower sent in federal troops to protect the black students and ensure their safe entry to the school
7. the federal troops stayed for a year and even patrolled the corridors of Central High School
8. despite the presence of the troops the black students faced verbal and physical abuse from white students at Central High School

63. *Candidates can be credited in a number of ways **up to a maximum of 5 marks**.*

Candidates must show a causal relationship between events.

Up to a **maximum of 5 marks in total**, **1 mark** should be given for each accurate, relevant reason, and a **second mark** should be given for reasons that are developed. Candidates may achieve full marks by providing five straightforward reasons, three developed reasons, or a combination of these.

Possible reasons may include:
1. predominantly white police forces led to resentment/ riots were sparked by police actions which were perceived by many black Americans to be unfair
2. discontent resulting from high levels of poverty/ unemployment in ghettos/those that did have work were frustrated that they earned so little
3. housing in the ghetto was overcrowded and of poor quality which further fuelled resentment amongst black Americans
4. black Americans were angry at the lack of health services in the ghetto
5. frustration at the lack of investment in ghetto schools/low educational standards which meant that black Americans saw no way out of the ghetto
6. high crime rates in the ghetto led to even greater feelings of despair
7. citizens of the ghettos were angry at a government which they believed to have ignored their needs for far too long
8. radical groups (eg the Black Panthers) encouraged direct action

Section 3, Context H, Appeasement and the Road to War, 1918–1939

64. *Candidates can be credited in a number of ways up to a maximum of 5 marks.*

Candidates must show a causal relationship between events.

Up to a **maximum of 5 marks in total**, **1 mark** should be given for each accurate, relevant reason, and a **second mark** should be given for reasons that are developed. Candidates may achieve full marks by providing five straightforward reasons, three developed reasons, or a combination of these.

Possible reasons may include:
1. many felt that the military terms of the Treaty of Versailles had been too harsh and Germany should be allowed to rearm
2. Hitler's claims that rearmament was merely required for security, helped soften opinion against German rearmament
3. Hitler's offer to disarm should other countries do so convinced others that military action was not required to halt German rearmament
4. cuts in defence spending and the weakness of the British armed forces restricted the opportunity for military action
5. given the horrors of World War One, there was little sign that British public opinion would have supported military action against Hitler
6. there was a thriving peace movement in Britain which further reduced support for military action
7. many within Britain saw a strong Germany as a useful barrier against the spread of communism and therefore supported German rearmament
8. the construction of the Maginot Line gave the French a defensive mentality and a sense of security that reduced fears of German rearmament

65. *Candidates can be credited in a number of ways up to a maximum of 5 marks.*

They may take different perspectives on the events and may describe a variety of different aspects of the events.

1 mark should be given for each accurate relevant key point of knowledge. A **second mark** should be given for each point that is developed, up to a maximum of **5 marks**. Candidates may achieve full marks by providing five straightforward points, by making three developed points, or a combination of these.

Possible points of knowledge may include:
1. the Austrian Nazi Party led by Seyss-Inquart had embarked on a series of activities which included mass demonstrations and bomb attacks
2. Chancellor Schuschnigg of Austria asked to meet Hitler to discuss the activities of the Austrian Nazis/Schuschnigg travelled to Berchtesgaden to meet Hitler
3. Schuschnigg expected to receive answers to his complaints about the Austrian Nazis but instead faced a display of temper, verbal aggression and threats from Hitler/Hitler demanded that Austrian Nazis be given important posts in the Austrian government and threatened to invade Austria if Schuschnigg did not agree
4. on his return to Austria, Schuschnigg decided to hold a plebiscite to ask the Austrian people if they wanted Austria to remain independent from Germany/Hitler was furious and plans were put in place for the invasion of Austria by Germany
5. Hitler demanded Schuschnigg's resignation and the cancellation of the plebiscite
6. Schuschnigg resigned and was replaced by Seyss-Inquart
7. Seyss-Inquart promptly invited the German Army in to Austria on the premise that they were required to help maintain law and order
8. on 12 March 1938, German soldiers crossed the border into Austria unopposed
9. German soldiers were greeted by crowds who cheered and threw flowers/Hitler himself received a rousing reception as he entered Linz in an open-topped Mercedes
10. The following day a new law was announced which incorporated Austria into the German Reich

66. *Candidates can be credited in a number of ways up to a maximum of 6 marks.*

Candidates must make an overall judgement about how fully the source explains the events. **1 mark** may be given for each valid point interpreted from the source or each valid point of significant omission provided.

A maximum of 2 marks may be given for answers which refer only to the source.

Possible points which may be identified in the source include:
1. the main reason was the invasion of Czechoslovakia which proved that Hitler was a liar and that he did not just want land where Germans lived
2. many were influenced by Churchill's speeches which meant appeasement was losing the support of the British people
3. Kristallnacht proved that the Nazi regime was evil and ought to be resisted
4. Rearmament had strengthened Britain's armed forces too and gave Chamberlain the confidence to tackle Nazi aggression

Possible points of significant omission may include:
5. the Pact of Steel showed that appeasement had failed to satisfy Hitler and that he was planning for war
6. the Oxford by-election showed that there were many British people who did not agree with appeasing Hitler and who would support military action against Nazi aggression
7. Fascists were growing in power across Europe – Franco came to power in Spain in February 1939 – and many felt that they had to be stopped
8. by March 1939, Britain was better prepared to protect its civilians against German attacks (eg a quarter of a million free air raid shelters are given to Londoners)

67. *Candidates can be credited in a number of ways up to a maximum of 4 marks.*

Candidates must make direct comparisons of the two sources, either overall or in detail. A simple comparison will indicate what points of detail or overall viewpoint they agree or disagree about and should be given **1 mark**. A developed comparison of the points of detail or overall viewpoint should be given **2 marks**. Candidates may achieve full marks by making four simple comparisons, two developed comparisons or by a combination of these.

Possible points of comparison may include:

Source B	Source C
Overall: The sources agree about the reasons why Stalin signed the Nazi-Soviet Non-Aggression Pact	
By signing the pact the Soviet Union gained time to prepare its defences against a future German attack	The pact gave the Soviet Union time to prepare for eventual German invasion
Stalin also gained the opportunity to take back lands Russia lost in the aftermath of the First World War	The chance to extend Soviet control over lands from which Russia had been excluded since the end of the First World War was another factor
The half-hearted attempt of the British to come to an agreement with the Soviet Union was another factor in Stalin's decision	The British were unenthusiastic about a possible Anglo-Soviet agreement, and this encouraged Stalin to sign the Nazi-Soviet Pact

Section 3, Context I, World War II, 1939–1945

68. *Candidates can be credited in a number of ways up to a maximum of 6 marks.*

Candidates must make an overall judgement about how fully the source explains the events. **1 mark** may be given for each valid point interpreted from the source or each valid point of significant omission provided.

A maximum of 2 marks may be given for answers which refer only to the source.

Possible points which may be identified in the source include:
1. Japan became increasingly angry with America for cutting off its oil supplies.
2. Japan was also determined to push American influence out of the Pacific
3. the attack was also intended to damage US military strength
4. Japan was confident of winning because the Japanese had rehearsed the attack for a year until they achieved an 80% hit rate

Possible points of significant omission may include:
1. Japan hoped to seize control in Asia and the Pacific and extend its Empire
2. the entire US Pacific fleet could be destroyed at Pearl Harbour giving Japan the upper hand
3. Japan hoped to crush US morale by destroying its prestigious naval fleet
4. Japan was angered after the First World War when the US placed immigration restrictions on it

69. *Candidates can be credited in a number of ways up to a maximum of 5 marks.*

They may take different perspectives on the events and may describe a variety of different aspects of the events.

1 mark should be given for each accurate relevant key point of knowledge. A **second mark** should be given for each point that is developed, up to a maximum of **5 marks**. Candidates may achieve full marks by providing five straightforward points, by making three developed points, or a combination of these.

Possible points of knowledge may include:
1. confiscation of Jewish property and businesses
2. Jews made to wear the Star of David
3. ghettos created for Jews in Poland and Eastern Europe
4. work camps, detention camps, transfer camps and concentration camps set up around Europe for the internment of Jews, gypsies, homosexuals, other religious minorities, asocials
5. in Eastern Europe mobile killing units were dispatched to eliminate Jews eg Lithuania, Latvia, Ukraine, Romania,
6. mobile gas chambers in vans appeared in Eastern occupied territories from late 1941 onwards
7. mass deportation of Jews and other prisoners from Western Europe to Eastern camps took place from 1942 onwards
8. liquidation of the ghettos
9. euthanasia of some minorities (eg the disabled)
10. used as slave labour

70. *Candidates can be credited in a number of ways up to a maximum of 4 marks.*

Candidates must make direct comparisons of the two sources, either overall or in detail. A simple comparison will indicate what points of detail or overall viewpoint they agree or disagree about and should be given **1 mark**. A developed comparison of the points of detail or overall viewpoint should be given **2 marks**. Candidates may achieve full marks by making four simple comparisons, two developed comparisons or by a combination of these.

Possible points of comparison may include:

Source B	Source C
Overall: The sources agree about collaboration in Nazi occupied Europe	
In many cases it was simply a way to survive such as doing the laundry of German soldiers to earn extra food for your family.	Other examples of collaboration involved civilians working for the Germans in order to earn extra money or gain extra food rations.
Others were more actively involved by informing the Germans of 'enemies' within the community.	Collaboration on a large scale occurred in Vichy France where the authorities supplied information to help the Nazis round up 'undesirables'.
Then there were those who supported the Nazi regime such as the local civilians and police who were recruited into the SS *death squads.*	Over 33,000 Jews were slaughtered there in September 1941 by Nazi SS forces, assisted by the Ukrainian police.

71. *Candidates can be credited in a number of ways **up to a maximum of 5 marks**.*

Candidates must show a causal relationship between events.

Up to a **maximum of 5 marks in total, 1 mark** should be given for each accurate, relevant reason, and a **second mark** should be given for reasons that are developed. Candidates may achieve full marks by providing five straightforward reasons, three developed reasons, or a combination of these.

Possible reasons may include:
1. the Allies had complete naval and air superiority of the area prior to the landings which allowed them to deliver supplies
2. Allied deception plans were successful because the German High command believed the attack would happen at Pas-de-Calais
3. strategic bombing of the area behind the lines prevented German Panzer forces being deployed to Normandy
4. the use of floating harbours (Mulberries) which were brought over from England by the Allies allowed more troops and supplies to be transported to the beach heads
5. Pluto, the undersea pipe line was able to deliver fuel to allow for the sustained attack on the beach heads and further into German occupied territory
6. the landing of airborne forces hindered a German counter-attack
7. the German Atlantic Wall was incomplete
8. assistance of French resistance (eg destroying German communications)

Section 3, Context J, The Cold War, 1945–1989

72. *Candidates can be credited in a number of ways **up to a maximum of 5 marks**.*

They may take different perspectives on the events and may describe a variety of different aspects of the events.

1 mark should be given for each accurate relevant key point of knowledge. A **second mark** should be given for each point that is developed, up to a maximum of **5 marks**. Candidates may achieve full marks by providing five straightforward points, by making three developed points, or a combination of these.

Possible points of knowledge may include:
1. the Soviets were disliked because they denied democratic freedoms
2. many hated Soviet control (eg the activities of the secret police)
3. many disliked Soviet control of education
4. many were angry at the suppression of religion (eg the Catholic Church)
5. many resented the Red Army as foreign occupiers
6. people were disappointed that Soviet central control had stifled economic growth/lowered living standards
7. some Hungarians supported the Soviets as they were committed Communists

73. *Candidates can be credited in a number of ways **up to a maximum of 5 marks**.*

Candidates must show a causal relationship between events.

Up to a **maximum of 5 marks in total, 1 mark** should be given for each accurate, relevant reason, and a **second mark** should be given for reasons that are developed. Candidates may achieve full marks by providing five straightforward reasons, three developed reasons, or a combination of these.

Possible reasons may include:
1. to prevent East Germans moving to the West
2. to reduce the possibility of flashpoints in Berlin which could cause war

3. to limit Western spying
4. to stop the embarrassment of people appearing to choose Capitalism over Communism
5. to shore up support for Communism elsewhere in Eastern Europe
6. to close the only gap in the Iron Curtain

74. *Candidates can be credited in a number of ways **up to a maximum of 6 marks**.*

Candidates must make an overall judgement about how fully the source explains the events. **1 mark** may be given for each valid point interpreted from the source or each valid point of significant omission provided.

A maximum of 2 marks may be given for answers which refer only to the source.

Possible points which may be identified in the source include:
1. they felt it was not America's job to fight a war thousands of miles from home
2. many remembered the Second World War and did not want a repeat of the casualties suffered in this conflict
3. by 1967, as many as 160 American soldiers were being killed every week
4. some Americans opposed the conflict as they felt its huge cost meant the government was unable to spend money on health and housing

Possible points of significant omission may include:
1. many thought America was trying to suppress the democratic wishes of the Vietnamese people
2. many were uncomfortable supporting the corrupt South Vietnamese regime
3. the revelation of US involvement in atrocities such as the My Lai massacre caused unease
4. people were uncomfortable with aerial bombing of civilians
5. many felt the Vietcong had the support of the Vietnamese public
6. US media contributed to changing attitudes to the conflict
7. many afraid that the war was spreading to Laos, Cambodia etc

75. *Candidates can be credited in a number of ways **up to a maximum of 4 marks**.*

Candidates must make direct comparisons of the two sources, either overall or in detail. A simple comparison will indicate what points of detail or overall viewpoint they agree or disagree about and should be given **1 mark**. A developed comparison of the points of detail or overall viewpoint should be given **2 marks**. Candidates may achieve full marks by making four simple comparisons, two developed comparisons or by a combination of these.

Possible points of comparison may include:

Source B	Source C
Overall: The sources agree about the aims of the policy of Glasnost	
His intention was to give a boost to the Soviet economy, which was performing badly	the hope was that Glasnost could help strengthen the Soviet economy
The aim of Glasnost was to allow open discussion of social and economic issues	He wanted to find new solutions to problems by allowing people to express their views freely
Gorbachev hoped this would strengthen the Communist system	Gorbachev remained a committed Communist and hoped that Glasnost would increase support for the system

NATIONAL 5 HISTORY
2017 SPECIMEN QUESTION PAPER

Section 1, Context A, The Wars of Independence, 1286–1328

1. *Candidates can be credited in a number of ways up to a maximum of 5 marks.*

Candidates must evaluate the extent to which a source is useful by commenting on evidence such as the author, type of source, purpose, timing, content or omission. For a mark to be awarded, the candidate must identify an aspect of the source <u>and</u> make a comment which shows why this aspect makes the source more or less useful.

A **maximum of 4 marks** can be awarded for evaluative comments relating to the author, type of source, purpose and timing. A **maximum of 2 marks** may be awarded for evaluative comments relating to the content of the source. A **maximum of 2 marks** may be awarded for evaluative comments relating to points of significant omission.

Examples of aspects of the source and relevant comments:

Aspect	Possible comment(s)
Author: Modern historian	Useful because he has expert knowledge/has studied a range of relevant sources
Type of Source: Textbook	Useful because it contains straightforward information without bias/well researched
Purpose: To inform	Useful because it provides detailed information
Timing: 2011	Useful because it has the benefit of hindsight

Content	Possible comment(s)
Balliol argued this because he was descended from the eldest daughter in the family of David, Earl of Huntingdon, brother of King William the Lion.	Useful as this is accurate (as Balliol claimed being descended from David's eldest daughter he should be the next king).
According to Balliol it didn't matter that he was a generation younger than Bruce because the feudal law of primogeniture always supported the eldest line of a family.	Useful as this is accurate (as Balliol argued that the feudal law of primogeniture meant he should be Scotland's next king).
Bruce argued the feudal law of primogeniture did not apply to kingdoms.	Useful as this is accurate (as Bruce said the law of primogeniture didn't apply when determining Scotland's next king).

Possible points of significant omission may include:
1. Bruce said that Imperial Law supported him because he was one generation closer to the Earl of Huntingdon's family than Balliol
2. many nobles thought that they should be the next ruler of Scotland (eg thirteen competitors/factionalism amongst the Scottish nobility over the succession)
3. concerns that the succession problem could threaten law and order in Scotland
4. fears that a civil war could break out over the succession issue.

Any other valid point of omission

2. *Candidates can be credited in a number of ways up to a maximum of 6 marks.*

Candidates must make a number of points that make the issue plain or clear, for example by showing connections between factors or causal relationships between events or ideas. These should be key reasons but there is no need for any evaluation or prioritising of these reasons.

Up to a maximum of 6 marks in total, **1 mark** should be awarded for each accurate, relevant reason, and a **second mark** should be awarded for reasons that are developed. Candidates may achieve full marks by providing six straightforward reasons, three developed reasons (or any combination of these).

Possible reasons may include:
1. Balliol had accepted Edward as his overlord, so weakening his authority
2. he was inexperienced in Scottish affairs as he was essentially an English noble
3. Balliol was unable to stop Edward interfering in the government of Scotland
4. Edward undermined him by summoning him to appear at court/before his parliament
5. Edward heard Scottish legal appeals which angered the Scots
6. Edward sent direct orders to the Scottish nobles which undermined Balliol as king
7. Edward forced him to appoint an Englishman as his Chancellor, further humiliating him
8. Balliol had been defeated by Edward at the Battle of Dunbar, which weakened his power
9. Edward had stripped John Balliol of his crown and title publicly, so humiliating him
10. Edward took Balliol away as a prisoner, leaving Scotland without a king
11. Bruce and other nobles had never supported Balliol, which weakened his authority
12. the Community of the Realm of Scotland made John Balliol share power with 12 Scottish Guardians, which showed little faith in him.

Any other valid reason

3. *Candidates can be credited in a number of ways up to a maximum of 4 marks.*

They may take different perspectives on the events and may describe a variety of different aspects of the events. Candidates must make a number of relevant, factual points. These should be key points. These do not have to be in any particular order.

1 mark should be awarded for each accurate relevant key point of knowledge. A **second mark** should be awarded for each point that is developed, **up to a maximum of 4 marks.** Candidates may achieve full marks by providing four straightforward points, by making two developed points (or any combination of these).

Possible points of knowledge may include:
1. murdered Sheriff of Lanark which made him an outlaw and forced him into open rebellion
2. his use of guerrilla tactics was very successful against the English
3. he united people under his leadership as Guardian
4. he organised the army of Scotland
5. worked with Andrew Moray to defeat the English at the Battle of Stirling Bridge
6. tried to establish trade with the Low Countries
7. when he was defeated at the Battle of Falkirk he resigned the Guardianship
8. he continued to resist Edward till he was executed.

Any other valid point of knowledge

4. *Candidates can be credited in a number of ways up to a maximum of 6 marks.*

Candidates must make a judgement about the extent to which the source provides a full description or explanation of a given event or development.

Up to a maximum of 6 marks in total, 1 mark should be awarded for each valid point selected from the source or each valid point of significant omission provided.

Candidates should be awarded up to 3 marks for their identification of points from the source which support their judgement. Candidates should be awarded up to 4 marks for their identification of points of significant omission, based on their own knowledge, that support their judgement. A maximum of 2 marks may be awarded for answers in which no judgement has been made or which refer only to the source.

Possible points which may be identified from the source include:

1. gave the much larger English army no room to move because they were surrounded by marshes and streams
2. Bruce decided to take advantage of this mistake and to attack them
3. the English were so jammed together and so tangled up that their leaders struggled to organise any defence
4. they lost all confidence in Edward II for leading them into this trap.

Possible points of significant omission may include:

5. Bruce organised the Scots into schiltrons which was an effective defensive formation
6. Bruce chose the higher ground which gave the Scots a positional advantage
7. Bruce trained his schiltrons to move which allowed them to respond to attacks
8. the death of de Bohun demoralised the English
9. the English had been arguing among themselves and could not agree on a plan
10. many English were trapped by the ditches by the Pelstream and Bannock burns and drowned.

Any other valid point of significant omission

5. *Candidates can be credited in a number of ways up to a maximum of 4 marks.*

Candidates must interpret the evidence and make direct comparisons between sources. Candidates are expected to compare content directly on a point-by-point basis. They may compare the details in the sources and/or compare the viewpoints overall.

A simple comparison will indicate what points of detail or viewpoint the sources agree or disagree on and should be awarded 1 mark. A developed comparison of the points of detail or overall viewpoint should be awarded a second mark. Candidates may achieve full marks by making four simple comparisons, two developed comparisons (or by any combination of these).

Possible points of comparison may include:

Source C	Source D
Overall: The sources disagree about how much support Bruce had in 1320.	
...all the Scots thought Robert Bruce was their rightful king.	...some Scottish nobles were plotting against Robert Bruce.

(...by saving Scotland from being taken over by England) he proved that he was worthy of being King of Scotland.	(They felt he was a ruthless thug who had murdered his main rival in a church and) so he was unworthy of being King of Scots.
They argued Bruce had royal blood.	Other Scottish nobles claimed their blood ties meant they were more closely related to the Scottish royal family than Robert Bruce.

Section 1, Context B, Mary Queen of Scots and the Scottish Reformation, 1542–1587

6. *Candidates can be credited in a number of ways up to a maximum of 4 marks.*

They may take different perspectives on the events and may describe a variety of different aspects of the events. Candidates must make a number of relevant, factual points. These should be key points. These do not have to be in any particular order.

1 mark should be awarded for each accurate relevant key point of knowledge. A second mark should be awarded for each point that is developed, up to a maximum of 4 marks. Candidates may achieve full marks by providing four straightforward points, by making two developed points (or any combination of these).

Possible points of knowledge may include:

1. the Scots broke the Treaty of Greenwich which stated that Mary would marry Edward, Henry VIII's son
2. Henry VIII ordered the Earl of Hertford to invade Scotland and burn Edinburgh
3. the English attacked Scotland and destroyed abbeys/towns in the south of Scotland
4. Battle of Pinkie Cleugh 1547 – large Scottish army defeated
5. the Palace of Holyrood in Edinburgh was looted/large parts of Edinburgh were burned/the pier at Leith in Edinburgh was destroyed
6. Berwick upon Tweed was attacked and burned
7. Scots received help from the French who sent a force to Edinburgh in 1548
8. Treaty of Haddington was signed by the Scots and French which agreed Mary would marry the heir to the French throne and Mary was then sent to France for protection.

Any other valid point of knowledge

7. *Candidates can be credited in a number of ways up to a maximum of 6 marks.*

Candidates must make a judgement about the extent to which the source provides a full description or explanation of a given event or development.

Up to a maximum of 6 marks in total, 1 mark should be awarded for each valid point selected from the source or each valid point of significant omission provided.

Candidates should be awarded up to 3 marks for their identification of points from the source which support their judgement. Candidates should be awarded up to 4 marks for their identification of points of significant omission, based on their own knowledge, that support their judgement. A maximum of 2 marks may be awarded for answers in which no judgement has been made or which refer only to the source.

Possible points which may be identified from the source include:
1. some Scots began to criticise the teachings of the Catholic Church
2. the distribution of English translations of the Bible which helped the growth of Protestantism in Scotland
3. religious pamphlets, smuggled into Scotland from Europe, also spread Protestant ideas
4. the "Good and Godly Ballads" encouraged the spread of Protestant ideas.

Possible points of significant omission may include:
5. increasing criticism of the wealth of the Catholic Church/not using its wealth properly, eg to support the poor, sick etc
6. some Scots began to resent payments to the church claiming they were excessive
7. some churchmen lived scandalous lives which brought the Catholic Church into disrepute
8. John Knox returned to Scotland and helped spread Protestantism
9. anger at the way some Protestant preachers had been treated (eg Wishart)
10. resentment of French/Catholic influence over Scotland.

Any other valid point of significant omission

8. *Candidates can be credited in a number of ways up to a maximum of 4 marks.*

Candidates must interpret the evidence and make direct comparisons between sources. Candidates are expected to compare content directly on a point-by-point basis. They may compare the details in the sources and/or compare the viewpoints overall.

A **simple comparison** will indicate what points of detail or viewpoint the sources agree or disagree on and **should be awarded 1 mark**. A **developed comparison** of the points of detail or overall viewpoint **should be awarded a second mark**. Candidates may achieve full marks by making four simple comparisons, two developed comparisons (or by any combination of these).

Possible points of comparison may include:

Source B	Source C
Overall: The sources disagree about how well Mary, Queen of Scots ruled Scotland	
...she neglected the government of Scotland.	...to begin with, Mary had been a successful ruler in Scotland/had established a successful government.
...Mary was happy to leave the running of the country to a group of Protestant nobles.	...she had defeated the Protestant nobles who challenged her authority.
...she showed little interest in the issue of religion in Scotland.	...she decided that she would tolerate Scotland's new Protestant church.

9. *Candidates can be credited in a number of ways up to a maximum of 5 marks.*

Candidates must evaluate the extent to which a source is useful by commenting on evidence such as the author, type of source, purpose, timing, content or omission. For a mark to be awarded, the candidate must identify an aspect of the source <u>and</u> make a comment which shows why this aspect makes the source more or less useful.

A **maximum of 4 marks** can be awarded for evaluative comments relating to the author, type of source, purpose

and timing. A **maximum of 2 marks** may be awarded for evaluative comments relating to the content of the source. A **maximum of 2 marks** may be awarded for evaluative comments relating to points of significant omission

Examples of aspects of the source and relevant comments:

Aspect	Possible comment(s)
Author: Modern historian	Useful because has expert knowledge/ has studied a range of relevant sources
Type of Source: Textbook	Useful because it contains straightforward information without bias/well researched
Purpose: To inform	Useful because it provides detailed information
Timing: 2007	Useful because it has the benefit of hindsight

Content	Possible comment(s)
Some Scots simply did not want to be ruled by a woman, as they believed that only men should be in positions of power.	Useful as this is accurate (as many Scots believed that a woman was too weak to rule a country properly).
Others were suspicious of Mary's religion...	Useful as this is accurate (as Mary was a Catholic while most Scots were Protestant).
...the Earl of Moray, forced her into giving up her power...	Useful as this is accurate (as Mary's brother, the Earl of Moray, made her give up the throne).

Possible points of significant omission may include:
1. many Scots blamed her for the murder of Darnley/people would not accept being ruled by a murderess
2. she had caused a scandal by marrying Bothwell shortly after the murder of Darnley
3. Mary's Protestant critics disapproved of her frivolity (criticised Mary for dancing)
4. Scottish nobles, mainly Protestant, rebelled against Mary.

Any other valid point of significant omission

10. *Candidates can be credited in a number of ways up to a maximum of 6 marks.*

Candidates must make a number of points that make the issue plain or clear, for example by showing connections between factors or causal relationships between events or ideas. These should be key reasons but there is no need for any evaluation or prioritising of these reasons.

Up to a maximum of 6 marks in total, **1 mark** should be awarded for each accurate, relevant reason, and a **second mark** should be awarded for reasons that are developed. Candidates may achieve full marks by providing six straightforward reasons, three developed reasons (or any combination of these).

Possible reasons may include:
1. Catholics plotted to kill Elizabeth and to make Mary Queen of England, which convinced English Protestants Mary was a menace
2. Mary claimed that she was the true, Catholic Queen of England, which worried English Protestants
3. Mary was Elizabeth's heir and she didn't trust Mary/saw Mary as a threat
4. Elizabeth was afraid if Mary got free she would return to Scotland where she could cause trouble for Elizabeth by making it a base for French and Roman Catholic activities

5. Mary's son, who was next in line to the English crown, was a Protestant, so Mary's death would ensure England remained Protestant
6. 1580: the Pope's policy of encouraging plots against Elizabeth persuaded many Protestants that Mary was a threat
7. 1585: after several plots, the English government passed a law stating that Mary would be executed if she was actively involved in any plot against Elizabeth
8. Mary had not been involved in any of these plots but the law was changed to make beneficiaries of plots liable to the death penalty
9. 1586: Babington contacted Mary to inform her of his plans to kill Elizabeth and help Mary to escape and Mary replied agreeing to Elizabeth's death
10. the incriminating letter was intercepted by Elizabeth's spies which proved she was plotting against Elizabeth
11. Elizabeth hesitated to execute her cousin but the death warrant was concealed amongst a pile of letters all of which Elizabeth signed.

Any other valid reason

Section 1, Context C, The Treaty of Union, 1689–1715

11. *Candidates can be credited in a number of ways **up to a maximum of 6 marks.***

Candidates must make a number of points that make the issue plain or clear, for example by showing connections between factors or causal relationships between events or ideas. These should be key reasons but there is no need for any evaluation or prioritising of these reasons.

Up to a maximum of 6 marks in total, **1 mark** should be awarded for each accurate, relevant reason, and a **second mark** should be awarded for reasons that are developed. Candidates may achieve full marks by providing six straightforward reasons, three developed reasons (or any combination of these).

Possible reasons may include:
1. Scots were excluded from trading with England's colonies which offered great wealth
2. the monarch was in England but was out of touch with the wishes of the Scots
3. many Scots, loyal to the House of Stewart, felt that King James was their rightful king
4. the wars between England and France had damaged Scottish trade with France
5. Scotland gained nothing from peace treaties at the end of these wars
6. the Scots blamed the English for the failure of the Darien Scheme as they offered no financial, military or political support
7. Queen Anne found it difficult to govern Scotland from Westminster
8. Scots accused Queen Anne of policies which were damaging to Scotland
9. the Worcester Affair turned ordinary Scots against what they regarded as English pirates
10. England feared a French threat in the future if the discontented Scots ever wanted to revive the Auld Alliance
11. the English were angry that the Scots were intruding into their colonies/markets
12. the religious differences between Scotland and England caused mistrust.

Any other valid reason

12. *Candidates can be credited in a number of ways **up to a maximum of 4 marks.***

Candidates must interpret the evidence and make direct comparisons between sources. Candidates are expected to compare content directly on a point-by-point basis. They may compare the details in the sources and/or compare the viewpoints overall.

A **simple comparison** will indicate what points of detail or viewpoint the sources agree or disagree on and **should be awarded 1 mark**. A **developed comparison** of the points of detail or overall viewpoint **should be awarded a second mark**.

Candidates may achieve full marks by making four simple comparisons, two developed comparisons (or by any combination of these).

Possible points of comparison may include:

Source A	Source B
Overall: The sources disagree about Scottish attitudes to a possible Union of the Parliaments	
Supporters of the Union saw it as a way of settling the Protestant Succession and closing the door to the Jacobite claimant to the throne.	The Jacobites encouraged opposition to the Union in the hope of restoring their king to his throne.
Other Scots saw the economic benefits of gaining access to England's colonies.	They feared that Scotland's economy would be ruined by cheap goods flooding up from England.
They weren't worried about wanting a closer relationship with England.	Many Scots disliked the idea of entering a Union with "the Auld Enemy".

13. *Candidates can be credited in a number of ways **up to a maximum of 4 marks.***

They may take different perspectives on the events and may describe a variety of different aspects of the events. Candidates must make a number of relevant, factual points. These should be key points. These do not have to be in any particular order.

1 mark should be awarded for each accurate relevant key point of knowledge. A **second mark** should be awarded for each point that is developed, **up to a maximum of 4 marks**. Candidates may achieve full marks by providing four straightforward points, by making two developed points (or any combination of these).

Possible points of knowledge may include:
1. when the draft of the treaty was made public there were riots on the streets of Scottish towns and cities
2. violent demonstrations took place outside Parliament House in Edinburgh
3. the Edinburgh mob threatened and insulted judges and Members of the Scottish Parliament
4. serious riots took place in Glasgow
5. in Glasgow, Dumfries and Lanark people had taken up arms
6. there were protests and demonstrations against the Union in many Scottish burghs
7. in Edinburgh a huge crowd marched up the High Street shouting, "No Union, No Union"
8. the Edinburgh mob threw stones at house windows which showed a light.

Any other valid point of knowledge

14. *Candidates can be credited in a number of ways up to a maximum of 6 marks.*

Candidates must make a judgement about the extent to which the source provides a full description or explanation of a given event or development.

Up to a maximum of 6 marks in total, **1 mark** should be awarded for each valid point selected from the source or each valid point of significant omission provided.

Candidates should be awarded **up to 3 marks** for their identification of points from the source which support their judgement. Candidates should be awarded **up to 4 marks** for their identification of points of significant omission, based on their own knowledge, that support their judgement. A **maximum of 2 marks** may be awarded for answers in which no judgement has been made **or** which refer only to the source.

Possible points which may be identified from the source include:

1. Hamilton however was indecisive and unreliable/he suddenly changed sides
2. there was widespread belief that, like many, Hamilton had been bribed to support the Union
3. Hamilton's activities kept the opponents of the Union disorganised
4. opponents of the Union were unable to overcome the ruthless methods used by supporters of the Union.

Possible points of significant omission may include:

5. the government had sent Argyll and then Queensberry/ secret agents, to organise and promote support for the Union
6. the government threatened Scottish trade if the Union was not passed
7. government officials in Scotland were warned they would not be paid wage arrears unless they supported the Union
8. the Church of Scotland was won over to the Union by guaranteeing its position
9. the Equivalent, which made money available to Scotland, won over many people
10. people were offered titles and jobs in return for supporting the Union.

Any other valid point of significant omission

15. *Candidates can be credited in a number of ways up to a maximum of 5 marks.*

Candidates must evaluate the extent to which a source is useful by commenting on evidence such as the author, type of source, purpose, timing, content or omission. For a mark to be awarded, the candidate must identify an aspect of the source **and** make a comment which shows why this aspect makes the source more or less useful.

A **maximum of 4 marks** can be awarded for evaluative comments relating to the author, type of source, purpose and timing. A **maximum of 2 marks** may be awarded for evaluative comments relating to the content of the source. A **maximum of 2 marks** may be awarded for evaluative comments relating to points of significant omission.

Examples of aspects of the source and relevant comments:

Aspect	Possible comment(s)
Author: Modern historian	Useful because has expert knowledge/has studied a range of relevant sources
Type of Source: Textbook	Useful because it contains straightforward information without bias/well researched

| **Purpose:** To inform | Useful because it provides detailed information |
| **Timing:** 1994 | Useful because it has the benefit of hindsight |

Content	Possible comment(s)
The Church of Scotland was outraged when patronage was reintroduced into the church and Episcopalians were to be tolerated.	Useful as this is accurate (because the reintroduction of church patronage angered the Church of Scotland)
Many Scots thought these changes also broke the terms of the Treaty of Union.	Useful as this is accurate (because Scots were disappointed with the results of the Treaty of Union and believed they'd been cheated)
They were unhappy with the introduction of the Malt Tax...	Useful as this is accurate (because Scots opposed having to pay tax on malt)

Possible points of significant omission may include

1. were soon disillusioned because the Union did not bring immediate prosperity
2. they disliked the changes in Scotland's weights, measures, money, etc
3. nobles and important politicians had left Edinburgh for London
4. some believed that English imports were ruining Scottish businesses.

Any other valid point of omission

Section 1, Context D, Migration and Empire, 1830–1939

16. *Candidates can be credited in a number of ways up to a maximum of 6 marks.*

Candidates must make a judgement about the extent to which the source provides a full description or explanation of a given event or development.

Up to a maximum of 6 marks in total, **1 mark** should be awarded for each valid point selected from the source or each valid point of significant omission provided.

Candidates should be awarded **up to 3 marks** for their identification of points from the source which support their judgement. Candidates should be awarded **up to 4 marks** for their identification of points of significant omission, based on their own knowledge, that support their judgement. A **maximum of 2 marks** may be awarded for answers in which no judgement has been made **or** which refer only to the source.

Possible points which may be identified from the source include:

1. the Irish potato famine of the mid-1840s led to a sharp increase in numbers moving to Scotland
2. others left for Scotland as some landlords evicted those who could not pay their rent
3. transport costs were cheap making it easy to travel to Scotland
4. The Irish were attracted to the west of Scotland as wages were higher than those in Ireland.

Possible points of significant omission may include:

5. some Irish already had family in Scotland who helped them with the cost of emigrating/encouraged them to come to Scotland

6. poverty of Irish tenants encouraged them to leave home
7. work was available for unskilled workers in factories eg jute mills and cotton mills
8. building railways and canals/work in the coal and iron ore mines provided employment for many Irish
9. seasonal labour on farms also provided a lot of jobs for the Irish
10. housing was available/often better (not 'good') in Scotland's growing towns and cities.

Any other valid point of significant omission

17. *Candidates can be credited in a number of ways* ***up to a maximum of 4 marks.***

They may take different perspectives on the events and may describe a variety of different aspects of the events. Candidates must make a number of relevant, factual points. These should be key points. These do not have to be in any particular order.

1 mark should be awarded for each accurate relevant key point of knowledge. A **second mark** should be awarded for each point that is developed, **up to a maximum of 4 marks.** Candidates may achieve full marks by providing four straightforward points, by making two developed points (or any combination of these).

Possible points of knowledge may include:
1. Empire cultures and religions brought to Scotland
2. provided raw materials for factories, such as cotton, jute and sugar
3. many jobs were created in manufacturing industries to produce goods for export to the Empire eg locomotives and ships
4. trade with the Empire increased the wealth/population of cities such as Glasgow
5. profits from the Empire led to impressive new public buildings and mansions being built
6. provided jobs for Scots in the Empire (such as in the armed forces and civil service)
7. immigrant workers provided a cheap labour force which kept wages down
8. later the Empire became a source of competition to Scottish economy: farm produce from Australia, Jute mill development in India, etc.

Any other valid point of knowledge

18. *Candidates can be credited in a number of ways* ***up to a maximum of 4 marks.***

Candidates must interpret the evidence and make direct comparisons between sources. Candidates are expected to compare content directly on a point-by-point basis. They may compare the details in the sources and/or compare the viewpoints overall.

A **simple comparison** will indicate what points of detail or viewpoint the sources agree or disagree on and **should be awarded 1 mark.** A **developed comparison** of the points of detail or overall viewpoint **should be awarded a second mark.** Candidates may achieve full marks by making four simple comparisons, two developed comparisons (or by any combination of these).

Possible points of comparison may include:

Source B	Source C
Overall: The sources disagree about Scottish attitudes to Irish immigration.	
Newspapers were eager to describe the violent activities of groups of Irish men.	...the Irish are of good character and behave very well.
They were also blamed for being dirty and responsible for spreading disease.	When they first came over they were, in general, very clean.
...Irish however were accused of being too lazy to work (and for relying on charity)	...the Irish are always ready to work hard for their pay.

19. *Candidates can be credited in a number of ways* ***up to a maximum of 5 marks.***

Candidates must evaluate the extent to which a source is useful by commenting on evidence such as the author, type of source, purpose, timing, content or omission. For a mark to be awarded, the candidate must identify an aspect of the source <u>and</u> make a comment which shows why this aspect makes the source more or less useful.

A **maximum of 4 marks** can be awarded for evaluative comments relating to the author, type of source, purpose and timing. A **maximum of 2 marks** may be awarded for evaluative comments relating to the content of the source. A **maximum of 2 marks** may be awarded for evaluative comments relating to points of significant omission.

Examples of aspects of the source and relevant comments:

Aspect	Possible comment(s)
Author: Modern historian	Useful because has expert knowledge/ has studied a range of relevant sources
Type of Source: Textbook	Useful because it contains straightforward information without bias/well researched
Purpose: To inform	Useful because it provides detailed information
Timing: 1992	Useful because it has the benefit of hindsight

Content	Possible comment(s)
Many Scots had farms which they could sell to raise funds for emigration.	Useful as this is accurate (many Scots farmers sold their land to pay for the cost of emigrating)
...many emigrants were happy to help pay for relatives to come and join them.	Useful as this is accurate (as Scots who had prospered were willing to help pay for other family members to emigrate)
The journey became much easier and cheaper with the development of faster and more efficient steam ships.	Useful as this is accurate (as improvements in steam ships made the journey more affordable for Scots)

Possible points of significant omission may include
1. landowners, especially in Highlands, were willing to help pay for their tenants to emigrate/landlords wrote off rent arrears so that emigrants had money to emigrate
2. various Scottish societies provided support for poorer Scots to emigrate
3. the government gave help after the First World War to those who wanted to emigrate/1922 Empire Settlement Act – money for travel, trading and land purchase
4. charities such as Barnardos, Quarriers and the YMCA assisted with passages.

Any other valid point of significant omission

20. *Candidates can be credited in a number of ways* ***up to a maximum of 6 marks.***

Candidates must make a number of points that make the issue plain or clear, for example by showing connections between factors or causal relationships between events or ideas. These should be key reasons but there is no need for any evaluation or prioritising of these reasons.

Up to a maximum of 6 marks in total, **1 mark** should be awarded for each accurate, relevant reason, and a **second mark** should be awarded for reasons that are developed. Candidates may achieve full marks by providing six straightforward reasons, three developed reasons (or any combination of these).

Possible reasons may include:

1. Scottish emigrants usually had a good level of education which helped them succeed
2. most Scots spoke English which helped them settle in the USA and countries of the Empire
3. some Scots had great financial and business skills which they used to develop a variety of industries
4. many Scots brought capital with them to start farms and businesses
5. they made their fortune from developing businesses, banks and trading companies
6. Scottish farmers were successful as they were skilled at working more difficult land/developed sheep farming in Australia
7. Scots were entrepreneurial and had a reputation for hard work which helped them succeed
8. Scots were imaginative and came up with new ideas eg William Davidson organised the first shipment of frozen meat from New Zealand to Britain
9. Scots founded many industries eg paper-making in New Zealand (credit examples such as wool/brewing/steel) which made them rich
10. money from Scottish banks was skilfully invested in business and industry
11. Scottish emigrants helped each other by providing work and housing
12. tradesmen such as stonemasons were in demand to work in the building industry in USA.

Any other valid reason

Section 1, Context E, The Era of the Great War, 1900–1928

21. *Candidates can be credited in a number of ways up to a maximum of 4 marks.*

They may take different perspectives on the events and may describe a variety of different aspects of the events. Candidates must make a number of relevant, factual points. These should be key points. These do not have to be in any particular order.

1 mark should be awarded for each accurate relevant key point of knowledge. A **second mark** should be awarded for each point that is developed, **up to a maximum of 4 marks.** Candidates may achieve full marks by providing four straightforward points, by making two developed points (or any combination of these).

Possible points of knowledge may include:

1. poison gas was used to cause confusion/disable enemy during an attack
2. gas was unreliable as a change in wind direction could blow it back
3. chlorine gas caused choking, while mustard gas caused burns and blindness
4. the development of gas masks helped protect soldiers from poison gas

5. tanks crushed barbed wire/provided cover for advancing soldiers
6. tanks frequently broke down, ran out of fuel or got stuck in the mud
7. range and speed of machine guns meant they could kill large numbers of attacking soldiers
8. aircraft could spot enemy activity/take aerial photographs to help plan more effective attacks/drop bombs on enemy trenches.

Any other valid point of knowledge

22. *Candidates can be credited in a number of ways up to a maximum of 5 marks.*

Candidates must evaluate the extent to which a source is useful by commenting on evidence such as the author, type of source, purpose, timing, content or omission. For a mark to be awarded, the candidate must identify an aspect of the source <u>and</u> make a comment which shows why this aspect makes the source more or less useful.

A **maximum of 4 marks** can be awarded for evaluative comments relating to the author, type of source, purpose and timing. A **maximum of 2 marks** may be awarded for evaluative comments relating to the content of the source. A **maximum of 2 marks** may be awarded for evaluative comments relating to points of significant omission.

Examples of aspects of the source and relevant comments:

Aspect	Possible comment(s)
Author: Modern historian	Useful because has expert knowledge/ has studied a range of relevant sources
Type of Source: Textbook	Useful because it contains straightforward information without bias/well researched
Purpose: To inform	Useful because it provides detailed information
Timing: 1984	Useful because it has the benefit of hindsight

Content	Possible comment(s)
British Summer Time was introduced to give more daylight working hours.	Useful as this is accurate (the government did this to increase daylight working hours and so increase food production)
Pub opening hours were limited to prevent drunkenness.	Useful as this is accurate (as the government restricted drinking hours to try and reduce drunkenness damaging war production)
(High casualties on the Western Front) led to conscription, forcing unmarried men between 18 and 41 to join the armed forces,	Useful as this is accurate (the government made it compulsory for single men between 18–41 to fight for their country)

Possible points of significant omission may include:

1. the government censored newspapers to keep morale high
2. restrictions were imposed on aliens (foreign citizens) to protect Britain from spies
3. rationing was introduced to ensure everyone got a fair share of the food
4. government took greater control over essential industries to ensure strikes didn't damage essential war production.

Any other valid point of significant omission

23. *Candidates can be credited in a number of ways up to a maximum of 4 marks.*

Candidates must interpret the evidence and make direct comparisons between sources. Candidates are expected to compare content directly on a point-by-point basis. They may compare the details in the sources and/or compare the viewpoints overall.

A **simple comparison** will indicate what points of detail or viewpoint the sources agree or disagree on and **should be awarded 1 mark.** A **developed comparison** of the points of detail or overall viewpoint **should be awarded a second mark.** Candidates may achieve full marks by making four simple comparisons, two developed comparisons (or by any combination of these).

Possible points of comparison may include:

Source B	Source C
Overall: The sources disagree about the impact of the First World War on employment opportunities for women	
From the outbreak of war there was a steady increase in the female workforce...	At the beginning of the war, thousands of women were unemployed.
The vital role they played in the war helped change many people's attitude to women.	Despite women's contribution to the war effort, it didn't change deep-seated beliefs many people had about the role of women.
When the war ended, many women voluntarily gave up their jobs to men returning from the fighting.	Many women wanted to keep their jobs but when the fighting ended, large numbers of women were sacked.

24. *Candidates can be credited in a number of ways up to a maximum of 6 marks.*

Candidates must make a judgement about the extent to which the source provides a full description or explanation of a given event or development.

Up to a maximum of 6 marks in total, **1 mark** should be awarded for each valid point selected from the source or each valid point of significant omission provided.

Candidates should be awarded **up to 3 marks** for their identification of points from the source which support their judgement. Candidates should be awarded **up to 4 marks** for their identification of points of significant omission, based on their own knowledge, that support their judgement. A **maximum of 2 marks** may be awarded for answers in which no judgement has been made **or** which refer only to the source.

Possible points which may be identified from the source include:
1. when the war ended, there was a sharp drop in demand for Clyde-built warships
2. this decline of shipbuilding in the 1920s had a damaging effect on the iron and steel industries
3. Scotland's manufacturers failed to invest in new technology
4. overseas markets lost during the war often preferred to stay with their new suppliers.

Possible points of significant omission may include:
5. pre-war lack of investment left Scottish shipyards using outdated methods/facilities/bad management

6. the slump of the 1920s had led to a drop in demand for merchant ships
7. industrial unrest (strikes) damaged the reputation of Scottish industries
8. overseas competitors continued to produce quality goods more cheaply than Scottish industries could after the war
9. increased use of electricity and oil cut demand for coal
10. new textiles such as rayon and nylon cut demand for traditional textiles such as cotton and wool.

Any other valid point of significant omission

25. *Candidates can be credited in a number of ways up to a maximum of 6 marks.*

Candidates must make a number of points that make the issue plain or clear, for example by showing connections between factors or causal relationships between events or ideas. These should be key reasons but there is no need for any evaluation or prioritising of these reasons.

Up to a maximum of 6 marks in total, **1 mark** should be awarded for each accurate, relevant reason, and a **second mark** should be awarded for reasons that are developed. Candidates may achieve full marks by providing six straightforward reasons, three developed reasons (or any combination of these).

Possible reasons may include:
1. the women's campaigns for the vote had gradually gained momentum before the War
2. Suffragist peaceful campaign of persuasion gained support from across the social spectrum including men as well as women
3. women had gained voting rights in local elections and showed they could use it sensibly
4. there was a gradual widening of the franchise to men and a sense that it was only a matter of time before women were given the vote
5. the Suffragette militant campaigns kept the issue in the public eye/gained a lot of publicity
6. hunger strikes/force feeding in prison won public sympathy for votes for women
7. by calling off their campaign during the war, the women's groups gained a lot of respect and support for them being given the vote
8. women's work during the war was recognised as significant and persuaded many men that women deserved the vote
9. militant actions such as the Glasgow Rent Strikes reminded the government that women could resume their pre-war campaigning if ignored
10. voting laws had to be changed to allow returning soldiers the vote, which created the opportunity to give the vote to some women in 1918.

Any other valid reason

Section 2, Context A, The Creation of the Medieval Kingdoms, 1066–1406

26. *Candidates can be credited in a number of ways up to a maximum of 5 marks.*

Candidates must evaluate the extent to which a source is useful by commenting on evidence such as the author, type of source, purpose, timing, content or omission. For a mark to be awarded, the candidate must identify an aspect of the source <u>and</u> make a comment which shows why this aspect makes the source more or less useful.

A **maximum of 4 marks** can be awarded for evaluative comments relating to the author, type of source, purpose and timing. A **maximum of 2 marks** may be awarded for evaluative comments relating to the content of the source. A **maximum of 2 marks** may be awarded for evaluative comments relating to points of significant omission.

Examples of aspects of the source and relevant comments:

Aspect	Possible comment(s)
Author: William's priest	Useful because he would have been an eyewitness/well placed to see what William was doing
Type of Source: Chronicle	Useful because it was a detailed record of events
Purpose: To inform	Useful because it was written to inform about William's role in trying to control England/perhaps less useful because he would have been biased in favour of William
Timing: 1077	Useful because it is a primary source written from the time William was attempting to bring England under his control

Content	Possible comment(s)
The remaining English Earls were confirmed in their lands and titles.	Useful because it is accurate (William allowed the other English Earls to keep their land and titles)
...his loyal Norman lords undertook a programme of castle building to maintain their hold on the kingdom.	Useful because it is accurate (Norman lords built castles to strengthen their control of England)
He gave rich fiefs to the men he had brought over from France...	Useful because it is accurate (William did reward his loyal supporters who came over from France)

Possible points of significant omission may include:
1. no mention of William's cruelty/military campaigns against the Saxons/"Harrying of the North" following rebellion there
2. severe taxation was applied
3. replacing Saxon lords killed at Hastings with Norman barons
4. Tower of London built to intimidate the capital.

Any other valid point of significant omission

27. *Candidates can be credited in a number of ways **up to a maximum of 9 marks**.*

Candidates must make a judgement about the extent to which different factors contributed to an event or development, or its impact. They are required to provide a balanced account of the influence of different factors and come to a reasoned conclusion based on the evidence presented.

Up to 5 marks can be awarded for relevant, factual, key points of knowledge used to support factors, with **1 mark** awarded for each point (but **one mark should be deducted** if the correct process is not clear in at least two factors). If **only one factor is presented, a maximum of 3 marks should be awarded** for relevant points of knowledge. A **further 4 marks** can be awarded for providing the answer in a structured way and coming to a reasoned conclusion.

Possible factors	Key points of knowledge to support this factor may include:
Corruption in the legal system	1. there was no uniform law in the kingdom/sheriffs decided the law in their local area 2. Sheriffs were corrupt/could not be trusted by the king 3. Barons held the office of sheriff and abused their position/had set up their own law courts 4. Barons were keeping the fines collected from criminals, instead of giving them to the king.
Barons had become too powerful during the civil war	5. castles had been built without the king's permission which increased the Barons' power/king's authority had been reduced 6. some Barons openly challenged Henry eg Earl of York, Scarborough Castle 7. Barons had private armies/hired mercenaries 8. Barons were stealing land from their weaker neighbours and increasing their power.
Henry ruled over a wide area	9. Henry ruled from the Pyrenees to the Scottish border a huge area which was difficult to control effectively 10. there was no common language or traditions in Henry's empire to help hold it together.
Authority of the Church increased	11. the Church had gained more power and its clergy were not tried in the king's court if they were suspected of a crime 12. Church courts had become powerful/were using their own laws instead of the kings.

Up to **4 marks** should be awarded for presenting the answer in a structured way, leading to a conclusion which addresses the question, as follows:

1 mark for an introduction (which places the question in its historical context or outlines relevant factors).

1 mark for the answer being presented in a structured way (with knowledge being organised in support of different factors).

1 mark for a conclusion with a valid judgement (or overall summary).

1 mark for a reason in support of the judgement (a summary cannot be supported).

Any other valid factor

28. *Candidates can be credited in a number of ways **up to a maximum of 6 marks**.*

Candidates must make a number of points that make the issue plain or clear, for example by showing connections between factors or causal relationships between events or ideas. These should be key reasons but there is no need for any evaluation or prioritising of these reasons.

Up to a maximum of 6 marks in total, **1 mark** should be awarded for each accurate, relevant reason, and a **second mark** should be awarded for reasons that are developed. Candidates may achieve full marks by providing six straightforward reasons, three developed reasons (or any combination of these).

Possible reasons may include:
1. provided centres of worship for communities
2. offered support and comfort in difficult times/ encouraged people not to give up/hope that life after death would be better
3. offered spiritual guidance on how to be a good Christian
4. provided guidelines/controlled how people should live their lives
5. carried out important rituals eg baptism, marriage, last rites
6. the Church was a place of education and was used to train boys who wished to become priests
7. kept one third of its tithe/crops to give to the parish in times of need
8. canon law had a major impact on people's lives eg whom you could marry, holidays, no red meat on Fridays
9. had political power – it could excommunicate a king or place a country under interdict
10. had great economic importance; it owned land and made a profit from this
11. held its own court and enforced Canon Law
12. employed large number of people from the local community.

Any other valid reason

29. *Candidates can be credited in a number of ways up to a maximum of 6 marks.*

Candidates must make a judgement about the extent to which the source provides a full description or explanation of a given event or development.

Up to a maximum of 6 marks in total, **1 mark** should be awarded for each valid point selected from the source or each valid point of significant omission provided.

Candidates should be awarded **up to 3 marks** for their identification of points from the source which support their judgement. Candidates should be awarded **up to 4 marks** for their identification of points of significant omission, based on their own knowledge, that support their judgement. A **maximum of 2 marks** may be awarded for answers in which no judgement has been made **or** which refer only to the source.

Possible points which may be identified from the source include:
1. one in three of the population of England died
2. Lords, who relied on their peasants to farm their land, became desperate to retain them
3. Lords were forced to pay more to keep each peasant on their land
4. some peasants left their own Lord's land in search of higher pay elsewhere.

Possible points of significant omission may include:
5. Black Death led to a lack of shepherds/farm workers/ labourers
6. some villages became derelict
7. disastrous effects on agriculture eg animals died, crops rotted in the fields
8. trade was seriously interrupted
9. affected the attitudes of survivors eg less deferential towards the church
10. led to worsening relations between peasants and landowners.

Any other valid point of significant omission

Section 2, Context B, War of the Three Kingdoms, 1603–1651

30. *Candidates can be credited in a number of ways up to a maximum of 9 marks.*

Candidates must make a judgement about the extent to which different factors contributed to an event or development, or its impact. They are required to provide a balanced account of the influence of different factors and come to a reasoned conclusion based on the evidence presented.

Up to 5 marks can be awarded for relevant, factual, key points of knowledge used to support factors, with **1 mark** awarded for each point (but **one mark should be deducted** if the correct process is not clear in at least two factors). If **only one factor is presented, a maximum of 3 marks should be awarded** for relevant points of knowledge. A **further 4 marks** can be awarded for providing the answer in a structured way and coming to a reasoned conclusion.

Possible factors	Key points of knowledge to support this factor may include:
Financial grievances	1. James was viewed as extravagant by Parliament/by some as overgenerous to his favourites 2. Parliament was dismissed in 1610 because of arguments over finances and the failure of the Great Contract 3. the 'Addled Parliament' was dismissed in 1614 due to arguments over impositions (extra customs tax) and subsidies 4. Crown and Parliament quarrelled over the sale of monopolies.
Religious differences	5. the Millenary Petition of 1603 requested changes to be made to practices in the Church of England; James rejected most of the changes 6. James licensed Archbishop Bancroft's Canons which stated that the clergy had to follow 39 articles and the Prayer Book, which annoyed the clergy 7. James gave bishops more control in the Church (Direction of Preachers, 1622) which worried Puritans 8. Parliament was suspicious of James' perceived Catholic sympathies.
Political disputes	9. James' belief in the Divine Rights of Kings offended many in Parliament 10. James was criticised for neglecting Parliament in favour of leisure pursuits 11. quarrels over the King's choice of leading ministers eg Duke of Buckingham 12. James rules without Parliament from 1614 to 1621.

Up to 4 marks should be awarded for presenting the answer in a structured way, leading to a conclusion which addresses the question, as follows:

1 mark for an introduction (which places the question in its historical context or outlines relevant factors).

1 mark for the answer being presented in a structured way (with knowledge being organised in support of different factors).

1 mark for a conclusion with a valid judgement (or overall summary).

1 mark for a reason in support of the judgement (a summary cannot be supported).

Any other valid interpretation

31. *Candidates can be credited in a number of ways up to a maximum of 6 marks.*

Candidates must make a number of points that make the issue plain or clear, for example by showing connections between factors or causal relationships between events or ideas. These should be key reasons but there is no need for any evaluation or prioritising of these reasons.

Up to a maximum of 6 marks in total, **1 mark** should be awarded for each accurate, relevant reason, and a **second mark** should be awarded for reasons that are developed. Candidates may achieve full marks by providing six straightforward reasons, three developed reasons (or any combination of these).

Possible reasons may include:
1. resentment of Charles as an absentee monarch
2. many Scots were suspicious that Charles wanted to be an absolute monarch
3. the General Assembly was not allowed to meet which caused resentment
4. resentment at Charles' money raising methods (eg Ship Money)
5. Scottish nobles resented Charles' Act of Revocation whereby church lands which had been alienated since 1540 had to be returned to the Crown
6. Charles' coronation in Edinburgh was a High Church ceremony based on Anglican forms and Scottish Presbyterians were suspicious of Anglican ideas
7. Charles demanded that Scottish Ministers accept and use the new English Prayer Book which caused a great deal of resentment and some riots in Edinburgh
8. Scottish clergy opposed Laud's Canons and their requirement to wear gowns and surplices because it seemed too Catholic
9. Bishops were to be introduced into the Scottish Church which was resented by the Scots
10. rejection of the Canons was included in the National Covenant for the Defence of True Religion in 1638 and was signed by thousands because they wanted to protect Scottish religious practices.

Any other valid reason

32. *Candidates can be credited in a number of ways up to a maximum of 5 marks.*

Candidates must evaluate the extent to which a source is useful by commenting on evidence such as the author, type of source, purpose, timing, content or omission. For a mark to be awarded, the candidate must identify an aspect of the source <u>and</u> make a comment which shows why this aspect makes the source more or less useful.

A **maximum of 4 marks** can be awarded for evaluative comments relating to the author, type of source, purpose and timing. A **maximum of 2 marks** may be awarded for evaluative comments relating to the content of the source. A **maximum of 2 marks** may be awarded for evaluative comments relating to points of significant omission.

Examples of aspects of the source and relevant comments:

Aspect	Possible comment(s)
Author: Sir John Eliot, a Member of Parliament	Useful as it is from an eyewitness/had first-hand experience of the dispute with the king
Type of Source: A letter	Useful as it is likely to give an honest/accurate description of the growing opposition to the reign of King Charles I
Purpose: To inform	Useful as it provides a detailed account of the growing opposition/less useful as it may be biased as Eliot was an outspoken critic of Charles
Timing: 1630s	Useful because it is a primary source from the time when there was growing opposition to the reign of King Charles I

Content	Possible comment(s)
Members of Parliament complained that the terms of Charles' marriage contract included unacceptable concessions to English Catholics.	Useful because it is accurate (Parliament was suspicious of any concessions given to Catholics)
In addition we were suspicious of Charles' foreign policy which meant Parliament was reluctant to grant him funds.	Useful because it is accurate (Parliament didn't trust Charles' foreign policy and was unwilling to fund it)
...launching a fierce criticism of Charles' favourite, Buckingham's mismanagement of the Cadiz expedition.	Useful because it is accurate (many MPs criticised Buckingham's disastrous Cadiz campaign)

Possible points of significant omission may include:
1. growing opposition to Charles' belief in the Divine Right of Kings
2. anger at Charles' refusal to let Parliament meet in 1629/ MPs arrived to find the doors locked
3. Protestants were upset at his marriage to Henrietta Maria – a Catholic
4. criticised for his spending habits eg paintings and expensive clothes.

Any other valid point of significant omission

33. *Candidates can be credited in a number of ways up to a maximum of 6 marks.*

Candidates must make a judgement about the extent to which the source provides a full description or explanation of a given event or development.

Up to a maximum of 6 marks in total, **1 mark** should be awarded for each valid point selected from the source or each valid point of significant omission provided.

Candidates should be awarded **up to 3 marks** for their identification of points from the source which support their judgement. Candidates should be awarded **up to 4 marks** for their identification of points of significant omission, based on their own knowledge, that support their judgement. A **maximum of 2 marks** may be awarded for answers in which no judgement has been made **or** which refer only to the source.

Possible points which may be identified from the source include:

1. Parliament was dismissed in 1640 because MPs would not give Charles what he wanted/He still didn't get the money he wanted
2. Charles faced growing criticism in Parliament from Pym and other Puritan MPs regarding his religious policies
3. Parliament accused the king's chief minister, Strafford, of treason and executed him
4. many MPs were unhappy with the way Pym twisted the laws to get Strafford executed, which led to further disputes in Parliament.

Possible points of significant omission may include:

5. activities of the Long Parliament angered the King eg arrest and imprisonment of Archbishop Laud
6. the Grand Remonstrance in November 1641 divided the House of Commons in support for the King
7. attempted arrest of 5 Members of Parliament in January 1642 angered Parliament
8. Parliament's decision to throw bishops out of the House of Lords in February 1642 divided the House of Commons
9. Parliament took control of the army in March 1642 without the King's assent
10. the Nineteen Propositions of June 1642 were rejected by Charles, this divided Parliament and the King's supporters left London.

Any other valid point of significant omission

Section 2, Context C, The Atlantic Slave Trade, 1770–1807

34. *Candidates can be credited in a number of ways up to a maximum of 5 marks.*

Candidates must evaluate the extent to which a source is useful by commenting on evidence such as the author, type of source, purpose, timing, content or omission. For a mark to be awarded, the candidate must identify an aspect of the source and make a comment which shows why this aspect makes the source more or less useful.

A **maximum of 4 marks** can be awarded for evaluative comments relating to the author, type of source, purpose and timing. A **maximum of 2 marks** may be awarded for evaluative comments relating to the content of the source. A **maximum of 2 marks** may be awarded for evaluative comments relating to points of significant omission.

Examples of aspects of the source and relevant comments:

Aspect	Possible comment(s)
Author: Slave ship doctor	Useful as he is an eyewitness/has first-hand experience
Type of Source: Diary	Useful as it is an honest personal account
Purpose: To record	Useful as it is a private record and is likely to tell the truth
Timing: 1788	Useful as it was written during the period of the slave trade

Content	Possible comment(s)
...led to diarrhoea and fevers among the slaves.	Useful because it is accurate (the terrible conditions meant disease was common on ships and it spread very quickly below deck)
...the apartments became so extremely hot (as to be only bearable for a very short time).	Useful because it is accurate (conditions in the hold of the ship were often very hot and stuffy with little or no fresh air)
The floor of the place where the slaves lay was covered in blood and diarrhoea (which had come from them because of their sickness).	Useful because it is accurate (as the floor of the hold where the slaves were kept was covered in human waste which was seldom cleaned)

Possible points of significant omission may include:

1. slaves were held on board using tight pack/loose pack system
2. crew were often cruel towards slaves/female slaves often suffered sexual abuse
3. food was limited and bland/unfamiliar to slaves – some had to be force fed
4. slaves taken above deck and whipped to make them exercise.

Any other valid point of omission

35. *Candidates can be credited in a number of ways up to a maximum of 6 marks.*

Candidates must make a judgement about the extent to which the source provides a full description or explanation of a given event or development.

Up to a maximum of 6 marks in total, **1 mark** should be awarded for each valid point selected from the source or each valid point of significant omission provided.

Candidates should be awarded **up to 3 marks** for their identification of points from the source which support their judgement. Candidates should be awarded **up to 4 marks** for their identification of points of significant omission, based on their own knowledge, that support their judgement. A **maximum of 2 marks** may be awarded for answers in which no judgement has been made **or** which refer only to the source.

Possible points which may be identified from the source include:

1. (the slaves outnumbered the white population about 20 to 1 which) created a fear of rebellion among the white population
2. fear of a slave uprising led to the introduction of a legal system which supported slavery
3. slave laws were introduced which allowed slave owners to brutally punish or even execute slaves
4. the concentration on sugar production did lasting damage to the Jamaican economy.

Possible points of significant omission may include:

5. many of the native people, the Arawaks, were killed or cleared off their land by white settlers
6. new diseases were introduced to the islands by the slaves
7. small farms were replaced by large plantations
8. slave uprisings caused damage and destruction to the Caribbean
9. natural beauty, vegetation and wildlife damaged by the growth of plantations
10. slave trade brought racist attitudes to the Caribbean
11. island economies stifled by slave trade.

Any other valid point of significant omission

36. *Candidates can be credited in a number of ways up to a maximum of 6 marks.*

Candidates must make a number of points that make the issue plain or clear, for example by showing connections between factors or causal relationships between events or ideas. These should be key reasons but there is no need for any evaluation or prioritising of these reasons.

Up to a maximum of 6 marks in total, **1 mark** should be awarded for each accurate, relevant reason, and a **second mark** should be awarded for reasons that are developed. Candidates may achieve full marks by providing six straightforward reasons, three developed reasons (or any combination of these).

Possible reasons may include:
1. slaves were controlled by strict laws or codes which scared them from resisting
2. slave risings lacked effective leadership making planning resistance difficult
3. slave resistance was crushed by the better armed and organised whites/the slaves had no weapons
4. plantation owners often used black overseers to help them maintain control
5. captured slaves were subjected to brutal torture or even put to death and this acted as a powerful warning to other slaves
6. slaves lived in fear of being sold off/separated from their families if they broke the rules
7. slaves had little or no education and could be brainwashed into accepting plantation life/the slaves didn't think they could succeed
8. many islands were small and it was difficult for slaves to evade capture
9. plantation owners offered large rewards for the capture of escaped slaves
10. escaped slaves could easily be identified by brandings or lack of legal papers
11. plantation owners used bounty hunters/bloodhounds to track down runaway slaves.

Any other valid reason

37. *Candidates can be credited in a number of ways up to a maximum of 9 marks.*

Candidates must make a judgement about the extent to which different factors contributed to an event or development, or its impact. They are required to provide a balanced account of the influence of different factors and come to a reasoned conclusion based on the evidence presented.

Up to 5 marks can be awarded for relevant, factual, key points of knowledge used to support factors, with **1 mark** awarded for each point (but **one mark should be deducted** if the correct process is not clear in at least two factors). If **only one factor is presented, a maximum of 3 marks should be awarded** for relevant points of knowledge. A **further 4 marks** can be awarded for providing the answer in a structured way and coming to a reasoned conclusion.

Possible factors	Key points of knowledge to support this factor may include:
Role of Olaudah Equiano	1. Equiano was a freed slave who travelled throughout the country speaking against slavery 2. his first-hand account of his experiences as a slave persuaded many people about the evils of slavery 3. his was the only book to be written by an African telling about his experiences as a slave and it persuaded many people to support the abolition of the slave trade.
Wilberforce	4. Wilberforce used evidence gathered by abolitionists to try to persuade Parliament to abolish the African slave trade 5. Wilberforce regularly introduced anti-slavery bills in Parliament 6. Wilberforce made speeches which brought great publicity to the cause of the abolition of the slave trade.
Clarkson	7. Thomas Clarkson collected information about the terrible conditions on slave ships/displayed equipment used on the slave ships, such as iron handcuffs and branding irons, to demonstrate the barbarity of the slave trade.
Newton	8. John Newton had been a slave ship captain who campaigned against the slave trade/his book provided an eyewitness account of the slave trade/wrote the song Amazing Grace.
Anti-slave trade groups	9. the Society for the Abolition of the Slave Trade had campaigned, with growing support for many years 10. women played an important role in persuading grocers to stop selling sugar produced by slaves and campaigned to get people to stop eating it.
Changing attitudes	11. people had begun to think of Africans as fellow human beings making them regard the slave trade as unacceptable 12. Christian teaching led people to change their attitude to the slave trade.

Up to **4 marks** should be awarded for presenting the answer in a structured way, leading to a conclusion which addresses the question, as follows:

1 mark for an introduction (which places the question in its historical context or outlines relevant factors).

1 mark for the answer being presented in a structured way (with knowledge being organised in support of different factors).

1 mark for a conclusion with a valid judgement (or overall summary).

1 mark for a reason in support of the judgement (a summary cannot be supported).

Any other relevant factor

Section 2, Context D, Changing Britain, 1760–1914

38. *Candidates can be credited in a number of ways up to a maximum of 9 marks.*

Candidates must make a judgement about the extent to which different factors contributed to an event or development, or its impact. They are required to provide a balanced account of the influence of different factors and come to a reasoned conclusion based on the evidence presented.

Up to 5 marks can be awarded for relevant, factual, key points of knowledge used to support factors, with **1 mark** awarded for each point (but **one mark should be deducted** if the correct process is not clear in at least two factors). If **only one factor is presented, a maximum of 3 marks should be awarded** for relevant points of knowledge. A **further 4 marks** can be awarded for providing the answer in a structured way and coming to a reasoned conclusion.

Up to **4 marks** should be awarded for presenting the answer in a structured way, leading to a conclusion which addresses the question, as follows:

1 mark for an introduction (which places the question in its historical context or outlines relevant factors).

1 mark for the answer being presented in a structured way (with knowledge being organised in support of different factors).

1 mark for a conclusion with a valid judgement (or overall summary).

1 mark for a reason in support of the judgement (a summary cannot be supported).

Possible factors	Key points of knowledge to support this factor may include:
Medical advances	1. after 1858 all doctors had to be fully qualified/improved standard of nursing/midwifery 2. building of more hospitals/cleaner hospitals reduced infection 3. vaccination against killer diseases such as smallpox/antiseptics/anaesthetics.
Better diet	4. farming improvements led to better, more varied, nutritious diet eg fresh vegetables and fruit, meat, dairy products 5. railways transported fresh food and milk to towns 6. improved food standards reduced illness caused by adulterated food.
Improvements in public health	7. Public Health Acts gave councils power to improve conditions 8. improved sewerage systems/proper drainage reduced spread of germs/diseases 9. provision of fresh, clean water reduced the threat of disease.
Improvements in hygiene	10. cheaper soap kept people cleaner/reduced risk of disease 11. wash houses and public baths introduced in 1878 which helped improve hygiene.

Any other relevant factor

39. *Candidates can be credited in a number of ways up to a maximum of 6 marks.*

Candidates must make a judgement about the extent to which the source provides a full description or explanation of a given event or development.

Up to a maximum of 6 marks in total, **1 mark** should be awarded for each valid point selected from the source or each valid point of significant omission provided.

Candidates should be awarded **up to 3 marks** for their identification of points from the source which support their judgement. Candidates should be awarded **up to 4 marks** for their identification of points of significant omission, based on their own knowledge, that support their judgement. A **maximum of 2 marks** may be awarded for answers in which no judgement has been made **or** which refer only to the source.

Possible points which may be identified from the source include:
1. powered machines went on hour after hour and many workers struggled to keep up with them
2. owners had very strict rules and workers had to do what they were told to do
3. wages were usually better than farm work
4. if business became slow then workers were laid off, with no income at all.

Possible points of significant omission may include:
5. poor ventilation/air was full of harmful dust particles which damaged lungs/caused TB
6. bending over all day led to children becoming deformed
7. working long hours led to tiredness and accidents
8. children pulled into machines and seriously injured/machines were dangerous as they were unfenced
9. new machinery made work easier/machines easy to operate
10. changing rooms provided in some mills/water was available for workers/there was decent sanitation in some mills.

Any other valid point of significant omission

40. *Candidates can be credited in a number of ways up to a maximum of 5 marks.*

Candidates must evaluate the extent to which a source is useful by commenting on evidence such as the author, type of source, purpose, timing, content or omission. For a mark to be awarded, the candidate must identify an aspect of the source <u>and</u> make a comment which shows why this aspect makes the source more or less useful.

A **maximum of 4 marks** can be awarded for evaluative comments relating to the author, type of source, purpose and timing. A **maximum of 2 marks** may be awarded for evaluative comments relating to the content of the source. A **maximum of 2 marks** may be awarded for evaluative comments relating to points of significant omission.

Examples of aspects of the source and relevant comments:

Aspect	Possible comment(s)
Author: Railway engineer	Useful as it was written by an eyewitness to the events
Type of Source: Diary	Useful as it's an honest personal account
Purpose: To record	Useful as it's a private record/less likely to tell lies
Timing: 1840s	Useful as it was written during the early period of railway expansion

Content	Possible comment(s)
Lady Seafield very decidedly told us that she hated railways/"Cheap travel brought together such an objectionable variety of people".	Useful because it is accurate (many landowners objected to railways/they would bring industrial workers out to the countryside).
The railway would frighten away the grouse from his moors.	Useful because it is accurate (there was concern that railways would spoil hunting on estates).
What would become of the men employed who float timber down the river Spey to the sea?	Useful because it is accurate (many people were worried railways would take away people's jobs).

Possible points of significant omission may include:

1. factory owners saw the advantages of cheaper transport for their goods
2. farmers were happy they could sell their goods further afield
3. working class pleased about the job opportunities on the railways/could go away on day trips to seaside or the countryside
4. workers in other forms of transport such as stage coaches and canals saw railways as a threat to their jobs.

Any other valid point of significant omission

41. *Candidates can be credited in a number of ways up to a maximum of 6 marks.*

Candidates must make a number of points that make the issue plain or clear, for example by showing connections between factors or causal relationships between events or ideas. These should be key reasons but there is no need for any evaluation or prioritising of these reasons.

Up to a maximum of 6 marks in total, **1 mark** should be awarded for each accurate, relevant reason, and a **second mark** should be awarded for reasons that are developed. Candidates may achieve full marks by providing six straightforward reasons, three developed reasons (or any combination of these).

Possible reasons may include:

1. need to include middle classes in government because they were key to generating the country's wealth
2. political reform was no longer seen as a threat to the country's stability
3. campaigns by groups such as the National Reform League put pressure on the government to give more people the vote
4. fear of revolution helped convince many politicians it would be dangerous to deny giving the vote to some of the working class
5. increasingly obvious skilled workers were vital to Britain's economic success/many of whom were better educated and respectable therefore deserved the vote
6. better education in towns made it more reasonable to extend the franchise
7. development of railways and growth of cheap popular newspapers raised political awareness of the working class
8. spread of radical ideas and moral arguments; equality became more of an issue
9. political benefits at Westminster for parties; they saw potential voters
10. population growth in the towns made politicians more politically sensitive

11. Hyde Park riots put more pressure on the government
12. Chartist movement provided organised political pressure for change.

Section 2, Context E, The Making of Modern Britain, 1880–1951

42. *Candidates can be credited in a number of ways up to a maximum of 5 marks.*

Candidates must evaluate the extent to which a source is useful by commenting on evidence such as the author, type of source, purpose, timing, content or omission. For a mark to be awarded, the candidate must identify an aspect of the source <u>and</u> make a comment which shows why this aspect makes the source more or less useful.

A **maximum of 4 marks** can be awarded for evaluative comments relating to the author, type of source, purpose and timing. A **maximum of 2 marks** may be awarded for evaluative comments relating to the content of the source. A **maximum of 2 marks** may be awarded for evaluative comments relating to points of significant omission.

Examples of aspects of the source and relevant comments:

Aspect	Possible comment(s)
Author: Social investigator	Useful as would be an eyewitness/has expertise
Type of Source: Report	Useful because reports are usually well researched
Purpose: Inform/persuade	Useful because it provides a detailed description of the effects of poverty/less useful as could exaggerate to try to bring about improvements
Timing: 1892	Useful because it was from a time of widespread poverty in Britain

Content	Possible comment(s)
The two room apartment on the ground floor is occupied by Fletcher, a pedlar, his wife and six of his children.	Useful as it is accurate (because many people lived in very overcrowded conditions).
In most of the apartments the walls and ceilings are black with filth.	Useful as it is accurate (because in many rooms the wall and ceilings were very dirty).
In these buildings it is a common occurrence to find sewage running down the walls.	Useful as it is accurate (because it wasn't unusual to find sewage seeping through the walls).

Possible points of significant omission may include:

1. many people lived in poor quality housing which was often damp/lacked good ventilation/little sunlight
2. lack of fresh, clean water made it difficult to keep themselves/houses clean
3. poor sanitation led to frequent outbreaks of disease
4. poor diet/children often malnourished which contributed to poor health.

Any other valid point of significant omission

43. *Candidates can be credited in a number of ways up to a maximum of 6 marks.*

Candidates must make a judgement about the extent to which the source provides a full description or explanation of a given event or development.

Up to a maximum of **6 marks** in total, **1 mark** should be awarded for each valid point selected from the source or each valid point of significant omission provided.

Candidates should be awarded **up to 3 marks** for their identification of points from the source which support their judgement. Candidates should be awarded **up to 4 marks** for their identification of points of significant omission, based on their own knowledge, that support their judgement. A **maximum of 2 marks** may be awarded for answers in which no judgement has been made or which refer only to the source.

Possible points which may be identified from the source include:
1. medical care was only provided for the worker, it did not cover his wife or children
2. other benefits were only to last for a short period of time
3. the amounts paid as benefits were not enough to live on
4. as the pension only applied to people over 70, many elderly still received no help.

Possible points of significant omission may include:
5. not compulsory for local authorities to introduce free school meals
6. school medical inspections did not provide treatment (until school clinics in 1912)
7. amount of old age pensions was not enough to prevent poverty
8. health insurance lasted only 13 weeks at 10s, 5s weekly for next 13 weeks
9. unemployment insurance only covered certain/seasonal industries
10. no attempts were made to tackle poor housing.

Any other valid point of significant omission

44. *Candidates can be credited in a number of ways* **up to a maximum of 6 marks.**

Candidates must make a number of points that make the issue plain or clear, for example by showing connections between factors or causal relationships between events or ideas. These should be key reasons but there is no need for any evaluation or prioritising of these reasons.

Up to a **maximum of 6 marks** in total, **1 mark** should be awarded for each accurate, relevant reason, and a **second mark** should be awarded for reasons that are developed. Candidates may achieve full marks by providing six straightforward reasons, three developed reasons (or any combination of these).

Possible reasons may include:
1. bombing broke down barriers between middle and working classes eg bomb shelters, war work and people began to have more sympathy for each other
2. during the war, classes were mixing in society who previously had little in common which led to greater sympathy towards helping those in need/a greater sense of "community" was created
3. evacuation exposed continuing poverty in cities and created desire for Government action to improve things
4. in wartime the Government took more responsibility for the nation's health eg free milk and vitamins/free medical care for those who were victims of war and people saw the benefit of this
5. rationing during the war helped encourage the idea of universal sharing of the nation's food supply and people wanted this to continue
6. during the war the Government interfered more in people's lives eg conscription, direction of labour and many wanted this to continue
7. as a result of people's experience during the war, Government assistance was no longer seen as shameful

8. suffering of war caused a determination to create a better society once the war was over/the public expected the Government to do more for them since they had worked together to achieve victory during the war
9. Beveridge Report produced in 1942 was well received by the public and encouraged Government involvement in solving the problems of society
10. Beveridge Report showed the true nature of poverty and had widespread support
11. changing expectations of Government involvement in easing the problems of society since everyone was suffering hardship
12. Labour Party's socialist ideology said there should be redistribution of wealth.

Any other valid reason

45. *Candidates can be credited in a number of ways* **up to a maximum of 9 marks.**

Candidates must make a judgement about the extent to which different factors contributed to an event or development, or its impact. They are required to provide a balanced account of the influence of different factors and come to a reasoned conclusion based on the evidence presented.

Up to 5 marks can be awarded for relevant, factual, key points of knowledge used to support factors, with **1 mark** awarded for each point (but **one mark should be deducted** if the correct process is not clear in at least two factors). If **only one factor is presented, a maximum of 3 marks should be awarded** for relevant points of knowledge. A **further 4 marks** can be awarded for providing the answer in a structured way and coming to a reasoned conclusion.

Possible factors	Key points of knowledge to support this factor may include:
National Health Service	1. National Health Service Act provided free medical treatment for everyone 2. National Health Service offered many services eg hospitals, dentistry, opticians, prescriptions, vaccinations.
National Insurance	3. National Insurance Act provided comprehensive insurance for all workers eg sickness and unemployment benefit, pensions 4. National Assistance Act provided benefits for those not covered by the National Insurance Act 5. maternity and widows' benefits ensured that families were also covered 6. Family Allowance Act provided extra financial help to families with more than one child.
Housing	7. 200,000 homes built a year between 1948 and 1951 8. New Towns Act laid plans for 14 new towns in Britain which helped ease overcrowding in cities and create healthier living conditions.
Education	9. Education Act made secondary education compulsory up to the age of 15 which improved education opportunities/made secondary education a reality for all 10. massive school building programme was started which improved access to education.
Employment	11. the government promoted a policy of full employment 12. nationalisation of key industries eg electricity, gas, iron and steel, kept unemployment levels down to 2.5%.

Up to **4 marks** should be awarded for presenting the answer in a structured way, leading to a conclusion which addresses the question, as follows:

1 mark for an introduction (which places the question in its historical context or outlines relevant factors).

1 mark for the answer being presented in a structured way (with knowledge being organised in support of different factors).

1 mark for a conclusion with a valid judgement (or overall summary).

1 mark for a reason in support of the judgement (a summary cannot be supported).

Any other relevant factor

Section 2, Context A, The Cross and the Crescent: the Crusades, 1071–1192

46. *Candidates can be credited in a number of ways up to a maximum of 6 marks.*

Candidates must make a judgement about the extent to which the source provides a full description or explanation of a given event or development.

Up to a maximum of 6 marks in total, **1 mark** should be awarded for each valid point selected from the source or each valid point of significant omission provided.

Candidates should be awarded **up to 3 marks** for their identification of points from the source which support their judgement. Candidates should be awarded **up to 4 marks** for their identification of points of significant omission, based on their own knowledge, that support their judgement. A **maximum of 2 marks** may be awarded for answers in which no judgement has been made **or** which refer only to the source.

Possible points which may be identified from the source include:
1. castles became a key symbol of power
2. were also the administrative centres of each town
3. an ideal base for the local garrison carrying out guard duty
4. during times of attack when food, drink and other supplies could be stored there.

Possible points of significant omission may include:
5. castles were used as a court where local law was enforced
6. castles were used to defend and protect the lord's lands and the people who lived on them
7. used as a home for the lord's family
8. centre of entertainment eg feasts and banquets
9. peasants' taxes would be paid in produce and this was often stored in the grounds of the castle
10. castles were used as a place to keep criminals/prisoners.

Any other valid point of significant omission

47. *Candidates can be credited in a number of ways up to a maximum of 4 marks.*

Candidates must interpret the evidence and make direct comparisons between sources. Candidates are expected to compare content directly on a point-by-point basis. They may compare the details in the sources and/or compare the viewpoints overall.

A **simple comparison** will indicate what points of detail or viewpoint the sources agree or disagree on and **should be awarded 1 mark**. A **developed comparison** of the points of detail or overall viewpoint **should be awarded a second mark**. Candidates may achieve full marks by making four simple comparisons, two developed comparisons (or by any combination of these).

Possible points of comparison may include:

Source B	Source C
Overall: The sources agree about what happened to Jews during the First Crusade.	
Many Crusaders were poor and hungry so they began stealing food and possessions from the Jews.	(In the riot that followed) Jewish houses were robbed and valuables stolen.
Some forced the Jews to change religion and become Christian.	Those Jews who survived the massacre were forced to give up their faith and become Christians.
Others, against the orders of Peter the Hermit, slaughtered the Jews.	Immediately Peter the Hermit's army began attacking and killing Jewish men, women and children.

48. *Candidates can be credited in a number of ways up to a maximum of 9 marks.*

Candidates must make a judgement about the extent to which different factors contributed to an event or development, or its impact. They are required to provide a balanced account of the influence of different factors and come to a reasoned conclusion based on the evidence presented.

Up to 5 marks can be awarded for relevant, factual, key points of knowledge used to support factors, with **1 mark** awarded for each point (but **one mark should be deducted** if the correct process is not clear in at least two factors). If **only one factor is presented, a maximum of 3 marks should be awarded** for relevant points of knowledge. A **further 4 marks** can be awarded for providing the answer in a structured way and coming to a reasoned conclusion.

Possible factors	Key points of knowledge to support this factor may include:
Muslim divisions	1. Muslims refused to join together and only thought of their own land 2. Muslims frequently fought against each other so weakening their cause 3. a Muslim was bribed to let the Crusaders into Antioch 4. Muslim communities didn't attack the Crusaders/gave them money to keep the peace.
Crusaders' military advantages	5. Crusaders had effective leaders in Bohemond of Taranto and Raymond of Toulouse who were experienced knights/both men were involved in key victories eg Antioch/Jerusalem 6. Crusaders used effective tactics to defeat the Muslims eg siege towers used at Jerusalem 7. the knights were militarily superior to the Muslim forces eg the knights' tactics of charging at Dorylaeum/Antioch secured victory.
Crusading ideals	8. many Christians believed that it was their duty to recapture Jerusalem/believed they were doing God's work 9. Crusaders were inspired by the promise that all their sins would be forgiven if they took part in the Crusade.
Support for Crusaders	10. the Crusaders received help from Italian ports eg cities such as Pisa/Genoa/Venice supplied timber for siege machines 11. the Crusaders received help from Emperor Alexius eg provided Crusaders with additional soldiers/supplies at Constantinople etc 12. secured important trade routes ensuring Crusaders had access to vital supplies.

Up to **4 marks** should be awarded for presenting the answer in a structured way, leading to a conclusion which addresses the question, as follows:

1 mark for an introduction (which places the question in its historical context or outlines relevant factors).

1 mark for the answer being presented in a structured way (with knowledge being organised in support of different factors).

1 mark for a conclusion with a valid judgement (or overall summary).

1 mark for a reason in support of the judgement (a summary cannot be supported).

Any other relevant factor

49. *Candidates can be credited in a number of ways up to a maximum of 6 marks.*

Candidates must make a number of points that make the issue plain or clear, for example by showing connections between factors or causal relationships between events or ideas. These should be key reasons but there is no need for any evaluation or prioritising of these reasons.

Up to a maximum of 6 marks in total, **1 mark** should be awarded for each accurate, relevant reason, and a **second mark** should be awarded for reasons that are developed. Candidates may achieve full marks by providing six straightforward reasons, three developed reasons (or any combination of these).

Possible reasons may include:
1. Crusaders were divided eg Guy de Lusignan and Reynald of Chatillon hated each other
2. Crusaders had different ideologies towards the Muslims eg the Hawks and the Doves
3. death of Baldwin IV meant that Jerusalem did not have a strong ruler
4. King Guy made a tactical error by leaving Jerusalem with the Crusader army
5. Crusaders were defeated at the Battle of Hattin where most of the nobility were taken prisoner, including King Guy
6. Crusaders lacked resources to defend Jerusalem once the army was defeated
7. when a portion of the wall was mined, it collapsed and the Crusaders were unable to push Saladin's troops back from the breach
8. by the end of September there were only a few dozen knights and a handful of remaining men-at-arms capable of bearing arms and defending the wall
9. Muslims were united under Saladin's leadership making them stronger
10. Saladin's army outnumbered the Crusaders.

Any other valid reason

50. *Candidates can be credited in a number of ways up to a maximum of 4 marks.*

They may take different perspectives on the events and may describe a variety of different aspects of the events. Candidates must make a number of relevant, factual points. These should be key points. These do not have to be in any particular order.

1 mark should be awarded for each accurate relevant key point of knowledge. A **second mark** should be awarded for each point that is developed, **up to a maximum of 4 marks.** Candidates may achieve full marks by providing four straightforward points, by making two developed points (or any combination of these).

Possible points of knowledge may include:
1. In July 1192 Saladin laid siege to the town of Jaffa
2. Saladin's soldiers successfully stormed the walls after three days of bloody clashes
3. the Crusaders however held out in Jaffa's citadel
4. Richard gathered a small army (of knights, a few hundred infantrymen, and about 2,000 crossbowmen) and led them into battle
5. The Muslim army panicked at the sudden attack/fled the city in disarray
6. Saladin launched a counter attack on Jaffa
7. Richard ordered the infantry and knights to form a defensive hedge of spears, with the crossbowmen behind
8. Saladin's cavalry repeatedly charged but suffered heavy casualties so he ordered it to withdraw.

Any other valid point of knowledge

Section 3, Context B, "Tea and Freedom": the American Revolution, 1774–1783

51. *Candidates can be credited in a number of ways up to a maximum of 9 marks.*

Candidates must make a judgement about the extent to which different factors contributed to an event or development, or its impact. They are required to provide a balanced account of the influence of different factors and come to a reasoned conclusion based on the evidence presented.

Up to 5 marks can be awarded for relevant, factual, key points of knowledge used to support factors, with **1 mark** awarded for each point (but **one mark should be deducted** if the correct process is not clear in at least two factors). If **only one factor is presented, a maximum of 3 marks should be awarded** for relevant points of knowledge. A **further 4 marks** can be awarded for providing the answer in a structured way and coming to a reasoned conclusion.

Up to **4 marks** should be awarded for presenting the answer in a structured way, leading to a conclusion which addresses the question, as follows:

1 mark for an introduction (which places the question in its historical context or outlines relevant factors).

1 mark for the answer being presented in a structured way (with knowledge being organised in support of different factors).

1 mark for a conclusion with a valid judgement (or overall summary).

1 mark for a reason in support of the judgement (a summary cannot be supported).

Possible factors	Key points of knowledge to support this factor may include:
Raising revenue	1. the Revenue Act (the Sugar Act) – cut duty on molasses but it was now more strictly enforced 2. the Stamp Act – all legal documents, commercial papers, newspapers and pamphlets had to be officially stamped 3. Townshend Duties – taxes on tea, lead, glass, paper and paint 4. colonists resented being taxed without representation.
George III	5. colonists were angry at George III's desire to exert greater control over colonies/was accused of becoming a tyrant 6. George III was blamed for refusing to introduce sensible laws/a fair justice system in the colonies.
British troops	7. colonists were unhappy with the continuing presence of British soldiers in the colonies following the defeat of the French in 1763 8. colonists were further angered by the passing of The Quartering Act.
British restrictions	9. some colonists were frustrated that the British were stopping them from moving west 10. some colonists felt that the policies of the British government were damaging trade.
Outbreaks of violence	11. the Boston Massacre increased tension between Britain and the colonists 12. fighting at Lexington and Concord in April 1775 led to formation of Continental Army.

Any other relevant factor

52. *Candidates can be credited in a number of ways up to a maximum of 6 marks.*

Candidates must make a number of points that make the issue plain or clear, for example by showing connections between factors or causal relationships between events or ideas. These should be key reasons but there is no need for any evaluation or prioritising of these reasons.

Up to a maximum of 6 marks in total, **1 mark** should be awarded for each accurate, relevant reason, and a **second mark** should be awarded for reasons that are developed. Candidates may achieve full marks by providing six straightforward reasons, three developed reasons (or any combination of these).

Possible reasons may include:
1. many colonists had become wealthy through trade with Britain/merchants feared damage to their trade if the colonists won
2. King George III still commanded some respect among many colonists/some colonists had a great loyalty to the King/saw the monarchy as important
3. some colonists feared law and order would break down if British rule was overthrown
4. some loyalists felt their power and influence had increased under British rule

5. some colonists greatly feared the spread of revolutionary ideas if the colonists won
6. loyalists were mainly conservative and feared change if the British lost
7. many loyalists believed in the importance of the Empire and opposed any threat to it
8. individuals like Flora McDonald encouraged Scots colonists to remain loyal to Britain
9. some hoped to win favour with the British Government by remaining loyal
10. most colonists were of British descent and were proud of being British
11. some loyalists felt that the conflict was the colonists' fault and had no sympathy for them.

Any other valid reason

53. *Candidates can be credited in a number of ways up to a maximum of 6 marks.*

Candidates must make a judgement about the extent to which the source provides a full description or explanation of a given event or development.

Up to a maximum of 6 marks in total, **1 mark** should be awarded for each valid point selected from the source or each valid point of significant omission provided.

Candidates should be awarded **up to 3 marks** for their identification of points from the source which support their judgement. Candidates should be awarded **up to 4 marks** for their identification of points of significant omission, based on their own knowledge, that support their judgement. A **maximum of 2 marks** may be awarded for answers in which no judgement has been made **or** which refer only to the source.

Possible points which may be identified from the source include:
1. the American forces were often led by inefficient, even incompetent, commanders who fought muddled campaigns
2. the men gathering in Boston were very enthusiastic
3. they were however badly armed and lacking supplies
4. most men were part-time and served for only a few months at a time

Possible points of significant omission may include:
5. many American officers lacked proper military training/training in the different types of warfare
6. American forces were short of artillery and cavalry
7. many soldiers lacked experience in battle/needed practice with their weapons
8. many soldiers didn't even have a uniform
9. troops grew exhausted and sick as the campaign went on
10. troops suffered from poor food/shortages of food and cold weather during winter campaigns.

Any other valid point of significant omission

54. *Candidates can be credited in a number of ways up to a maximum of 4 marks.*

They may take different perspectives on the events and may describe a variety of different aspects of the events. Candidates must make a number of relevant, factual points. These should be key points. These do not have to be in any particular order.

1 mark should be awarded for each accurate relevant key point of knowledge. A **second mark** should be awarded for each point that is developed, **up to a maximum of 4 marks.** Candidates may achieve full marks by providing four straightforward points, by making two developed points (or any combination of these).

Possible points of knowledge may include:
1. British plan was to link their two armies to defeat the colonists
2. Burgoyne's army invaded from Canada
3. colonists cut down trees and blocked British army's progress
4. colonists destroyed crops and other potential food supplies
5. Native Americans deserted the British
6. St Leger's British army was defeated/he retreated
7. British at Saratoga outnumbered and surrounded by colonists
8. Burgoyne's army unable to break out so he surrendered (6,000 men and 30 cannon) to colonists.

Any other valid point of knowledge

55. *Candidates can be credited in a number of ways* **up to a maximum of 4 marks.**

Candidates must interpret the evidence and make direct comparisons between sources. Candidates are expected to compare content directly on a point-by-point basis. They may compare the details in the sources and/or compare the viewpoints overall.

A **simple comparison** will indicate what points of detail or viewpoint the sources agree or disagree on and **should be awarded 1 mark.** A **developed comparison** of the points of detail or overall viewpoint **should be awarded a second mark.** Candidates may achieve full marks by making four simple comparisons, two developed comparisons (or by any combination of these).

Possible points of comparison may include:

Source B	Source C
Overall: The sources agree about the events of the Battle of Yorktown	
Cornwallis moved into Virginia and began to build a base at Yorktown.	...Cornwallis's British forces set up camp at Yorktown.
By late summer, Cornwallis's position at Yorktown was deteriorating fast.	Yorktown however turned out to be a poor position and his situation became more serious.
...American forces prevented him from moving inland...	..American troops moved quickly into the area to surround him and keep him there.

Section 3, Context C, USA 1850–1880

56. *Candidates can be credited in a number of ways* **up to a maximum of 6 marks.**

Candidates must make a number of points that make the issue plain or clear, for example by showing connections between factors or causal relationships between events or ideas. These should be key reasons but there is no need for any evaluation or prioritising of these reasons.

Up to a maximum of 6 marks in total, **1 mark** should be awarded for each accurate, relevant reason, and a **second mark** should be awarded for reasons that are developed. Candidates may achieve full marks by providing six straightforward reasons, three developed reasons (or any combination of these).

Possible reasons may include:
1. desire for good farmland/thought the land would be more fertile in the West

2. ranch owners realised the Great Plains could feed their huge herds of cattle
3. government publicity encouraged people to move West with promises of a better life
4. Government Acts eg Homestead Act, offered cheap/free land to settlers
5. to fulfil Manifest Destiny as many Americans saw it as their duty to spread their way of life
6. searching for gold/"California gold rush" attracted many hoping to become rich
7. railways encouraged many settlers to move West by providing quick transport
8. railway companies sold land cheaply to settlers which encouraged settlers to move
9. some settlers were attracted West by a sense of adventure
10. to be able to enjoy religious freedom away from other people eg Mormons
11. freed slaves headed West after 1865 to escape persecution.

Any other valid reason

57. *Candidates can be credited in a number of ways* **up to a maximum of 6 marks.**

Candidates must make a judgement about the extent to which the source provides a full description or explanation of a given event or development.

Up to a maximum of 6 marks in total, **1 mark** should be awarded for each valid point selected from the source or each valid point of significant omission provided. Candidates should be awarded **up to 3 marks** for their identification of points from the source which support their judgement. Candidates should be awarded **up to 4 marks** for their identification of points of significant omission, based on their own knowledge, that support their judgement. A **maximum of 2 marks** may be awarded for answers in which no judgement has been made **or** which refer only to the source.

Possible points which may be identified from the source include:
1. the Compromise of 1850 was created by Henry Clay and others to deal with the balance between slave and free states
2. the Kansas–Nebraska Act of 1854, however, increased tensions
3. Pro-slavery people of Missouri began to pour into Kansas to help force it to be a slave state
4. the fight over slavery even erupted on the floor of the Senate/Anti-slavery campaigner Charles Sumner was beat over the head by South Carolina's pro-slavery Senator Preston Brooks.

Possible points of significant omission may include:
5. Dred Scott case caused unhappiness among abolitionists and Northern States
6. attack on Harper's Ferry by John Brown heightened tension
7. South was alarmed by election of Lincoln who wanted to halt spread of slavery
8. Lincoln's election was seen as the last straw by Southern States
9. South Carolina seceded and other Southern States followed
10. Fort Sumter was besieged by Confederate troops/food supplies cut off
11. the Confederates opened fire on the fort which led to an outburst of patriotic fever in the North.

Any other valid point of significant omission

58. *Candidates can be credited in a number of ways up to a maximum of 4 marks.*

They may take different perspectives on the events and may describe a variety of different aspects of the events. Candidates must make a number of relevant, factual points. These should be key points. These do not have to be in any particular order.

1 mark should be awarded for each accurate relevant key point of knowledge. A **second mark** should be awarded for each point that is developed, **up to a maximum of 4 marks.** Candidates may achieve full marks by providing four straightforward points, by making two developed points (or any combination of these).

Possible points of knowledge may include:
  1. was set up to help newly freed slaves
  2. it helped provide food for poor freed slaves
  3. helped former slaves buy land for farming
  4. paid for schools/helped former slaves learn to read and write
  5. set up/paid for hospitals for former slaves
  6. provided temporary shelter for former slaves
  7. helped former slaves find employment.

Any other valid point of knowledge

59. *Candidates can be credited in a number of ways up to a maximum of 4 marks.*

Candidates must interpret the evidence and make direct comparisons between sources. Candidates are expected to compare content directly on a point-by-point basis. They may compare the details in the sources and/or compare the viewpoints overall.

A **simple comparison** will indicate what points of detail or viewpoint the sources agree or disagree on and **should be awarded 1 mark.** A **developed comparison** of the points of detail or overall viewpoint **should be awarded a second mark.** Candidates may achieve full marks by making four simple comparisons, two developed comparisons (or by any combination of these).

Possible points of comparison may include:

Source B	Source C
Overall: The sources agree about what happened during Reconstruction	
Hostility was shown to the school teachers like me who taught in schools for blacks.	Teachers in schools for black Americans became key figures so they were frequently intimidated.
They came at night and gave these warnings.	These attacks usually took place at night...
...they were whipping me...	...they whipped, mutilated and murdered black people.

60. *Candidates can be credited in a number of ways up to a maximum of 9 marks.*

Candidates must make a judgement about the extent to which different factors contributed to an event or development, or its impact. They are required to provide a balanced account of the influence of different factors and come to a reasoned conclusion based on the evidence presented.

Up to 5 marks can be awarded for relevant, factual, key points of knowledge used to support factors, with **1 mark** awarded for each point (but **one mark should be deducted** if the correct process is not clear in at least two factors).

If **only one factor is presented, a maximum of 3 marks should be awarded** for relevant points of knowledge. A **further 4 marks** can be awarded for providing the answer in a structured way and coming to a reasoned conclusion.

Possible factors	Key points of knowledge to support this factor may include:
Discovery of gold	1. Bozeman Trail was cause of conflict/triggered war: Native Americans opposed white men building road to gold mines 2. Trail passed through Yellowstone River/heart of Sioux hunting grounds 3. Custer's discovery of gold in Black Hills brought thousands of miners/Black Hills were sacred Sioux territory 4. grants to encourage gold prospecting alarmed Native Americans (Colorado and Montana in 1858 and the Black Hills in 1874).
Railways	5. railroads caused tension with Native Americans: opened up West/encouraged white settlers to buy prairie lands 6. building railways across the Plains disturbed the Native American hunting grounds/migration of the buffalo.
Buffalo	7. Native Americans feared destruction of bison/buffalo herds: reliance on buffalo for all their needs 8. railroad companies sent in hunters to kill buffalo.
Beliefs	9. Native Americans believed Great Spirit created land for their care; whites had a "property attitude" 10. white settlers believed in Manifest Destiny that they had the right to settle where they wanted.
Treaties	11. treaties with the Native Americans were broken/Native Americans felt betrayed due to broken promises.
Reservations	12. many white Americans favoured setting up reservations to keep Native Americans out of their way/Native American feared reservations would mean the destruction of their way of life.

Any other relevant information

Section 3, Context D, Hitler and Nazi Germany, 1919–1939

61. *Candidates can be credited in a number of ways up to a maximum of 4 marks.*

They may take different perspectives on the events and may describe a variety of different aspects of the events. Candidates must make a number of relevant, factual points. These should be key points. These do not have to be in any particular order.

1 mark should be awarded for each accurate relevant key point of knowledge. A **second mark** should be awarded for each point that is developed, **up to a maximum of 4 marks.** Candidates may achieve full marks by providing four straightforward points, by making two developed points (or any combination of these).

Possible points of knowledge may include:
  1. Von Kahr, Governor of Bavaria, was making a speech at a meeting in a Munich beer hall
  2. Nazi SA men surrounded the building

3. Hitler burst into the hall and ordered three Bavarian leaders, Von Kahr, Von Seisser and Von Lossow into a private/side room
4. Hitler claimed they had agreed to support him/announced a national revolution had begun
5. Ludendorff let the Bavarian leaders go once they had promised their support
6. once free the Bavarian leaders withdrew their support and ordered the putsch to be crushed
7. next day Hitler marched in centre of Munich with several thousand Nazis
8. police blocked their way and shooting broke out and a number of Nazis and policemen were killed.

Any other valid point of knowledge

62. *Candidates can be credited in a number of ways **up to a maximum of 9 marks**.*

Candidates must make a judgement about the extent to which different factors contributed to an event or development, or its impact. They are required to provide a balanced account of the influence of different factors and come to a reasoned conclusion based on the evidence presented.

Up to 5 marks can be awarded for relevant, factual, key points of knowledge used to support factors, with **1 mark** awarded for each point (but **one mark should be deducted** if the correct process is not clear in at least two factors). If **only one factor is presented, a maximum of 3 marks should be awarded** for relevant points of knowledge. A **further 4 marks** can be awarded for providing the answer in a structured way and coming to a reasoned conclusion.

Possible factors	Key points of knowledge to support this factor may include:
Weimar Republic	1. blamed for signing the hated Treaty of Versailles (November Criminals) and its harsh terms 2. criticised for the voting system, proportional representation, which produced weak coalition governments 3. unpopular as coalition governments lacked authority/seemed unable to solve problems facing Germany 4. blamed for economic hardships such as hyperinflation, the Wall Street Crash and mass unemployment.
Appeal of Hitler	5. Hitler appeared to offer strong, decisive leadership 6. Hitler was an outstanding orator who inspired people 7. had a clear, simple message which appealed to many people.
Nazi Policies	8. Nazis seemed to offer something to most groups/classes in Germany, such as jobs for the unemployed, crush Communism, remilitarisation, destroy Treaty of Versailles 9. promised to restore order to Germany after chaos of the Weimar period.
Nazi propaganda	10. Nazi use of propaganda eg posters, Nazi newspapers gained widespread support 11. held large public meetings, parades, rallies, eg Nuremberg, which excited and impressed people 12. use of SA to impress people/well-disciplined in times of chaos.

Up to **4 marks** should be awarded for presenting the answer in a structured way, leading to a conclusion which addresses the question, as follows:

1 mark for an introduction (which places the question in its historical context or outlines relevant factors).

1 mark for the answer being presented in a structured way (with knowledge being organised in support of different factors).

1 mark for a conclusion with a valid judgement (or overall summary).

1 mark for a reason in support of the judgement (a summary cannot be supported).

Any other relevant point

63. *Candidates can be credited in a number of ways **up to a maximum of 4 marks**.*

Candidates must interpret the evidence and make direct comparisons between sources. Candidates are expected to compare content directly on a point-by-point basis. They may compare the details in the sources and/or compare the viewpoints overall.

A **simple comparison** will indicate what points of detail or viewpoint the sources agree or disagree on and **should be awarded 1 mark**. A **developed comparison** of the points of detail or overall viewpoint **should be awarded a second mark**. Candidates may achieve full marks by making four simple comparisons, two developed comparisons (or by any combination of these).

Possible points of comparison may include:

Source A	Source B
Overall: The sources agree about the Nazi ideas on race	
...differences between the races was a matter of scientific fact.	...biological research had shown that there was a distinction between races.
...Aryan people of northern Europe were superior in every way.	...Aryans of Germany and Scandinavia were the Master Race.
It was logical that superior people like this should be in control of all other races.	This gave these superior races the authority to rule over the peoples of the world.

64. *Candidates can be credited in a number of ways **up to a maximum of 6 marks**.*

Candidates must make a number of points that make the issue plain or clear, for example by showing connections between factors or causal relationships between events or ideas. These should be key reasons but there is no need for any evaluation or prioritising of these reasons.

Up to a maximum of 6 marks in total, **1 mark** should be awarded for each accurate, relevant reason, and a **second mark** should be awarded for reasons that are developed. Candidates may achieve full marks by providing six straightforward reasons, three developed reasons (or any combination of these).

Possible reasons may include:

1. fear of the Nazi regime/intimidation by the SS deterred opposition
2. opposition groups often infiltrated by Gestapo/spies leading to their arrest
3. opponents scared by brutal treatment/hanging of opponents
4. opposition leaders were arrested and sent to concentration camps/outspoken individuals eg Bonhoeffer, Niemoller were arrested and sent to camps which weakened opposition groups

5. many opponents of the Nazis fearful for their lives fled abroad
6. opposition groups had to meet in secret, making meetings difficult/dangerous
7. all other political parties/trade unions were banned
8. little cooperation between the opposition groups as they didn't trust each other
9. Nazi control of the media made it difficult for opponents to publicise their views
10. Nazi propaganda brainwashed people into supporting the Nazis
11. there was widespread support for the Nazis and most Germans were impressed as Hitler was a strong leader/solving Germany's problems
12. Nazi control of the courts meant opponents were harshly punished.

Any other valid reason

65. *Candidates can be credited in a number of ways up to a maximum of 6 marks.*

Candidates must make a judgement about the extent to which the source provides a full description or explanation of a given event or development.

Up to a maximum of 6 marks in total, **1 mark** should be awarded for each valid point selected from the source or each valid point of significant omission provided.

Candidates should be awarded **up to 3 marks** for their identification of points from the source which support their judgement. Candidates should be awarded **up to 4 marks** for their identification of points of significant omission, based on their own knowledge, that support their judgement. A **maximum of 2 marks** may be awarded for answers in which no judgement has been made **or** which refer only to the source.

Possible points which may be identified from the source include:
1. the introduction of new Nazi textbooks
2. the number of PE periods was increased at the expense of religious education
3. competitive field games were added to curriculum
4. at the start of class, we had to raise our arms in the "Heil Hitler!" salute.

Possible points of significant omission may include:
5. indoctrination of Nazi ideas eg anti-Semitism/militarism
6. biology was used to 'prove' the Nazi belief in racial superiority/introduction of new subjects such as Racial Science/Eugenics
7. for girls emphasis on 'female' subjects (Kinder, Kirche, Kuche)
8. all teachers had to join the Nazi Teachers' League/teachers suspected of being disloyal to the Party were arrested/pictures of Hitler/Swastika flag in classrooms
9. Jewish children were humiliated/from 1938 only allowed to attend Jewish schools.

Any other valid point of significant omission

Section 3, Context E, Red Flag: Lenin and the Russian Revolution, 1894–1921

66. *Candidates can be credited in a number of ways up to a maximum of 4 marks.*

They may take different perspectives on the events and may describe a variety of different aspects of the events. Candidates must make a number of relevant, factual points. These should be key points. These do not have to be in any particular order.

1 mark should be awarded for each accurate relevant key point of knowledge. A **second mark** should be awarded

for each point that is developed, **up to a maximum of 4 marks.** Candidates may achieve full marks by providing four straightforward points, by making two developed points (or any combination of these).

Possible points of knowledge may include:
1. Tsar was an autocrat/not answerable to anyone
2. Orthodox Church preached that his rule was the will of God
3. the army was loyal and was used to put down any uprisings
4. secret police, Okhrana, kept watch on any suspected opponents
5. execution/prison/exile to Siberia extensively used as a deterrent
6. the press was censored
7. government ran the trades unions to maintain control of the workers
8. policy of Russification used to keep control of national minorities.

Any other valid point of knowledge

67. *Candidates can be credited in a number of ways up to a maximum of 6 marks.*

Candidates must make a number of points that make the issue plain or clear, for example by showing connections between factors or causal relationships between events or ideas. These should be key reasons but there is no need for any evaluation or prioritising of these reasons.

Up to a maximum of 6 marks in total, **1 mark** should be awarded for each accurate, relevant reason, and a **second mark** should be awarded for reasons that are developed. Candidates may achieve full marks by providing six straightforward reasons, three developed reasons (or any combination of these).

Possible reasons may include:
1. people hated the repressive policies of the Tsar and his government
2. most groups felt that their problems were being ignored by the government
3. peasants struggled to make a living off the land/high taxes/redemption debt
4. factory workers in the industrial cities faced terrible hardship, with long hours, low wages, dangerous working conditions, and terrible living conditions
5. the policy of Russification caused anger and discontent among national minorities
6. the economic problems people faced grew worse during the war with Japan
7. defeat by Japan led to unrest/strengthened the revolutionary movement
8. shortages of food, fuel and high unemployment in industrial cities made people desperate and angry
9. impact of Bloody Sunday angered people and led to discontent and strikes
10. workers and liberal middle classes united against Tsar
11. revolutionary groups became more organised eg formation of St Petersburg Soviet
12. discontent in the armed forces increased during the war.

Any other valid reason

68. *Candidates can be credited in a number of ways up to a maximum of 6 marks.*

Candidates must make a judgement about the extent to which the source provides a full description or explanation of a given event or development.

Up to a maximum of 6 marks in total, **1 mark** should be awarded for each valid point selected from the source or each valid point of significant omission provided.

Candidates should be awarded **up to 3 marks** for their identification of points from the source which support their judgement. Candidates should be awarded **up to 4 marks** for their identification of points of significant omission, based on their own knowledge, that support their judgement. A **maximum of 2 marks** may be awarded for answers in which no judgement has been made **or** which refer only to the source.

Possible points which may be identified from the source include:
1. the October Manifesto established a parliament or Duma elected by the people
2. it also allowed the Russian people basic rights, such as freedom of speech
3. his land reforms allowed peasants to become owners of their own land
4. he set up a peasants' bank to provide loans to help them buy the land.

Possible points of significant omission may include:
5. political parties were legalised
6. peasants no longer had to pay the redemption debt
7. peasants could consolidate the size of their land holdings
8. a system of health insurance introduced for industrial workers
9. introduced some improvements to working conditions in factories
10. thousands more primary schools established.

Any other valid point of significant omission

69. *Candidates can be credited in a number of ways up to a maximum of 4 marks.*

Candidates must interpret the evidence and make direct comparisons between sources. Candidates are expected to compare content directly on a point-by-point basis. They may compare the details in the sources and/or compare the viewpoints overall.

A **simple comparison** will indicate what points of detail or viewpoint the sources agree or disagree on and **should be awarded 1 mark**. A **developed comparison** of the points of detail or overall viewpoint **should be awarded a second mark**. Candidates may achieve full marks by making four simple comparisons, two developed comparisons (or by any combination of these).

Possible points of comparison may include:

Source B	Source C
Overall: The sources agree about the effects of the First World War on the Russian people	
Prices have gone up...	The shortages meant that food prices went up...
Food is hard to get.	...Russian cities suffered from a shortage of food.
They blame the Tsar and say "he does not care we might starve".	...urban workers faced terrible starvation...

70. *Candidates can be credited in a number of ways up to a maximum of 9 marks.*

Candidates must make a judgement about the extent to which different factors contributed to an event or development, or its impact. They are required to provide a balanced account of the influence of different factors and come to a reasoned conclusion based on the evidence presented.

Up to 5 marks can be awarded for relevant, factual, key points of knowledge used to support factors, with **1 mark**

awarded for each point (but **one mark should be deducted** if the correct process is not clear in at least two factors). If **only one factor is presented, a maximum of 3 marks should be awarded** for relevant points of knowledge. A **further 4 marks** can be awarded for providing the answer in a structured way and coming to a reasoned conclusion.

Possible factors	Key points of knowledge to support this factor may include:
Trotsky	1. Trotsky was a skilled commander of the Red Army who was decisive and ruthless 2. Trotsky disciplined the Red Army to be an effective fighting force/conscripted men to raise 5 million by 1920/raised the Red Cavalry to counter the Cossacks 3. Trotsky used experienced Tsarist officers, supervised by political commissars/used Cheka to discourage desertions.
Red Army	4. by the end of 1919 the Red soldiers outnumbered the Whites by ten to one 5. soldiers were well supplied (boots, food, tobacco) 6. energetic propaganda campaign boosted soldiers' morale.
Territorial advantage	7. Reds controlled a compact area in the centre of Russia (easier to defend) 8. Reds had control of the industrial centres/factories 9. Reds controlled the railways/had good communication/able to transport of munitions etc.
Weaknesses of Whites	10. Whites had weak leadership, many generals were corrupt/incompetent 11. White forces were split/never united their full strength/White generals did not co-ordinate their attacks/strategy 12. Whites held peripheral areas/did not control the industrial centre or rail networks making it difficult to supply troops.

Up to **4 marks** should be awarded for presenting the answer in a structured way, leading to a conclusion which addresses the question, as follows:

1 mark for an introduction (which places the question in its historical context or outlines relevant factors).

1 mark for the answer being presented in a structured way (with knowledge being organised in support of different factors).

1 mark for a conclusion with a valid judgement (or overall summary).

1 mark for a reason in support of the judgement (a summary cannot be supported).

Any other relevant point

Section 3, Context F, Mussolini and Fascist Italy, 1919–1939

71. *Candidates can be credited in a number of ways up to a maximum of 4 marks.*

Candidates must interpret the evidence and make direct comparisons between sources. Candidates are expected to compare content directly on a point-by-point basis. They may compare the details in the sources and/or compare the viewpoints overall.

A **simple comparison** will indicate what points of detail or viewpoint the sources agree or disagree on and **should be** awarded **1 mark**. A **developed comparison** of the points of detail or overall viewpoint **should be awarded a second mark**. Candidates may achieve full marks by making four simple comparisons, two developed comparisons (or by any combination of these).

Possible points of comparison may include:

Source A	Source B
Overall: The sources agree about the events which led to Mussolini's seizure of power in Italy in 1922.	
This put Mussolini in the position to challenge the government, which he did in what became known as the famous "March on Rome".	...Mussolini decided to seize the government when he and his followers marched on the capital, Rome.
The government decided to send in the army to try and stop Mussolini.	...the prime minister called out the army when the Fascists surrounded Rome.
The king, Victor Emmanuel III, however decided instead of using the army, to give in to Mussolini's demands.	...the pressure proved too much for the Italian King who refused to use the military to squash Mussolini's "march".

72. *Candidates can be credited in a number of ways up to a maximum of 6 marks.*

Candidates must make a judgement about the extent to which the source provides a full description or explanation of a given event or development.

Up to a maximum of 6 marks in total, **1 mark** should be awarded for each valid point selected from the source or each valid point of significant omission provided.

Candidates should be awarded **up to 3 marks** for their identification of points from the source which support their judgement. Candidates should be awarded **up to 4 marks** for their identification of points of significant omission, based on their own knowledge, that support their judgement. A **maximum of 2 marks** may be awarded for answers in which no judgement has been made **or** which refer only to the source.

Possible points which may be identified from the source include:
1. the leadership cult in Fascist Italy started almost as soon as Mussolini came to power in 1922
2. his role as Duce of Fascism and Head of the Government had been secured by changes to the law
3. Mussolini had undoubted charisma and political intelligence (with which to maintain his power over Fascism and the Italian people)
4. his main talents lay chiefly in the areas of acting and propaganda.

Possible points of significant omission may include:
5. the cult was intended to build popular support for the dictator and to secure support for the government
6. the media played an important role in establishing the cult of "Il Duce"
7. Mussolini was shown as a man chosen by destiny to save Italy and its people from Communism and Socialism
8. he was portrayed as the new Caesar/a man of genius/a man of action
9. he established "holy days" such as 23 March, to remind Italians of the advent of Fascism
10. newspapers were forbidden to mention any signs of illness and even his birthdays were to be ignored as this would reveal his age.

Any other valid point of significant omission

73. *Candidates can be credited in a number of ways up to a maximum of 6 marks.*

Candidates must make a number of points that make the issue plain or clear, for example by showing connections between factors or causal relationships between events or ideas. These should be key reasons but there is no need for any evaluation or prioritising of these reasons.

Up to a maximum of 6 marks in total, **1 mark** should be awarded for each accurate, relevant reason, and a **second mark** should be awarded for reasons that are developed. Candidates may achieve full marks by providing six straightforward reasons, three developed reasons (or any combination of these).

Possible reasons may include:
1. revaluation of the lira in 1927 led to decline in exports, causing discontent
2. increase in unemployment 1926–28. By 1933 unemployment had reached 2 million, causing unpopularity
3. high tariffs restricted imports, so people unhappy
4. real wages fell, so people were angry
5. many workers were unhappy when trade unions were outlawed
6. sick pay and paid holidays were not introduced until 1938, which disappointed people
7. the failure to make Italy self-sufficient contributed to growing unpopularity
8. as part of the Battle for Grain, land in central and southern regions was turned over to wheat production despite being unsuitable (traditional agricultural exports declined), unpopular in these areas
9. increasing government control of industry was resented.

Any other valid reason

74. *Candidates can be credited in a number of ways up to a maximum of 4 marks.*

They may take different perspectives on the events and may describe a variety of different aspects of the events. Candidates must make a number of relevant, factual points. These should be key points. These do not have to be in any particular order.

1 mark should be awarded for each accurate relevant key point of knowledge. A **second mark** should be awarded for each point that is developed, **up to a maximum of 4 marks**. Candidates may achieve full marks by providing four straightforward points, by making two developed points (or any combination of these).

Possible points of knowledge may include:
1. to make Italy a great world power/the dominant power in the Mediterranean
2. to expand Italy's colonial empire in Africa/take over Ethiopia
3. to increase Italian influence in the Balkans
4. to build up Italy's armed forces to make Italy feared
5. to make Albania into an Italian satellite state
6. to encourage the break-up of Yugoslavia
7. to improve relations with Britain
8. to contain Germany's influence in Austria.

Any other valid point of knowledge

75. *Candidates can be credited in a number of ways up to a maximum of 9 marks.*

Candidates must make a judgement about the extent to which different factors contributed to an event or development, or its impact. They are required to provide a balanced account of the influence of different factors and come to a reasoned conclusion based on the evidence presented.

Up to 5 marks can be awarded for relevant, factual, key points of knowledge used to support factors, with 1 mark awarded for each point (but one mark should be deducted if the correct process is not clear in at least two factors). If only one factor is presented, a maximum of 3 marks should be awarded for relevant points of knowledge. A further 4 marks can be awarded for providing the answer in a structured way and coming to a reasoned conclusion.

Possible factors	Key points of knowledge to support this factor may include:
Fear/use of violence	1. a secret police force was set up, the OVRA, which spied on opponents 2. many opponents of the regime were murdered/sent to concentration camps, which scared people 3. people were afraid of the Blackshirts and this ensured Italians didn't challenge Mussolini.
Mussolini	4. he seemed to provide the strong leadership which Italians longed for and who would restore Italy's greatness 5. he was the new Caesar/a man of genius/a man of action.
Weakness of opposition	6. after 1926, all rival political parties were declared illegal 7. opposition newspapers were banned in Italy making it difficult for them to get publicity 8. opposition groups were weakened by the inability to unite on a common platform.
Propaganda	9. radio and the cinema were also used to broadcast Fascist propaganda 10. censorship made it difficult to oppose Mussolini.
Popular support	11. he bought off key groups: the workers were promised an eight-hour day/the rich benefited from a reduction in death duties 12. got the support of the Roman Catholic Church by making religious education compulsory in all elementary schools/entering into the Lateran Treaty.

Up to 4 marks should be awarded for presenting the answer in a structured way, leading to a conclusion which addresses the question, as follows:

1 mark for an introduction (which places the question in its historical context or outlines relevant factors).

1 mark for the answer being presented in a structured way (with knowledge being organised in support of different factors).

1 mark for a conclusion with a valid judgement (or overall summary).

1 mark for a reason in support of the judgement (a summary cannot be supported).

Any other relevant factor

Section 3, Context G, Free at Last? Civil Rights in the USA, 1918–1968

76. Candidates can be credited in a number of ways up to a maximum of 9 marks.

Candidates must make a judgement about the extent to which different factors contributed to an event or development, or its impact. They are required to provide a balanced account

of the influence of different factors and come to a reasoned conclusion based on the evidence presented.

Up to 5 marks can be awarded for relevant, factual, key points of knowledge used to support factors, with 1 mark awarded for each point (but one mark should be deducted if the correct process is not clear in at least two factors). If only one factor is presented, a maximum of 3 marks should be awarded for relevant points of knowledge. A further 4 marks can be awarded for providing the answer in a structured way and coming to a reasoned conclusion.

Possible factors	Key points of knowledge to support this factor may include:
Fear of revolution	1. 'Red Scare' – many Americans were afraid that immigrants from Eastern Europe would bring in dangerous new ideas such as communism 2. growing fear of social unrest/violent revolution in America in the aftermath of Russian Revolution 3. 1919 huge wave of strikes in USA which Americans claimed were caused by revolutionary workers from Eastern Europe.
Self-interest	4. concern that immigrants would take jobs/depress wages/break strikes 5. concern that immigrants would create pressure on scarce housing 6. American workers saw immigrants as a threat to their standard of living.
Racism	7. old immigrants, especially the WASPs, had lived in USA for several generations and many thought the new immigrants were inferior 8. WASPs saw the new immigrants as a threat to the American way of life 9. immigrants were often blamed for crime, disease, alcoholism and other social problems in cities 10. WASPs argued America must not be turned into a second rate power by second rate people (new immigrants).
Social factors	11. there were religious differences – older immigrants mainly Protestant, new immigrants Catholic/Jewish 12. new immigrants often settled amongst people from their own countries leading to a perception that they were unwilling to mix with other Americans.

Up to 4 marks should be awarded for presenting the answer in a structured way, leading to a conclusion which addresses the question, as follows:

1 mark for an introduction (which places the question in its historical context or outlines relevant factors).

1 mark for the answer being presented in a structured way (with knowledge being organised in support of different factors).

1 mark for a conclusion with a valid judgement (or overall summary).

1 mark for a reason in support of the judgement (a summary cannot be supported).

Any other relevant factor

77. Candidates can be credited in a number of ways up to a maximum of 4 marks.

Candidates must interpret the evidence and make direct comparisons between sources. Candidates are expected to compare content directly on a point-by-point basis. They may compare the details in the sources and/or compare the viewpoints overall.

A **simple comparison** will indicate what points of detail or viewpoint the sources agree or disagree on and **should be awarded 1 mark**. A **developed comparison** of the points of detail or overall viewpoint **should be awarded a second mark**. Candidates may achieve full marks by making four simple comparisons, two developed comparisons (or by any combination of these).

Possible points of comparison may include:

Source A	Source B
Overall: The sources agree about the experience of immigrants in the USA during the 1920s	
They headed for the great cities (where there was a far better prospect of finding employment).	My family lived in the city of Chicago.
Few planned to stay in America for long, but wanted to return to Italy some day.	My father came from Monfalcone in Italy and always hoped to return there.
Italian Americans succeeded in jobs requiring little formal education.	(When I was 14 years old I started dodging school) and so didn't get much formal education.

78. *Candidates can be credited in a number of ways **up to a maximum of 4 marks**.*

They may take different perspectives on the events and may describe a variety of different aspects of the events. Candidates must make a number of relevant, factual points. These should be key points. These do not have to be in any particular order.

1 mark should be awarded for each accurate relevant key point of knowledge. A **second mark** should be awarded for each point that is developed, **up to a maximum of 4 marks**. Candidates may achieve full marks by providing four straightforward points, by making two developed points (or any combination of these).

Possible points of knowledge may include:
1. created a segregated society/enforced segregation between black and white people
2. some states made relationships/marriage between races illegal
3. separate schooling was enforced
4. separate toilets, washrooms and canteens
5. separate drinking fountains/hospital wards
6. transport facilities – trains and buses – were segregated
7. separate leisure and sporting facilities
8. black Americans were humiliated/made to feel inferior.

Any other valid point of knowledge

79. *Candidates can be credited in a number of ways **up to a maximum of 6 marks**.*

Candidates must make a number of points that make the issue plain or clear, for example by showing connections between factors or causal relationships between events or ideas. These should be key reasons but there is no need for any evaluation or prioritising of these reasons.

Up to a maximum of 6 marks in total, **1 mark** should be awarded for each accurate, relevant reason, and a **second mark** should be awarded for reasons that are developed. Candidates may achieve full marks by providing six straightforward reasons, three developed reasons (or any combination of these).

Possible reasons may include:
1. the groundwork for a Civil rights movement had been laid by early reformers such as du Bois, Garvey and Washington who inspired others to join the cause
2. the experience of black American servicemen during WW2 had made them aware of non-segregated societies and more determined to fight against discrimination
3. during WW2 all Americans were called upon to fight for freedom and democracy but black Americans felt that they were denied their basic rights in their own country leading to growing support for civil rights for black Americans
4. success of Philip Randolph and the 'Double V' campaign encouraged greater demands for civil rights
5. NAACP and other organisations effectively highlighted discrimination faced by black Americans and gained support of both black and white Americans in support of civil rights
6. black people in the South living under a system of segregation/were subjected to violent persecution, such as lynching, and demanded reform
7. concern at other inequalities faced by black Americans eg low wages, poor housing and growing demands for improvements
8. success of non-violent protests – eg Montgomery Bus Boycott, Birmingham march encouraged others to become involved
9. leadership of black leaders such as Martin Luther King/ Malcolm X inspired others to join the civil rights campaign
10. successes of non-violent movement encouraged black Americans to demand more
11. impact of more radical protests such as Nation of Islam attracted those who didn't believe peaceful methods were working
12. media coverage especially television heightened awareness and motivated many to support the campaign.

Any other valid reason

80. *Candidates can be credited in a number of ways **up to a maximum of 6 marks**.*

Candidates must make a judgement about the extent to which the source provides a full description or explanation of a given event or development.

Up to a maximum of 6 marks in total, **1 mark** should be awarded for each valid point selected from the source or each valid point of significant omission provided.

Candidates should be awarded **up to 3 marks** for their identification of points from the source which support their judgement. Candidates should be awarded **up to 4 marks** for their identification of points of significant omission, based on their own knowledge, that support their judgement. A **maximum of 2 marks** may be awarded for answers in which no judgement has been made **or** which refer only to the source.

Possible points which may be identified from the source include:
1. urged that it was now time to defend black Americans against this white aggression
2. (Huey Newton) he voiced the distrust many black Americans felt towards the police
3. self-help programmes organised by the Black Panthers
4. they also had a ten-point programme which included demands for better housing and education.

Possible points of significant omission may include:
5. Black Panthers condoned use of violence and this appealed to many blacks who were frustrated by the non-violent methods of the Civil Rights Movement

6. Black Panthers had charismatic leaders who gained attention and popularity
7. they demanded the release of black prisoners which had widespread support
8. Black Panthers gained support due to their efforts to give practical help to poor blacks such as breakfast clubs in schools and providing free health clinics
9. The Black Panthers encouraged blacks to be proud of the colour of their skin and their African American culture which appealed to many
10. Black Panthers gained much publicity from the support of athletes at the 1968 Olympic Games eg Black Power salute was a political demonstration conducted by African-American athletes, which inspired many other black Americans.

Any other valid point of significant omission

Section 3, Context H, Appeasement and the Road to War, 1918–1939

81. *Candidates can be credited in a number of ways up to a maximum of 6 marks.*

Candidates must make a number of points that make the issue plain or clear, for example by showing connections between factors or causal relationships between events or ideas. These should be key reasons but there is no need for any evaluation or prioritising of these reasons.

Up to a maximum of 6 marks in total, **1 mark** should be awarded for each accurate, relevant reason, and a **second mark** should be awarded for reasons that are developed. Candidates may achieve full marks by providing six straightforward reasons, three developed reasons (or any combination of these).

Possible reasons may include:
1. furious as it was far harsher than expected and would cripple Germany
2. expected a peace treaty based on Wilson's Fourteen Points and angry it wasn't
3. criticised it as a diktat/dictated peace as Germany had been denied any say in it
4. hated the shame of the War Guilt clause which Germany claimed was unfair
5. accused the Treaty of being based on Allies' desire for revenge
6. angry at having to pay reparations which Germany claimed it couldn't afford
7. resented the loss of German colonies which it said was unfair
8. angry at the loss of land containing many Germans, especially land lost to Poland
9. furious at the reduction in Germany's armed forces which it claimed left Germany defenceless
10. angry that Germans were denied self-determination
11. argued Germany did not deserve to be punished so severely since the Kaiser and generals were gone
12. new German Government was angry because it felt it had little chance of success after the terms were imposed.

Any other valid reason

82. *Candidates can be credited in a number of ways up to a maximum of 4 marks.*

Candidates must interpret the evidence and make direct comparisons between sources. Candidates are expected to compare content directly on a point-by-point basis. They may compare the details in the sources and/or compare the viewpoints overall.

A **simple comparison** will indicate what points of detail or viewpoint the sources agree or disagree on and **should be awarded 1 mark**. A **developed comparison** of the points of detail or overall viewpoint **should be awarded a second mark**. Candidates may achieve full marks by making four simple comparisons, two developed comparisons (or by any combination of these).

Possible points of comparison may include:

Source A	Source B
Overall: The sources agree about the work of League of Nations	
The refusal of the USA to join the League however greatly weakened it's ability to succeed.	The failure of several big powers, including the USA, to join the League badly damaged its effectiveness.
The League did manage to settle disputes between smaller nations who could be leaned on.	The League however did achieve some success in solving arguments between lesser countries.
When disputes involved larger countries, the League however often failed to act.	Actions against larger nations who challenged the League were inadequate and frequently half-hearted.

83. *Candidates can be credited in a number of ways up to a maximum of 4 marks.*

They may take different perspectives on the events and may describe a variety of different aspects of the events. Candidates must make a number of relevant, factual points. These should be key points. These do not have to be in any particular order.

1 mark should be awarded for each accurate relevant key point of knowledge. A **second mark** should be awarded for each point that is developed, **up to a maximum of 4 marks**. Candidates may achieve full marks by providing four straightforward points, by making two developed points (or any combination of these).

Possible points of knowledge may include:
1. to restore German power by breaking the Treaty of Versailles
2. to build up the German army/create a German air force
3. to remilitarise the Rhineland
4. to regain the territory that Germany had lost after World War One
5. to achieve Anschluss with Austria
6. to create a Greater Germany for all Germans
7. to gain Lebensraum/'living space' in Eastern Europe for the German people
8. to defeat Communism.

Any other valid point of knowledge

84. *Candidates can be credited in a number of ways up to a maximum of 9 marks.*

Candidates must make a judgement about the extent to which different factors contributed to an event or development, or its impact. They are required to provide a balanced account of the influence of different factors and come to a reasoned conclusion based on the evidence presented.

Up to 5 marks can be awarded for relevant, factual, key points of knowledge used to support factors, with **1 mark** awarded for each point (but **one mark should be deducted** if the correct process is not clear in at least two factors). If **only one factor is presented, a maximum of 3 marks should be awarded** for relevant points of knowledge. A

further 4 marks can be awarded for providing the answer in a structured way and coming to a reasoned conclusion.

Up to **4 marks** should be awarded for presenting the answer in a structured way, leading to a conclusion which addresses the question, as follows:

Possible factors	Key points of knowledge to support this factor may include:
Military concerns	1. chiefs of the armed forces advised that the British military was unprepared for war/Britain had failed to modernise her armed forces
	2. Britain was concerned about Germany's powerful army and air force
	3. Britain's air preparations were inadequate, with insufficient fighter planes, radar systems or anti-aircraft artillery
	4. there was fear of bombing from the air – "The Bomber will always get through", according to the government.
Public opinion	5. majority of the public were still fearful of war after the huge losses suffered during World War One
	6. public concerns over the cost of rearmament (welfare vs warfare)
	7. there was a significant pacifist movement in the 1930s which was strongly against war eg the 'Peace Ballot'.
Relations with Hitler	8. Chamberlain believed that Hitler had a genuine grievance over the Sudetenland/Versailles was unjust and Germans should have some form of self-determination
	9. Chamberlain felt Hitler had only limited demands/was a man he could do business with.
Lack of allies	10. France was unwilling to support conflict over the Sudetenland
	11. USA was following an isolationist policy
	12. Empire was unwilling to fight eg disturbances in India.

1 mark for an introduction (which places the question in its historical context or outlines relevant factors).

1 mark for the answer being presented in a structured way (with knowledge being organised in support of different factors).

1 mark for a conclusion with a valid judgement (or overall summary).

1 mark for a reason in support of the judgement (a summary cannot be supported).

Any other relevant factor

85. *Candidates can be credited in a number of ways up to a maximum of 6 marks.*

Candidates must make a judgement about the extent to which the source provides a full description or explanation of a given event or development.

Up to a maximum of 6 marks in total, **1 mark** should be awarded for each valid point selected from the source or each valid point of significant omission provided.

Candidates should be awarded **up to 3 marks** for their identification of points from the source which support their judgement. Candidates should be awarded **up to 4 marks** for their identification of points of significant omission, based on their own knowledge, that support their judgement. A **maximum of 2 marks** may be awarded for

answers in which no judgement has been made **or** which refer only to the source.

Possible points which may be identified from the source include:
1. In March 1939, German troops marched into Czechoslovakia
2. Slovakia broke away and became a pro-German 'puppet state'
3. Bohemia and Moravia became a German protectorate
4. Germany's aggression led to Great Britain and France abandoning the policy of appeasement.

Possible points of significant omission may include:
5. German demands to Poland eg return of Danzig/permission to build a road and railway line through Poland
6. Britain and France promise to defend Poland if she was attacked by Germany
7. Germany and Italy sign the 'Pact of Steel' which required them to help each other in time of war
8. August 1939, Germany and Russia sign the Nazi-Soviet Non-Aggression Pact, agreeing not to go to war with each other so Germany was safe in the east
9. September 1st, Germany invades Poland/didn't respond to Britain and France's ultimatum to withdraw German forces from Poland or face war
10. September 3rd, Britain and France declare war on Germany.

Any other valid point of significant omission

Section 3, Context I, World War II, 1939—1945

86. *Candidates can be credited in a number of ways up to a maximum of 6 marks.*

Candidates must make a number of points that make the issue plain or clear, for example by showing connections between factors or causal relationships between events or ideas. These should be key reasons but there is no need for any evaluation or prioritising of these reasons.

Up to a maximum of 6 marks in total, **1 mark** should be awarded for each accurate, relevant reason, and a **second mark** should be awarded for reasons that are developed. Candidates may achieve full marks by providing six straightforward reasons, three developed reasons (or any combination of these).

Possible reasons may include:
1. Hitler hated the Communist ideals of the USSR/thought Communism was a threat to Germany
2. Hitler believed in the expansion rights of the Master Race and wanted Russian land as Lebensraum (living space)/declared plans to invade in Mein Kampf
3. Hitler believed the Russian army would be easily defeated due to Russia's failure in the Finnish war/as well as the purge of Red Army
4. he believed USSR would be an easy target and would fall in 6 to 8 weeks
5. Hitler wanted to enslave the Russian people (untermenschen) to work for the German Master Race
6. Hitler wanted the valuable resources contained in Russia eg grain, oil, iron ore/Germany was running short of vital raw materials by 1940
7. Hitler believed Russia to be a threat to Germany's interests in the Balkans and Scandinavia
8. Stalin had resisted joining Germany, Italy and Japan in the Tripartite Pact of 1940
9. Nazi-Soviet Pact of 1939 was only an alliance of convenience so that Hitler could successfully invade Poland/Hitler did not really trust Stalin
10. Hitler believed the conquest of Russia would force Britain to surrender.

Any other valid reason

87. *Candidates can be credited in a number of ways up to a maximum of 4 marks.*

They may take different perspectives on the events and may describe a variety of different aspects of the events. Candidates must make a number of relevant, factual points. These should be key points. These do not have to be in any particular order.

1 mark should be awarded for each accurate relevant key point of knowledge. A **second mark** should be awarded for each point that is developed, **up to a maximum of 4 marks**. Candidates may achieve full marks by providing four straightforward points, by making two developed points (or any combination of these).

Possible points of knowledge may include:

1. as the last part of their plan to conquer a Pacific Empire, the Japanese decided to attack the American airbase on the Island of Midway
2. Japanese fighter aircraft launched repeated attacks on American aircraft on Midway
3. American torpedo bombers launched a fierce attack and fatally damaged two Japanese aircraft carriers
4. bombers from the Yorktown were then bombed and destroyed another Japanese carrier
5. Japanese dive bombers attacked the Yorktown resulting in the carrier having to be abandoned
6. the Americans counter-attacked and dive bombers from Enterprise mortally wounded the Japanese carrier Hiryu
7. this forced Admiral Yamamoto to abandon the Japanese Midway invasion plans
8. Battle of Midway resulted in the US Navy inflicting a huge defeat on the Japanese navy/Japanese Imperial Navy lost four large aircraft carriers, Americans only lost one.

Any other valid point of knowledge

88. *Candidates can be credited in a number of ways up to a maximum of 4 marks.*

Candidates must interpret the evidence and make direct comparisons between sources. Candidates are expected to compare content directly on a point-by-point basis. They may compare the details in the sources and/or compare the viewpoints overall.

A **simple comparison** will indicate what points of detail or viewpoint the sources agree or disagree on and **should be awarded 1 mark**. A **developed comparison** of the points of detail or overall viewpoint **should be awarded a second mark**. Candidates may achieve full marks by making four simple comparisons, two developed comparisons (or by any combination of these).

Possible points of comparison may include:

Source A	Source B
Overall: The sources agree about the work of the French Resistance	
Their methods included sabotage of the German rail network.	They destroyed trains carrying German troops and military equipment.
The help they gave the Allies was extremely important.	...the French Resistance scored key victories against the German occupation forces.
If members of the Resistance were caught they would almost certainly be tortured and executed.	These accomplishments carried a heavy price as many members of the Resistance paid for their bravery with their lives.

89. *Candidates can be credited in a number of ways up to a maximum of 9 marks.*

Candidates must make a judgement about the extent to which different factors contributed to an event or development, or its impact. They are required to provide a balanced account of the influence of different factors and come to a reasoned conclusion based on the evidence presented.

Up to 5 marks can be awarded for relevant, factual, key points of knowledge used to support factors, with **1 mark** awarded for each point (but **one mark should be deducted** if the correct process is not clear in at least two factors). If **only one factor is presented, a maximum of 3 marks should be awarded** for relevant points of knowledge. A **further 4 marks** can be awarded for providing the answer in a structured way and coming to a reasoned conclusion.

Up to 4 marks should be awarded for presenting the answer in a structured way, leading to a conclusion which addresses the question, as follows:

1 mark for an introduction (which places the question in its historical context or outlines relevant factors).

1 mark for the answer being presented in a structured way (with knowledge being organised in support of different factors).

1 mark for a conclusion with a valid judgement (or overall summary).

1 mark for a reason in support of the judgement (a summary cannot be supported).

Possible factors	Key points of knowledge to support this factor may include:
German mistakes	1. German High Command remained fixated on the Calais area even after the attack on Normandy had started
	2. a number of key German commanders were absent from their posts during the critical first hours of June 6, including Rommel who was in Germany
	3. communication problems caused German commanders to fail to react quickly enough to the assault
	4. many of the German coastal units were made up of conscripts from Nazi-conquered lands who did not wish to die for Hitler and surrendered the first chance they had
	5. the Luftwaffe's last remaining fighter squadrons in France had been moved far out of range from the Normandy beaches, thus missing the chance to spot the Allied build-up and being able to disrupt or destroy it.
Effective allied planning	6. deception plans led German intelligence to believe an attack would target Calais/use of dummy staging areas in Dover fooled the Germans
	7. Allies took advantage of bad weather to surprise the Germans.
Allied resources	8. use of Mulberry harbours allowed more troops and supplies to be brought to the beach heads
	9. use of Pluto – pipeline transporting fuel across the Channel to allow a sustained attack by the allies.
Allied military advantages	10. allied superiority in men and equipment
	11. paratroopers landed the night before to secure bridges and roads near the Normandy landing sites and hindered German counter attack
	12. members of the French Resistance and the British Special Operations Executive (SOE) provided intelligence and helped weaken German defences through sabotage.

Any other relevant point

90. *Candidates can be credited in a number of ways up to a maximum of 6 marks.*

Candidates must make a judgement about the extent to which the source provides a full description or explanation of a given event or development.

Up to **a maximum of 6 marks** in total, **1 mark** should be awarded for each valid point selected from the source or each valid point of significant omission provided. Candidates should be awarded **up to 3 marks** for their identification of points from the source which support their judgement. Candidates should be awarded **up to 4 marks** for their identification of points of significant omission, based on their own knowledge, that support their judgement. A **maximum of 2 marks** may be awarded for answers in which no judgement has been made **or** which refer only to the source.

Possible points which may be identified from the source include:
1. the Soviets sent him a birthday present in the form of an artillery barrage right into the heart of the Berlin
2. the Western Allies launched a massive air raid
3. young boys who had 'volunteered' to join the SS and die for their Führer in defence of Berlin
4. boys who were found hiding were hanged as traitors by the SS.

Possible points of significant omission may include:
5. before the main battle in Berlin commenced, the Russian army was able to encircle the city by mid-April due to their success in previous battles
6. the Russians advanced easily against poor German defences at the Oder River
7. the defence of the city of Berlin relied upon disorganised/poorly armed units from the German army and Hitler Youth members/elderly men
8. within a few days, the Soviets rapidly advanced through the city and reached the city centre where close combat raged
9. before the battle was over, Hitler and a number of his followers committed suicide
10. faced with overwhelming odds, the city's defenders finally surrendered on 2 May.

Any other valid point of significant omission

Section 3, Context J, The Cold War, 1945–1989

91. *Candidates can be credited in a number of ways up to a maximum of 4 marks.*

Candidates must interpret the evidence and make direct comparisons between sources. Candidates are expected to compare content directly on a point-by-point basis. They may compare the details in the sources and/or compare the viewpoints overall.

A **simple comparison** will indicate what points of detail or viewpoint the sources agree or disagree on and **should be awarded 1 mark**. A **developed comparison** of the points of detail or overall viewpoint **should be awarded a second mark**. Candidates may achieve full marks by making four simple comparisons, two developed comparisons (or by any combination of these).

Possible points of comparison may include:

Source A	Source B
Overall: The sources agree about the reasons why a Cold War broke out between the Soviet Union and the USA	
(Once World War Two was over) relations between the two allies deteriorated, to be replaced by a climate of suspicion between America and the Soviet Union.	As soon as the war ended the Soviet Union and the Americans developed open hostility towards each other.
Soviet and American leaders held opposing ideological views...	(The new American President Truman and Soviet leader Stalin seemed hostile to one another and) this emphasised their ideological divisions.
America's decision to develop and use the atomic bomb against the Japanese without consulting the Soviets placed further strain on relations.	The tension at Potsdam was increased by America's use of the atomic bomb against Japan.

92. *Candidates can be credited in a number of ways up to a maximum of 6 marks.*

Candidates must make a judgement about the extent to which the source provides a full description or explanation of a given event or development.

Up to a **maximum of 6 marks** in total, **1 mark** should be awarded for each valid point selected from the source or each valid point of significant omission provided.

Candidates should be awarded **up to 3 marks** for their identification of points from the source which support their judgement. Candidates should be awarded **up to 4 marks** for their identification of points of significant omission, based on their own knowledge, that support their judgement. A **maximum of 2 marks** may be awarded for answers in which no judgement has been made **or** which refer only to the source.

Possible points which may be identified from the source include:
1. a new East German labour law, which stopped workers from going on strike, had led to growing unrest in the factories
2. agriculture reforms had led to higher prices and food shortages
3. all of this led to a massive increase in the numbers of refugees fleeing to the West
4. in the six months up to June 1961, 103,000 East Germans had fled through Berlin.

Possible points of significant omission may include:
5. in June 1961 the Soviet Premier Khrushchev raised tensions by threatening to end the existing four-power agreements guaranteeing American, British, and French rights to access West Berlin
6. President Kennedy asked Congress for an additional $3 billion to increase America's armed forces
7. the Soviets accused the West of using Berlin as a centre of operations against East Germany and the Soviet Union

8. In August 1961 the East German government took the decision to close the border between East and West Berlin
9. East German troops and workers had begun to tear up streets running alongside the barrier to make them impassable to most vehicles, and to install barbed wire entanglements and fences around the three western sectors
10. East Germans then started building a wall to separate the east and west of the city.

Any other valid point of significant omission

93. *Candidates can be credited in a number of ways **up to a maximum of 6 marks**.*

Candidates must make a number of points that make the issue plain or clear, for example by showing connections between factors or causal relationships between events or ideas. These should be key reasons but there is no need for any evaluation or prioritising of these reasons.

Up to a maximum of **6 marks** in total, **1 mark** should be awarded for each accurate, relevant reason, and a **second mark** should be awarded for reasons that are developed. Candidates may achieve full marks by providing six straightforward reasons, three developed reasons (or any combination of these).

Possible reasons may include:
1. Cuban leader Castro had formed a close alliance with the Soviet Union which alarmed the USA
2. Castro had angered American businesses by nationalising key Cuban industries
3. there were fears that Castro would turn Cuba into a communist stronghold
4. Kennedy was looking for an opportunity to take revenge against Castro after the failure of the Bay of Pigs incident
5. Castro agreed to site Soviet missiles on Cuba which USA saw as a threat to US cities
6. US spy planes took photographs of missile bases being constructed on Cuba
7. Cuba was only a short distance from the American mainland so caused great concern in the USA
8. an American U2 spy plane was shot down over Cuba further increasing tension
9. America was furious at Soviets as they refused to remove their missiles from Cuba
10. Soviet ships sailing towards the American blockade around Cuba with additional missiles increased the tension
11. President Kennedy was under huge pressure to stand up to communist aggression
12. American public opinion would not accept the presence of Soviet missiles on Cuba.

Any other valid reason

94. *Candidates can be credited in a number of ways **up to a maximum of 9 marks**.*

Candidates must make a judgement about the extent to which different factors contributed to an event or development, or its impact. They are required to provide a balanced account of the influence of different factors and come to a reasoned conclusion based on the evidence presented.

Up to **5 marks** can be awarded for relevant, factual, key points of knowledge used to support factors, with **1 mark** awarded for each point (but **one mark should be deducted** if the correct process is not clear in at least two factors). If **only one factor is presented, a maximum of 3 marks**

should be awarded for relevant points of knowledge. A **further 4 marks** can be awarded for providing the answer in a structured way and coming to a reasoned conclusion.

Up to **4 marks** should be awarded for presenting the answer in a structured way, leading to a conclusion which addresses the question, as follows:

1 mark for an introduction (which places the question in its historical context or outlines relevant factors).

1 mark for the answer being presented in a structured way (with knowledge being organised in support of different factors).

1 mark for a conclusion with a valid judgement (or overall summary).

1 mark for a reason in support of the judgement (a summary cannot be supported).

Possible factors	Key points of knowledge to support this factor may include:
Vietcong tactics	1. Vietcong were expert in conducting guerrilla warfare 2. Vietcong made full use of local knowledge/knowledge of the terrain 3. Vietcong generally avoided large scale attacks/when they attacked it was with fanatical determination 4. Vietcong travelled light carrying few supplies and basic weapons.
American soldiers	5. American soldiers were poorly trained and ill-equipped for jungle warfare/did not cope with the guerrilla tactics 6. the draft system meant that there was a lack of experience among American forces 7. American soldiers had low morale and lacked respect for their officers – reduced their combat effectiveness.
Opposition in USA	8. increasingly people in the USA were tired of the war/the war was wasting young American lives 9. the media presented evidence of cruelty by American soldiers, war crimes such as the My Lai massacre, tactics of defoliation 10. welfare programmes in America were being dropped because of the cost of the war in Vietnam.
US military problems	11. failure of American tactics – strategic hamlets, carpet bombing, use of defoliants (Agent Orange) 12. the US was trying to supply a war 8000 miles from America which made it very difficult for them.

Any other relevant factor

95. *Candidates can be credited in a number of ways **up to a maximum of 4 marks**.*

They may take different perspectives on the events and may describe a variety of different aspects of the events. Candidates must make a number of relevant, factual points. These should be key points. These do not have to be in any particular order.

1 mark should be awarded for each accurate relevant key point of knowledge. A **second mark** should be awarded for each point that is developed, **up to a maximum of 4 marks**.

Candidates may achieve full marks by providing four straightforward points, by making two developed points (or any combination of these).

Possible points of knowledge may include:

1. a hotline between the Soviet and American leaders was established following the Cuban Missile Crisis
2. the Non-Proliferation Treaty, which aimed to prevent the spread of nuclear weapons, was signed in 1968
3. in 1971 Brezhnev announced the 'programme for peace' to improve relations between East and West
4. war in Vietnam was scaled down and then ended in the early 1970s and this had a positive influence on superpower relations
5. President Nixon's visit to Moscow in 1973 helped to reduce tension
6. USA and USSR signed Helsinki Accords in 1975 to improve relations between the Communist bloc and the West
7. both sides reached agreement to limit or reduce nuclear weapons – SALT II
8. trade agreements between both sides helped to improve relations/USA begins to sell the USSR wheat in 1970s.

Any other valid point of knowledge

Acknowledgements

Permission has been sought from all relevant copyright holders and Hodder Gibson is grateful for the use of the following:

Source A: An extract from 'Scotland and the Impact of the Great War 1914–1928' by John Kerr, published by Hodder Gibson, 2010 (2016 page 7);

Source A: An extract from www.bbc.co.uk/history/historic_figures/charles_i_king.shtml © BBC 2014 (2016 page 10);

Source B: An extract from 'Charles I' by C.N. Trueman, taken from www.historylearningsite.co.uk/stuart-england/charles-i/© The History Learning Site, 17 Mar 2015 & 16 Aug 2016 (2016 page 10);

Source B: An extract from 'Black Peoples of the Americas' by Bob Rees and Marika Sherwood, published by Heinemann Educational Publishers, 1992 (2016 page 13);

Source A: An extract from 'Cannibals All! Or, Slaves Without Masters' by George Fitzhugh, published by A. Morris, 1857, Richmond V.A. (2016 page 20);

Source B: An extract from 'Trotsky's Diary in Exile, 1935' by Leon Trotsky, published by Harvard University Press, 1958 (2016 page 22);

Source A: An extract from 'Access to History: Italy: The Rise of Fascism 1915–1945' by Mark Robson (3rd edition), published by Hodder Education 2006 (2016 page 23);

Source B: An extract from an article by Professor Neil Gregor in '20th Century History Review' published by Philip Allan Updates, 2008 (2016 page 25);

Source A: National Health Service leaflet, May 1948 (INF 2/66, page 15) www.nationalarchives.gov.uk/wp-content/uploads/2014/03/inf-2-66-f151.jpg. Contains public sector information licensed under the Open Government Licence v3.0 (www.nationalarchives.gov.uk/doc/open-government-licence/version/3/) (2017 page 12);

Source B: An extract adapted from 'The Glorious Cause: The American Revolution, 1763–1789', by Robert Middlekauff. Copyright © 1982, 2005 by Oxford University Press, Inc (2017 page 16);

Source A: An extract adapted from 'The Night of the Long Knives' by C.N. Trueman, taken from www.historylearningsite.co.uk/nazi-germany/the-night-of-the-long-knives/ © The History Learning Site, 9 Mar 2015 & 16 Aug 2016 (2017 page 20);

Source B: An extract adapted from 'The Savage Years: Tales From the 20th Century' by Rupert Colley © 2015 Rupert Colley (2017 page 20);

Source C: An extract adapted from 'Nazi Education' by C.N. Trueman, taken from www.historylearningsite.co.uk/nazi-germany/nazi-education/© The History Learning Site, 9 Mar 2015 & 16 Aug 2016 (2017 page 21);

Source A: An extract adapted from 'The Russian Revolution' by Anthony Wood. Published by Routledge. Copyright © 1976, 1986, Taylor & Francis (2017 page 22);

Source D: An extract from 'Lordship to Patronage: Scotland, 1603–1745' (New History of Scotland) by Rosalind Mitchison, published by Edinburgh University Press, 1990 (2017 SQP page 9);

Source A: An extract from 'Heinemann Scottish History for Standard Grade: International Cooperation and Conflict 1890s–1920s' by Elizabeth Trueland, published by Heinemann Educational Publishers, 2004 (2017 SQP page 12);

Source B: An extract from 'Empires and Citizens: Pupil's Book 2' by Ben Walsh, published by Nelson Thornes 2004 (2017 SQP page 17);

Source A: An extract from 'Top Causes of the Civil War' by Martin Kelly, ThoughtCo, Sep. 13, 2017 (thoughtco.com/top-causes-of-the-civil-war-104532) (2017 SQP page 28);

Source C: Extract from 'Civil Rights in the USA, 1863–1890' by David Paterson, Susan Willoughby and Doug Willoughby, published by Heinemann Educational Publishers, 2001 (2017 SQP page 29);

Source C: An extract from 'Europe's Changing Economy in the Second Half of the Nineteenth Century' by Sidney Pollard © Sempringham; www.ehistory.org.uk (2017 SQP page 35);

Source C: An extract from 'Laughter Wasn't Rationed: Remembering the War Years in Germany' by Dorothea (von Schwanenfluegel) Lawson, 1999 © Tricor Press (2017 SQP page 41).